THE WOMEN'S GUIDE

TRIATHLON

USA
TRIATHLON

HUMAN KINETICS

Library of Congress Cataloging-in-Publication Data

The women's guide to triathlon / USA Triathlon; Tara S. Comer, project Coordinator.
   pages cm
 Includes bibliographical references and index.
 1. Triathlon--Training. 2. Women athletes--Training of. I. Comer, Tara S. II. USA Triathlon.
 GV1060.73.W68 2015
 796.082--dc23

                                   2014045350

 ISBN: 978-1-4504-8115-1 (print)

The web addresses cited in this text were current as of February 2015, unless otherwise noted.

Acquisitions Editor: Tom Heine; **Developmental Editor:** Cynthia McEntire; **Managing Editor:** Nicole O'Dell; **USA Triathlon Editors:** Linda Cleveland, Jayme McGuire; **Copyeditor:** Joyce Sexton; **Permissions Manager:** Martha Gullo; **Graphic Designer:** Dawn Sills; **Cover Designer:** Charlie Jahner, USA Triathlon; **Photographs (interior):** Neil Bernstein, unless otherwise noted; **Visual Production Assistant:** Joyce Brumfield; **Photo Production Manager:** Jason Allen; **Art Manager:** Kelly Hendren; **Associate Art Manager:** Alan L. Wilborn; **Illustrations:** © Human Kinetics, unless otherwise noted; **Printer:** Sheridan Books

In the cover image, Sarah (Groff) True in the bike leg of her 2014 ITU World Triathlon Series win in Stockholm.

Human Kinetics books are available at special discounts for bulk purchase. Special editions or book excerpts can also be created to specification. For details, contact the Special Sales Manager at Human Kinetics.

Printed in the United States of America   10 9 8 7 6 5 4 3 2 1

The paper in this book is certified under a sustainable forestry program.

Human Kinetics
Website: www.HumanKinetics.com

United States: Human Kinetics
P.O. Box 5076
Champaign, IL 61825-5076
800-747-4457
e-mail: humank@hkusa.com

Canada: Human Kinetics
475 Devonshire Road Unit 100
Windsor, ON N8Y 2L5
800-465-7301 (in Canada only)
e-mail: info@hkcanada.com

Europe: Human Kinetics
107 Bradford Road
Stanningley
Leeds LS28 6AT, United Kingdom
+44 (0) 113 255 5665
e-mail: hk@hkeurope.com

Australia: Human Kinetics
57A Price Avenue
Lower Mitcham, South Australia 5062
08 8372 0999
e-mail: info@hkaustralia.com

New Zealand: Human Kinetics
P.O. Box 80
Torrens Park, South Australia 5062
0800 222 062
e-mail: info@hknewzealand.com

E6235

THE WOMEN'S GUIDE TO
TRIATHLON

CONTENTS

Introduction vi

CHAPTER 1   Gearing Up. 1
             Rachel Sears Casanta

CHAPTER 2   Tri-Specific Strength Training
             and Performance Testing. 19
             Sarah Haskins

CHAPTER 3   Fueling the Female Triathlete 35
             Stacy T. Sims, PhD

CHAPTER 4   Mental Training for the Inner Athlete 55
             Siri Lindley

CHAPTER 5   Alternative Exercises for Triathletes. 61
             Sage Rountree, PhD

CHAPTER 6   Streamlining Your Swim 79
             Sara McLarty

CHAPTER 7   Biking Strong. 91
             Lindsay Hyman

CHAPTER 8   Running Smart 101
             Margie Shapiro

CHAPTER 9   Progressing From Sprint to Half Ironman. 113
             Melissa Mantak, MA

CHAPTER 10   The Traveling Triathlete 149
             Tara S. Comer

CHAPTER 11 Race Day Strategy 159
Melissa Stockwell

CHAPTER 12 Injury Prevention and Recovery 169
Krista Austin, PhD, CSCS

CHAPTER 13 Coaching Options for Triathletes 193
Gale Bernhardt

CHAPTER 14 Training Through Different Life Stages 201
Wendy Francke, MD

CHAPTER 15 Integrating Triathlon Into Your Busy Life 211
Rebeccah Wassner and Laurel Wassner

CHAPTER 16 Starting Children in Triathlon 221
Shelly O'Brien

CHAPTER 17 Succeeding in Off-Road Triathlons 237
Melanie McQuaid

CHAPTER 18 Careers in Triathlon 247
Celeste Callahan and Brenda Barrera

References **261**
Index **263**
About USA Triathlon **269**
About the Project Coordinator **271**
About the Contributors **273**

INTRODUCTION

In 1982, USA Triathlon was formed, with 1,500 members joining in the first year—a modest number of athletes in a sport few had even heard about. History doesn't tell us how many of those pioneers were women, but our sport's popularity has increased dramatically since then, and women have been among the biggest drivers of its growth. As of 2013, nearly 50,000 athletes—37 percent of all USA Triathlon members—were women, representing a rapidly growing force for the future of the sport. In 2013, another milestone for female triathletes was achieved as the National Collegiate Athletic Association (NCAA) voted to accept triathlon as an Emerging Sport for Women, setting it on the path toward increased funding, support, and publicity for the many great collegiate female triathletes in competition and the thousands more who will follow in their footsteps.

It has been one of the great pleasures and proudest achievements of my life to be associated with the triathlon community for the past two decades, and it is a great honor to edit the work of the amazing authors you're about to read. My own journey began, as for many of you, with participation in women-only charity races, and seeing an 80-year-old breast cancer survivor cross the finish line was all the inspiration I could have hoped for. The community of female triathletes immediately welcomed me and set me on a course toward developing female athletes and growing our presence in the sport. Today, I am exceedingly proud to serve as chair of the USA Triathlon Women's Committee and focus attention on the great achievements we've made, support women for leadership posts in USA Triathlon Governance, and build programs to make triathlon accessible, supportive, and sustaining for new generations of female athletes. The intent of this book is to be relevant for the beginner as well as the elite athlete and to allow athletes of all ages and abilities to be safer, stronger, fitter, and faster while celebrating the wonderful group of athletes to which we all belong.

The book you're holding is intended to be the definitive companion for the female triathlete and will be an outstanding resource for all training, equipment, strategy, and recovery needs. A lot about triathlon can be unique for women, and it can be both confusing and frustrating to try to sort through information that might not fit your needs. Rest easy, we ladies will take care of our own. This book highlights triathlon training expertise from today's most accomplished female coaches and female athletes. Each chapter of the book, addressing a different topic specific to women's experiences in the sport, is written by one or more women who are acknowledged authorities in that area of triathlon.

I have been greatly honored to be asked to assemble the group of authors, and was thrilled with the enthusiasm, talent, and skill that they brought to sharing their wisdom with their fellow female triathletes. Our distinguished cast includes Olympians, world champions, and expert coaches whose decades of experience represent the history of women in triathlon, as well as the current technological breakthroughs and best training practices available to athletes.

This book is a wonderful opportunity to increase the bonds of community among women in triathlon, highlight the amazing contributions we've made to the sport, and advertise our deep roots and ongoing excellence. Community and support drew me to this sport, and I have been pushed, coached, and applauded by many incredible athletes. This project was an ideal way to sustain that feeling of strength and unity. I hope that it helps you with your journey through the great sport of triathlon and helps you realize your goals, helps you grow as an athlete, and speeds you to many healthy, exhilarating finishes.

Tara S. Comer
Chair, USA Triathlon Women's Committee

CHAPTER 1

Gearing Up

Rachel Sears Casanta

Keeping up with the latest developments in triathlon gear and technology can be an endurance race in itself. Triathlon requires training and racing equipment for the swim, bike, and run. Add women-specific products to the mix and you have a lot to consider. Evaluating the purpose and benefits tied to gear purchases and usage in training and on race day can help you sort through the options. Determining your personal needs and finding products that satisfy them will help ensure you get the most from your endurance-sport budget. In this chapter, we look at necessary equipment, women-specific options, and some of the latest high-tech gear used to train for and compete in triathlon as you advance in your multisport journey.

Swim

Even the most basic gear in swimming has important features to consider. The swim caps, goggles, and swimsuit you select can help you train smarter and with greater comfort. As you progress in your aquatic adventures, training tools such as swim paddles will help you develop and refine your swim technique. When you are ready to make the dive from pool to open-water swimming, you'll want to consider wetsuit offerings as well.

Swim Caps

Swim caps keep your eyes and mouth free of wayward locks by keeping your hair tucked neatly away and also protect your hair from the elements (figure 1.1*a*). In open water, brightly colored swim caps provide a measure of safety, making you more visible as you move through the water. Latex swim caps are the least expensive, while silicon caps are more durable and more comfortable, especially if you have longer hair. Swimming in cold water? A thermal or neoprene skull cap (figure 1.1*b*) can help with heat retention and energy conservation, helping you to stay in the water longer.

FIGURE 1.1   *(a)* TYR swim cap; *(b)* TYR neoprene cap.
Courtesy of TYR Sport, Inc.

Goggles

Goggles with cushioned eye sockets (figure 1.2) come in a variety of shapes and styles and are a popular choice among triathletes due to their versatility and comfort. Masks designed for swimming and triathlon offer the widest field of vision. This makes masks excellent for sighting and navigation but less hydrodynamic due to their larger profiles.

Go with the option that is comfortable and best fits your face

FIGURE 1.2   **TYR goggles.**
Courtesy of TYR Sport, Inc.

while creating a good seal. Many retail stores allow you to try on goggles to find the model that works best for you. You may want to try youth goggles if you have particularly petite features. When you've found a pair of goggles that suits you, choose a few pairs with different lens colors so you are prepared to swim in varying light conditions. Table 1.1 describes the color options for lenses and the conditions in which they work best.

Swimsuits

Swimsuits are made of polyester and nylon blends or Lycra and spandex blends. Polyester swimsuits are more durable under exposure to chlorine and retain their shape and integrity (they do not quickly become see-through), making them a good investment. Competition swimsuits are constructed of Lycra and Spandex blends, are tighter fitting, and create less drag, but the fabric can deteriorate more quickly with repeated exposure to chlorine. Choose a suit that fits well and helps you feel confident,

TABLE 1.1

Goggle Lens Colors and Light Conditions

Lens color	Conditions
Clear	Ideal for low light or overcast conditions. Use for indoor pool swimming and dark conditions.
Blue-violet	Provide good visibility in changing light conditions. Reduce surface glare from water.
Amber	Because they amplify existing light, amber lenses are good for low light conditions and indoor swimming. In bright sunshine, they reduce glare, helping to provide better vision.
Smoke	Ideal for direct sunshine and bright conditions.
Mirrored-metallized	Reduce brightness and glare.

too. You can use Lycra or polyester suits in open water, but you may find that a polyester suit will hold up a bit better with prolonged use in salt water.

A more recent high-tech entry into the triathlon swim gear world is the swimskin (figure 1.3). A swimskin is a high-tech swimsuit meant to be worn over a regular swimsuit or tri gear. It is hydrophobic, is constructed of high-tech materials, and minimizes drag as you move through the water. A swimskin is a serious investment, with models from top manufacturers ranging from $300 to $400. If you do the majority of your racing in warm water and every second counts, determine if the potential performance gains (perceived or actual) are worth your money.

Wetsuits

A wetsuit is not mandatory in triathlon. However, if you regularly participate in cold-water events or seek every competitive advantage, then the wetsuit is key. Wetsuits provide increased buoyancy and added warmth and help with energy conservation. At USA

FIGURE 1.3   **TYR swimskin.**
Courtesy of TYR Sport, Inc.

Triathlon–sanctioned events, triathletes competing for age-group awards are permitted to wear wetsuits when the water temperature is 78 degrees Fahrenheit (25.5 degrees Celsius) or below. For more specifics about the rules, visit www.usatriathlon.org.

Which Style Is Right for You?

A full wetsuit is the best option for cold-water swimming and provides the highest level of warmth, buoyancy, and performance advantages (figure 1.4*a*). Full wetsuits particularly benefit novice swimmers as the buoyancy of the suit helps compensate for various body position and technique flaws. As a rule, the more expensive the suit, the more flexible it is via paneling and gradations in neoprene thickness. More flexibility can lead to better efficiency and faster swim times. Full wetsuits range in price from $100 to $750 or more.

Strong swimmers sometimes lament that full wetsuits restrict the range of motion in their shoulders or become too warm during racing. For these athletes and those who regularly swim in warmer waters, a sleeveless wetsuit (figure 1.4*b*) is an option. Sleeveless wetsuits

FIGURE 1.4   *(a)* Full TYR wetsuit; *(b)* sleeveless TYR wetsuit.
Courtesy of TYR Sport, Inc.

fully cover the torso and legs, leaving the shoulders free and thus offering more range of motion. Though a sleeveless wetsuit offers a bit less buoyancy and warmth, it can be quicker to remove in transition than a full wetsuit. Sleeveless wetsuits range in price from $75 to $450 or more.

Wetsuit Fit

Women are no longer limited to making do with an ill-fitting men's wetsuit. Wetsuits designed specifically for women feature sizing options to fit petite as well as tall and larger-statured athletes. TYR, for example, offers 12 different options for women. Visit www.tyr.com for more information. A wetsuit should fit snugly, like a second skin, yet provide ample flexibility that allows you to breathe and move comfortably. Avoid a suit with excess material or folds in the neoprene.

Entry-level wetsuits fit the needs of most triathletes. However, when performance matters, the technical design and advanced materials of a more expensive wetsuit can be well worth the investment. The payoff is greater flexibility and faster swim splits.

Swim Training Tools

Training tools enable you to focus on a specific aspect of your swim technique and conditioning. Common training tools include pull buoys, paddles (figure 1.5), fins, kickboards, stretch cords, and snorkels. While it is nice to buy your own personal training tools, you can borrow entry-level implements at most pools. For more advanced tools such as specialty paddles or fins, you'll need to head to your local swim or tri shop.

FIGURE 1.5 **Refine your technique with the right set of TYR paddles.**
Courtesy of TYR Sport, Inc.

Bike

The bike is the most gear-intensive discipline in triathlon. Whether you're a novice or a seasoned veteran, choosing a bike and the seemingly endless associated gear can be intimidating. Take heart—as with other equipment, you can start with the basics. Match your experience and skill level to your purchases knowing that virtually every part of your bike can be upgraded when the time is right for you.

To determine the best bike for you, establish a bike-buying budget. Quality entry-level road and triathlon bikes can be purchased for between $1,200 and $1,500. When establishing your budget, remember to figure in costs for accessories. Basic equipment includes a helmet, pedals, air inflation device, spare tubes, patch kit, seat bag, water bottles, footwear, and clothing.

Your budget will narrow your bike search. You won't generally have to worry about which frame material is best to buy or whether the bike has specific components; the price range you choose will include or exclude many of those choices for you. As a rule, manufacturers have bikes along the cost spectrum to match an athlete's experience and skill level. As bikes get more expensive, they are geared toward an increasingly more experienced athlete. Regardless of whether you aim to purchase an entry-level or high-end bike, each part of a bike is upgradable. However, just because a part costs more does not mean it is the best choice for you. With the help of your bike shop pro, you can add, swap out, and upgrade components as your skill level progresses.

Road Bike or Triathlon Bike

Before we look at specific bike parts and what you should know, let's address the question of which bike to use—a road bike (figure 1.6) or a triathlon bike (figure 1.7). If you will own only one bicycle, the most versatile option is to purchase a road bike, especially if you use the bike outside of triathlon or live in a hilly area. Later you can add aerobars or racing wheels and potentially upgrade components.

FIGURE 1.6a Litespeed L1R Road Bike. The L1R is a UCI-approved frameset composed of 60T carbon fiber formed with Reactive Pressure Molding for optimal stiffness, light weight, and all-around performance. It was created with the philosophy of Shape-Specific Design in which every tube is crafted with attention to shape, weight, functionality, and stiffness.

Courtesy of American Bicycle Group.

FIGURE 1.6b Litespeed L1R Road Bike. "My Litespeed is like a rocket that can maneuver through a maze. I am comfortable, confident, and excited to go fast. Every ride is a blast on my Litespeed." - Chelsea Burns, USA Triathlon Collegiate Recruitment Program

USA Triathlon

In general, a road bike is the most versatile bike choice. Designed to be used across varied terrains, the neutral geometry and availability in many sizes make a road bike an excellent first choice for the multisport athlete.

The triathlon-specific bicycle is best used as a tri bike for riding in the aerobars on flat to moderate climbs. Everything about the modern tri bike is designed to be aero and fast and provides the optimal choice for racing. It can pose challenges for training if you live in a region with hilly or mountainous terrain. Table 1.2 compares the characteristics of road bikes and tri bikes.

FIGURE 1.7*a* **Quintana Roo PRsix Triathlon Bike.** The PRsix is a superbike with everything you need and nothing you don't. Aero, agile, simple, light. This bike is fully adjustable to fit your needs and requires only two wrenches to assemble, making it easy to transport to any race.

Courtesy of American Bicycle Group.

FIGURE 1.7*b* **Quintana Roo PRsix Triathlon Bike.** "The PRsix is fast, sleek, and practical. It's faster, more responsive, and more comfortable than any bike I've ever ridden, meaning that I always know I'm getting the most out of whatever engine I can provide!" - Pro Triathlete Jennie Hansen

Courtesy of American Bicycle Group.

TABLE 1.2

Road Bike Versus Tri Bike

	Road bike	Triathlon bike
Geometry	Designed for neutral handling and varied terrain	Designed for a more forward position with weight on the front end
Seat angle	72 to 75 degrees	76 to 80 degrees
Wheel size	700c (standard)	650c and 700c
Frame materials	Aluminum, carbon, steel, and titanium	Aluminum and carbon
Price range	$800 to $10,000+	$1,500 to $10,000+
Handlebars	Drop bars, multipositions	Base bar and aerobars
Small riders	Many choices for individuals under 5 ft 2 in.	Limited choices for riders under 5 ft 2 in.
Skill level	Beginner to professional	Advanced beginner to professional
Women-specific model	Many options	Limited options

Women-Specific Bikes and Bike Fit

As the participation of women in triathlon and cycling has grown in recent years, manufacturers have responded by offering more bikes designated as women specific (figure 1.8). For some of these brands, women-specific models are bikes painted in feminine color schemes and modified with shorter cranks, narrower handlebars, and a woman-specific saddle. Other bike companies have chosen to make women-specific geometries with corresponding women-specific components. These bikes are generally marketed to women who are under 5 feet 5 inches in height. Even with a women-specific bike, there is no guarantee that the cranks, handlebars, and saddle are right for you. Almost any bike can be customized with different length, width, height, and weight components to fit your needs. Here's how it works.

Stack and Reach

Bikes are traditionally sized in one of two ways. The first is a measurement using seat tube length, and the second is by top tube length. The issue with both of these measurements is that manufacturers independently decide how the two lengths are measured. As a result, the parity of measurement between bike brands is inconsistent at best. To achieve parity, a method of standardizing sizing, called stack and reach (figure 1.9), was developed by industry veteran Dan Empfield. Today most bike professionals use stack and reach to compare bike sizes and determine fit.

Reach is the horizontal length from the center of the crank spindle to the center-top of the head tube. Stack is vertical height between these two points. Stack and reach numbers can be measured and compared across any bike brand and model. This means that you are free to choose from any bike brand, regardless of female–male designation. With the help of a professional bike fitter you'll be able to customize your bike, setting it up with an appropriate saddle, handlebars, and other parts to best fit

FIGURE 1.8*a*   Women-specific bike. The CD0.1 Camo uses QR's exclusive 18-millimeter offset downtube shift that diverts concentrated airflow away from the drive side to produce a measurable bike-course advantage for every athlete at every level.

Courtesy of American Bicycle Group.

FIGURE 1.8*b*   Women-specific bike. "The CD0.1 Camo is not only pretty, but the stability that shift technology provides creates an easy transition from bike to run." - Pro Triathlete Cait Snow.

Courtesy of American Bicycle Group.

you and your riding needs. While a women-specific bike might feature a color scheme that you like, unless you are particularly petite you do not have to purchase a women-specific bike. Compare bikes of similar prices, test ride, and go with the bike you like best, regardless of female–male designation.

Bike Fit

While all women do not need a women-specific bike, all women can benefit from working with a trained bike fit professional (figure 1.10). Being properly fitted reduces the potential for injury, increases performance, and is crucial to comfort, pain-free riding, and secure handling. Bike fit can be the single most cost-effective way to improve aerodynamics. Table 1.3 outlines specific parts of the bike and the considerations for female cyclists.

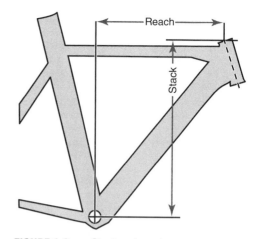

FIGURE 1.9 **Stack and reach.**

Adapted, by permission, from D. Empfield, 2003, Stack and reach primer: Chapter one. [Online.] Available: www.slowtwitch.com/Bike_Fit/Choosing_a_Tri_Bike_via_Stack_and_Reach/Stack_Reach_Primer_Chapter_One_95.html [January 13, 2015].

FIGURE 1.10 **Sarah True during a Retül bike fit.**
Courtesy of Retül.

TABLE 1.3

Bike Parts and Special Considerations for the Female Cyclist

Bike part	Considerations
Saddle	Women contact the saddle in a different location than men, and soft-tissue may be more sensitive for some women. Don't feel locked into a women-specific saddle. Some of the most popular saddles are not specific, including ISM, Cobb, and SMP.
Handlebars	Many women need narrower bars to match their shoulder width than what comes stock with a new bike. Shallower drops and short reach are also excellent features. When adding aerobars, adjustability is key.
Brake levers	For smaller hands, seek adjustable-reach brake levers.
Shift levers	Some shift levers can be difficult to use, requiring a large amount of wrist movement. Handlebar shape can also affect how much movement a shifter makes. Consider return-to-center or electronic shifters if you have hand or wrist dexterity issues.
Crank length	Many women require cranks shorter than stock length. Your position and leg length will determine the correct crank length for you.
Wheel size	Smaller-stature individuals may be better suited to a smaller (650c) wheel size for improved handling and control.
Pedals	Women with wider hips may need a pedal that allows for a wider stance.

Aerobars

Arguably the most iconic piece of triathlon equipment is the aerobar. Aerobars enable you to ride for extended periods of time in a position that reduces drag forces and cheats the wind. Aerobars come in varying shapes and styles and are made of aluminum or carbon. Some aerobar setups feature arm rests that flip up (figure 1.11*a*), providing

FIGURE 1.11   Aerobars with *(a)* elbow pads that flip up and *(b)* elbow pads that are stationary.
Courtesy of Profile Design.

more hand positions; others have stationary arm rests (figure 1.11*b*). Aerobars with a considerable amount of adjustability are important when it comes to fitting. Costs range from $50 to $1,300 for complete carbon front-end setups. Along with proprietary setups, popular brands are 3T, FSA, HED, Profile Design, Syntace, Vision, and Zipp.

Work with a bike fit specialist to determine which aerobar setup to purchase. Your fitter will help mate function and budget and, most importantly, help select which aerobars will work best for you and your setup. After all, if you are not comfortable riding in the aero position, the benefits of any potential savings in aerodynamics can be lost. Your position on the bike determines which aerobars are best to buy.

Components

You won't usually need to decide which components come on your bike, as your budget will determine that for you. However, should you decide to upgrade, more expensive components tend to weigh less, can be more durable, and offer higher performance. There are nuances of each groupset, often related to maintenance, which will likely mean more to your mechanic than to you unless you are doing your own wrenching. A safe bet is to choose the midlevel componentry unless you have needs or desires for pricier options. Talking with your bike sales professional will help you determine the best convergence of money spent and benefits gained.

Electronics

Currently, electronic shifting systems are available from Shimano (Di2) and Campagnolo (EPS). Electronic shifting enables you to shift from gear to gear by pressing a button on the shift lever to move the derailleurs. Electronic shifting has many advantages, including the ability to shift at any time, whether you are seated, standing, or under load. Faster and more precise than mechanical shifting, which is actuated via cables, electronic shifting is virtually silent. For women, the ability to adjust the shifting mechanism to reach small hands is a significant plus, and the push-button mechanism is also easier to manipulate for athletes with hand strength or dexterity issues. Though costs continue to come down, expect to pay between $1,200 and $3,000 more for an electric versus a mechanical bike with the same components.

Wheels

Athletes commonly train and race on the same set of wheels in the early phases of their multisport adventures. Most new road and triathlon bikes come with good, quality alloy wheels that will meet performance needs. Later, however, comes the call of carbon and the potential of faster bike splits. Race wheels are the next step. After aerobars, wheels are the investment that can result in the greatest performance gains, assuming that the wheelset chosen mates with your fitness, ability, and needs. High-performance race wheels come in a variety of rim styles, materials, depths, weights, and widths. Taking these features into consideration can help direct your wheelset purchase. Table 1.4 summarizes key characteristics to consider when you are choosing wheels.

TABLE 1.4

Choosing Wheels

RIM STYLES	
Style	**Comments**
Clincher	Most common, least expensive, and available in all materials. Can be converted to tubeless. Most choices in tires and features.
Tubeless	Special type of clincher designed to eliminate the need for a tube. Limited rim and tire options and more expensive. Excellent flat protection and ride quality. Very fast. Sealant tends to stop most punctures.
Tubular	Traditional glue-on tire, with the tire glued to the rim. Best performance, lightest weight, most expensive. Tire changing is more difficult. Typically used only in races.
WHEEL MATERIALS	
Material	**Comments**
Aluminum	Most common material, least expensive, can be lightweight, excellent braking surface. Very durable.
Carbon	More expensive, lighter weight. Requires special brake pads. May have reduced brake quality especially in wet conditions.
Mixed	Aluminum outer rim and brake surface bonded to carbon rim. Less costly than full carbon, same braking quality as aluminum, can be converted to tubeless.
WHEEL SPECIFICATIONS	
Specification	**Comments**
Rim depth	Rims can come in different depths. Generally the deeper the rim, the more aerodynamic but the more difficult to control in side winds. Lighter riders may want to avoid deep rims due to control issues.
Weight	Modern wheels are fairly light, with carbon the lightest in class. Lighter tends to be better for climbing and accelerating, but light wheels can be less durable.
Rim width	Rims come in different widths. Wider rims tend to be more comfortable, offer better road grip, and can be more aerodynamic.
OTHER CONSIDERATIONS	
Brands	American Classic, HED, Lightweight, Mad Fiber, Mavic, Profile Design, Reynolds, Ursus, Zipp
Price range	$350 to $3,000+

Helmets

There are helmets specifically designed for mountain biking (figure 1.12*a*), road riding (figure 1.12*b*), and for the aerodynamics of triathlon (figure 1.12*c*). Mountain bike (MTB) helmets generally have a removable, plastic visor and are more substantial for crash protection. Road helmets feature numerous vents and are lightweight and more aerodynamic than MTB helmets. Either road or MTB helmets will do in triathlon. Selecting a helmet that coordinates with your bike is fun, but be sure to choose a comfortable model that fits securely.

Aero helmets can improve a rider's aerodynamics and are increasingly popular in triathlon. Aero helmets have fewer vents and extend around the back of the head to the shoulders, typically ending in a point. An aero helmet that doesn't suit your position can be slower than a road helmet. For performance gains, you must ride consistently in an aerodynamic position, keeping your head still. Moving your head up or down or side to side causes you to leak aerodynamics, as the profile of the aero helmet can catch the wind and increase drag, erasing benefits gained from cheating the wind.

The helmet that is best for you is the one that fits your aero position. Look for helmets with ample adjustability in the retention system and neck strap and internal padding to ensure the best fit. There is some truth to the adage "If you feel fast, you'll ride fast," so if you desire an aero helmet, prepare to spend between $100 and $500. Always check helmets for a Consumer Product Safety Commission (CPSC) sticker, which is required by USA Triathlon for participation in USA Triathlon-sanctioned events.

Cycling Training Tools

When you start training, the most basic goal is simply to ride your bike. After you've had some time to learn fundamental handling skills and discover local training routes, and are generally comfortable with riding your bike, it may be time to consider investing in training tools and gadgets. Training tools can help you train more efficiently so you make the most of your time in the saddle. Power meters, stationary trainers, and gadgets each offer feedback that can help both self-coached and coach-guided athletes train smarter and get fit faster.

FIGURE 1.12*a* **Rudy Project Airstorm mountain bike helmet.**
Courtesy of Rudy Project North America.

FIGURE 1.12*b* **Rudy Project Windmax road bike helmet.**
Courtesy of Rudy Project North America.

FIGURE 1.12*c* **Rudy Project Wing57 aerodynamic helmet.**
Courtesy of Rudy Project North America.

Power Meters

When training according to perceived exertion, cadence, and heart rate is no longer serving your needs, it may be time to consider power. Power meters offer multiple benefits for athletes seeking to advance performance. Power meters provide instant feedback of various metrics including wattage output, which enables the fine-tuning of training efforts for maximum results. Power meters are also excellent pacing tools, effectively helping an athlete stay within prescribed wattage parameters. The robust data collected by a power meter make it an excellent tool for analysis, as it can record metrics associated with left and right balance, energy expenditure, and pedal force. Power meters are also excellent for repeatable and reliable performance testing. Keep in mind, though, that the sheer volume of data generated by a power meter can be overwhelming and that successful usage requires the expertise to interpret the data. Application of the information collected is what will help you get the most from your investment.

Power meters can be placed in four locations on the bike: rear wheel, crank arm spider, crank arm, and pedals. There are limitations to each type of power meter, including how it fits on your bike. In selecting a power meter, you'll want to enlist the help of your coach and your local bike shop to decide which models are compatible with your bike and meet your individual needs. If you are ready to move beyond cadence- or heart rate–based training, training with power may be the next step in advancing your cycling performance. Among the brands to consider are Garmin, Pioneer, Polar, PowerTap, Quarq, Rotor, SRM, and Stages. Costs range from $600 to $4,000 or more.

Stationary Trainers

Equipment that enables one to train indoors includes stationary trainers, computer-based trainers, rollers, and spin bikes. Matching your needs with equipment features, benefits, and costs will help determine the best option for you. Table 1.5 outlines different options.

Gadgets

A basic bike computer and trusty wristwatch with a timer are the least expensive gadgets you can use for timing training sessions. When you're ready to invest in technology to obtain more information such as speed, distance, cadence, or heart rate, take a look at Global Positioning System (GPS) and heart rate monitor watches. These gadgets can be like a coach on your wrist, providing motivation and helping you maximize the effectiveness of your workouts.

GPS watches provide instant feedback and can track speed, measure distance, and record myriad metrics including data for swim, bike, and run. Other features such as alarms and countdown timers can remind you to hydrate or fuel during training sessions. Data storage capacity is important for analysis, as is the ability to upload to your preferred training software. Think about how you (or your coach) will interpret data to get the most from your investment. When choosing which gadget to purchase, determine if you want data in swim, bike, and run or in run only. GPS watches intended for use in multisport have additional adaptors and sensors for the bike (to gather cadence–speed information) and for the run (to collect cadence–stride rate), and prices scale up accordingly.

TABLE 1.5

Indoor Training Equipment

Option	Brands	Cost	Comments
Stationary trainers	Kurt Kinetic, CycleOps, Blackburn, Tacx, Elite	$150 to $450+	Easy to use, stable, portable, can come with power.
Rollers	Blackburn, Elite, Tacx, Kreitler	$150 to $400+	Portable. Improve handling skills and fitness simultaneously. Greater learning curve for use, as rollers require more balance. The narrower the frame and smaller the drums, the more skill required.
Spin bikes	BH Fitness, Kettler, Lemond, Peloton, ProForm, Schwinn	$800 to $2,000+	Attempt to mimic the position of riding a road bike with a forward-leaning position but are quite different from a road or tri bike. Heavy flywheel forces more use of hamstrings and less overall energy to sustain momentum. Triathletes benefit most from riding their own bikes in training.
Computer-based trainers	CompuTrainer, Velotron	$1,500 to $2,000+	Based on stationary trainer. Connect to computer. Incorporate direct resistance. Course simulations. Expensive.

The Garmin Forerunner 920XT (see figure 1.13) packs a fleet of high-end training features into a sleek watch that is wetsuit-friendly and about 15 percent lighter than its predecessor, the Forerunner 910XT. It boasts a high-resolution color display; flexible, hinged bands and a watch mode, so you can wear it all day. The activity tracking feature measures your steps, sleep, and calories burned all day, giving you a more complete picture of your daily activity. Look for watches like this one that provide the data you need with an easy-to-use interface and the ability to download information. Other brands to check out include Polar, Suunto, Timex, and TomTom.

FIGURE 1.13   A Garmin Forerunner 920XT GPS watch.
Courtesy of Garmin International, Inc.

Apparel

There is no shortage of training and racing apparel options for women today in cycling and running; you'll find gear for virtually every taste and need. The most recent, significant entry into the apparel landscape in multisport is compression clothing. You'll see compression socks, calf sleeves, leg sleeves, shorts, and tights on athletes during traveling, training, racing, and pre- and post-workout. Through the use of gradient compression, compression apparel supports muscles and helps to improve circulation, reducing the risk of deep vein thrombosis (DVT), an important consideration for athletes traveling long distances. Compression gear also aims to reduce muscle fatigue and soreness and accelerate recovery, which can lead to improved performance. If you don't feel goofy donning knee-high compression socks or sporting calf sleeves, you can jump into the compression parade with products from companies such as EC3D as well as 2XU, CEP, SLS3, RecoFit, and Zensah.

Depending on the distance you are racing and what suits your needs, you will find that a great deal of your training gear transitions nicely to racing. The clothing you wear on race day should fit well, feel good, and make you feel confident as you progress from swim to bike to run. In today's marketplace, there are ample manufacturers offering selections of women's one- and two-piece trisuits. Considerations before you buy include these:

- Short-course versus long-course racing
- Access for bathroom breaks (a two-piece suit is easier and quicker than a one-piece suit with a rear zipper)
- Placement and size of pockets for nutrition, supplements, or other supplies
- Length of inseam of the bottoms (longer equals more support, possibly less chafing)
- Presence or absence of a built-in bra
- Chamois type

Test your race gear in training and remember the sunscreen! Trisuits cost $100 to $200 or more.

Cycling Shoes

There are shoes designed specifically for cycling and triathlon racing. Regular road shoes commonly feature a combination of Velcro strap and ratchet closures to ensure a customized, snug fit. Triathlon cycling shoes are designed for the unique demands of the sport and feature heel pull tabs (for quick transitions), are often vented (for quick drying), and have one or two Velcro straps that open to the outside of the shoe and away from the bike drive train. Triathlon shoes are intended for racing and can wear out quickly under the demands of daily training. Both cycling and triathlon shoes feature stiff soles that provide excellent energy transfer, protect your feet, and offer support that can reduce cramping and fatigue. You can wear your regular cycling shoes in a triathlon, but you may sacrifice time in transition fussing with a ratchet closure. Cycling shoes that feature a two- or three-strap Velcro closure may be a good compromise between fit and speed, enabling you to purchase one pair of shoes for both training and racing.

Running Shoes

Investing in running shoes that suit you is key to comfortable and injury-free training. When choosing your footwear, consider the shape and width of your feet; whether you pronate, underpronate, or overpronate; your mileage; and your budget. There are stability shoes, shoes with lots of cushioning, and motion-control models as well as lightweight trainers, shoes for trail running, minimalist and zero-drop shoes, racing flats, and triathlon-specific racing shoes. Many stores offer gait analysis and will work with you to determine your best options. To start, you may want to purchase a good all-around midweight training shoe and use elastic laces so you can use the same shoes for race day. However, a pair of eye-catching, lightweight triathlon racing shoes designed for fast transitions might be just the edge you need on race day!

Eyewear for the Bike and Run

Eyewear is a must for shielding and protecting your eyes from the elements and debris. While the sunglasses you wear when cycling can easily be used for running as well, be mindful that some options marketed specifically to runners may not have the coverage you need while riding a bike. Sunglasses for use while cycling have a larger profile to protect your eyes from debris and a wide variety of lens colors to match varying

FIGURE 1.14   Rudy Project Rydon prescription sunglasses with interchangeable lenses.
Courtesy of Rudy Project North America.

light conditions. Sunglasses with interchangeable lenses offer the most flexibility in a convenient package and can do double duty for cycling and running. Companies such as Rudy Project offer sunglasses with prescription lenses as well (figure 1.14). Better sunglasses are scratch resistant, well vented, and fog resistant. As the price increases, you can expect a better fit through more adjustability, as well as improved optics.

Accessories

Other items you may want to consider for your gear bag include a race number belt or number–nutrition belts that feature snaps, loops, and pockets to carry gels and other nutrition, elastic laces for speedy transitions, and visors or hats to protect your eyes, face, and skin.

Skin Lubricants

A good chamois or skin cream can make your training and racing more comfortable and enjoyable. Even with the ideal bike fit, saddle, and technical shorts, being on the bike for long durations can lead to discomfort. Many products exist in the body-lubricant category, but choosing one made specifically for women is highly recommended. Ingredients in many creams that are not female specific may create uncomfortable sensations or cause discomfort to sensitive female anatomy. Try products such as Body Glide, the original, never greasy, anti-chafing balm.

Recovery Tools

Being able to train consistently is key to improving fitness. Equipment that helps you recover quickly can be invaluable. Tools that can help you do that include foam rollers, massage sticks, and compression units.

Foam rollers are an economical alternative to deep tissue massage. Using your own body weight, you use a foam roller to help increase blood flow and circulation to tissues, decrease muscle tension, break up muscle adhesions, and relieve tight fascia. Massage sticks are rolled on muscles to reduce stiffness and soreness and speed up recovery. Like foam rollers, massage sticks are portable and help improve flexibility.

The latest high-tech recovery tools on the market are compression units (figure 1.15) that sequentially inflate and deflate with air and help promote circulation (and thus recovery). These portable units are low maintenance and are intended to facilitate faster recovery, enabling you to bounce back and tackle your next training session. Check out category leader NormaTec, the Official Recovery System of USA Triathlon, and Recovery Pump, both makers of recovery boots. Expect to invest between $1,200 and $2,000 or more for a compression unit.

FIGURE 1.15 **NormaTec recovery boots.**
Courtesy of NormaTec.

Conclusion

Shopping for and selecting your triathlon gear can be a sport in itself. Be prepared for the adventure by outlining your personal needs. Clearly define your goals and what you want to achieve using your equipment in multisport. Ask yourself: How often will I use it? What will it do for me? Do I need this now, or is it something I can grow into down the road? Match your needs with products that satisfy them, and you'll already be on the straightaway to a successful finish in the race to get geared up!

CHAPTER 2

Tri-Specific Strength Training and Performance Testing

Sarah Haskins

An athlete's coach mentions that she would like to complete some testing in the next week. Immediately, the athlete's heart begins to pound and the nerves begin to set in. The word "test" is associated with things like good or bad, pass or fail, and brings unwelcome emotions. Testing for the purpose of triathlon training is simply the opposite of what most athletes think. It is important for athletes to realize the purpose and function of testing. Once they understand the why, many of the nerves and the unnecessary stress will dissipate and they can focus on the task at hand.

Many types of testing for triathlon athletes are available, and the testing is individualized to help each athlete become more knowledgeable about and specific in her training. Some are just simple perceived exertion tests and others are more complicated. A rating of perceived exertion (RPE) scale, such as the Borg RPE scale, allows an athlete to measure her own effort level during physical activity. This scale reflects how intense the exercise feels while the athlete is training. It takes into account all the feelings that her body is experiencing. Athletes are asked what their RPE is during tests and at the end of every stage. The RPE scale is from 6 to 20, with 6 being very easy and 20 being maximal effort.

Lactate Profiling

One of the more sophisticated types of testing is blood lactate profiling. This test is used to measure the lactate in the athlete's blood at progressive intervals while the activity increases in intensity. The athlete's finger is pricked every 3 to 4 minutes, depending on the demands of the test. While she progresses to the next stage or intensity level, her blood is tested to see how much lactate is produced in the body and how much is being processed. Coaches may choose to repeat this test two or three times per year and then build training zones based on the testing numbers.

The test uses the RPE scale, the athlete's heart rate, power for the bike, and pace for the run as the increased load components.

The bike test starts at 100 watts. Every 3 minutes, the test increases in intensity by 20 watts. A finger prick is performed, and a small amount of blood is extracted and run through a lactate analyzer device to measure the lactate accumulation in the athlete's bloodstream. During the process, the body produces and uses lactic acid as energy at an aerobic state. The more intensely the athlete exercises, the less oxygen is available to process the lactic acid. As the lactic acid starts to accumulate in the blood, an acidic environment is produced inside the muscle cells, causing the muscles cells to burn out, making them unable to contract. This is the state at which an athlete goes from aerobic exercise to anaerobic exercise. The main goal of the test is to find out when an athlete starts to accumulate lactate in her bloodstream.

Figure 2.1 shows the results of my 2005 bike test at the Chula Vista Olympic Training Center. My blood lactate was taken and measured at every L marker. The H line represents my heart rate (HR), and the R line represents my RPE. The point at which the lactate started to accumulate in my bloodstream was at around 265 watts with a HR of 170 and a RPE of 14.

Figure 2.2 shows the results of my 2005 run test at the Chula Vista Olympic Training Center. Blood lactate was taken and measured at every L marker. The H line represents my HR, and the R line represents my RPE. The point at which the lactate started to

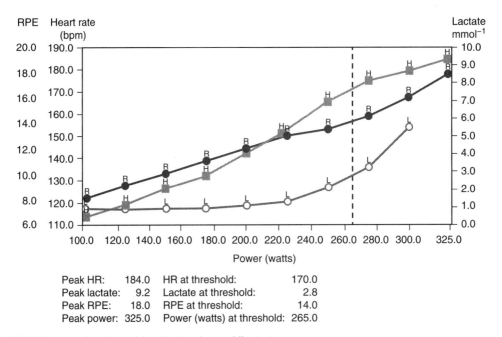

Peak HR:	184.0	HR at threshold:	170.0
Peak lactate:	9.2	Lactate at threshold:	2.8
Peak RPE:	18.0	RPE at threshold:	14.0
Peak power:	325.0	Power (watts) at threshold:	265.0

FIGURE 2.1 **Results on blood lactate from a bike test.**

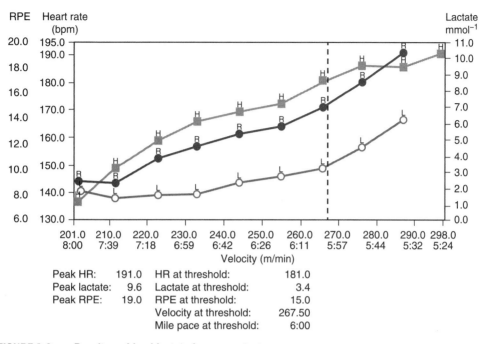

FIGURE 2.2   Results on blood lactate from a run test.

accumulate in my bloodstream was at around a 6 minutes per mile pace (3.7 minutes per kilometer) with a HR of 181 and a RPE of 15.

Field Testing

Currently I use more field testing than blood lactate profiling. The field tests I use are simple ramp tests that measure HR, RPE, and pace for running or power for cycling. In a ramp test, the effort gets increasingly harder. A power ramp test on the bike would start at 100 watts and get harder by 10 watts every 2 minutes. Comparing HR to pace or power and RPE helps me see how I am progressing in training and allows me to track my fitness and improvements over time. Field tests are performed every 3 to 4 weeks. My coach can then make adjustments to my training plan based on what he sees and what I need to work on. These are simple tests and do not require equipment such as a lactate analyzer device.

The field test is performed much like a lab test but without the lactate analyzer device and the finger pricks. A ramp test is just an increase in load over time. I use the Computrainer for a bike test, and it takes only about 45 minutes to complete. A Computrainer is an electromagnetic-powered ergometer that is hooked up via USB (Universal Serial Bus) to a computer. It controls the load placed on the rear wheel that provides resistance.

Bike Field Test

Figure 2.3 shows a field test that used 2-minute stages increasing in load by 10 watts. I found my functional lactate threshold around 22 minutes at 252 watts with a HR of 159 and a RPE of 16. Functional lactate threshold is the level at which the body starts to accumulate more lactate in the bloodstream than can be processed through the Cori cycle. The Cori cycle is the metabolic process where lactate produced by anaerobic glycolysis in the muscle travels to the liver and is converted to glucose, which then goes back into the bloodstream to fuel the muscles and be turned back into lactate. This creates an acidic state in the muscle cells that starts to heat the muscles and makes them less efficient at contraction. The body goes from an aerobic state to an anaerobic state in which it requires more oxygen than it can metabolize to process the lactic acid. A great example of this is the 400-meter sprinter. These runners are running to the point of acidosis, causing their muscles to become less and less efficient at contracting. In an anaerobic state, the human body can go for about 90 seconds without oxygen. After that time the body requires oxygen to process the by-products of glycolysis, the consumption of glycogen by the muscle cell. I determined that at 22 minutes into the test, I was going from an aerobic state to an anaerobic state. Even though I was able to keep going beyond this point, my respiration rate really increased and the effort became much more difficult. If I were to have continued at this pace, I would have lasted only another stage or so before my muscles reached an acidic state and I would be unable to produce the power to keep the effort going.

Workout: 15-min warm-up
Each stage is 2 min starting at 160 watts; increase by 10 watts each stage; Duration (min).

Interval	Duration (min)	Watts goal	Watts avg. off PM	HR (bpm)	RPE (6-20)
1	15:00				
1	2:00	130	153	125	10
2	4:00	140	160	128	11
3	6:00	150	169	132	11
4	8:00	160	181	138	11.5
5	10:00	170	191	140	12
6	12:00	180	203	144	13
7	14:00	190	213	147	13.5
8	16:00	200	223	148	13.5
9	18:00	210	232	151	14.5
10	20:00	220	243	156	15
11	22:00	230	252	159	16
12	24:00	240	264	162	17
13	26:00	250	273	165	18
14	28:00	260	284	166	18.5

Note: This was a test at the beginning of the season. Athlete just finished a 4-week break after her last race of the year in October. Athlete was near her lactate threshold around 250 watts and a HR of 159 bpm. Her RPE was around 16 indicating the test was becoming harder as she started to accumulate more lactic acid.

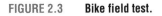

FIGURE 2.3   **Bike field test.**

Run Field Test

On the run field test (figure 2.4), I used 2-minute stages, increasing in load by .5 mile per hour (mph), or .8 kilometer per hour (km/h). This test was done on a treadmill at a 3 percent incline. I found my functional lactate threshold around 2 minutes at 9.6 mph with a HR of 170 beats per minute (bpm) and a RPE of 15.5. To determine that my functional lactate threshold was around 170 bpm, I took into account my respiration pattern, my RPE, and my previous experiences with training and the same test. Field tests do require you to have some experience in order to find your functional lactate threshold as you learn more about how your body feels during these tests. Even though I was able to go beyond this point, my respiration rate really increased and the effort became much harder.

Swim Field Test

For testing in the pool, USA Triathlon uses a standard test. The protocol is 200 meters at a hard pace followed by 800 meters at race pace. This protocol provides an average pace per 100 meters, which for me was around 1:16. This test is very applicable to open-water 1,500-meter swimming. The more I raced the 1,500 in the open water, the more I learned that it was about strength rather than speed. This type of test will

Warm-up:	10-min warm-up 3% grade starting at 5 mph, increasing speed by 5 mph every 2 min				
Interval	Duration (min)	MPH	HR	RPE (6-20)	Recovery HR (bpm)
1	10:00	Any			
1	2:00	6.0	109	9.5	
2	2:00	6.4	112	10	
3	2:00	6.8	119	10	
4	2:00	7.2	126	10.5	
5	2:00	7.6	133	11	
6	2:00	8	141	11.5	
7	2:00	8.4	150	12.5	
8	2:00	8.8	156	13.5	
9	2:00	9.2	163	14.5	
10	2:00	9.6	170	15.5	
11	2:00	10	175	17	
12	2:00	10.1	176	19	
13	2:00	10.8			111
14	2:00	11.2			
15	2:00	11.6			
16	2:00	12.0			

Note: Recovery HR was taken after 2 min; it dropped to 111. Athlete's test demonstrated she was very strong aerobically. For training, athlete should focus on gaining strength at the HR of 155-165 for the majority of her runs. If she runs slower than this, she will work on aerobic capacity, which is already very developed. For athlete to improve speed in the 10k, she needs to work primarily in the 165-170 range, combining this with anaerobic power intervals such as 1- and 2-min all-out efforts.

FIGURE 2.4 **Run field test.**

give you a parameter for pacing while training in the pool for open-water swimming. The goal is to have top-end race speed at the start during open-water swims, but then be able to hold a high pace and hold or clear lactate acid. The goal is to exit the swim without having a high amount of lactate in your body so that you can execute the bike stage well.

Ultimately, speed is most important in racing, but the best outcome in racing results from training the aerobic strength side of the swim. This is very different from dryland strength training.

Strength Training

Many triathletes are unsure about how important strength training is and whether they should include it in their weekly programs. If you decide to add strength training, you may be confused about what type is best for triathletes. Weight training, functional strength, Yoga, Pilates, and active and passive stretching are just a few types of strength training.

I have tried all types of strength training. My conclusion is that each athlete is individual and needs to find the mix of strength training that works best for her. One common theme, however, is that strength training is an important component of triathlon. If this area is neglected, over time, athletes will not perform to their potential and may even suffer compensation injuries.

Triathlon relies heavily on the large muscle groups. Once the large muscles fatigue, the small stabilizer muscles have to work really hard. If those muscles have not been trained, form begins to break down, which may lead to injury. Many athletes do not realize how important the trunk and core are in swim, bike, and run. The core is one of the most important areas to stabilize and strengthen in order to get the most out of triathlon training and racing.

I have focused on core strength in the past, but my 5 to 10 minutes spent on core three times a week was not enough for me. After I had a baby, I took a Pilates class and began to realize what core strength and stability meant for a triathlete. Two or three times a week, I focused on an intense hour-long class that emphasized core stability and hip flexor, glute, and back strength. Over time, I noticed how much more connected I felt while running. It was amazing to see the crossover between Pilates and the increased amount of strength during running.

At the same time I began Pilates, I also was seeing a physical therapist (PT). I was determined to correct the compensation issues I had developed over 10 years of bike crashes, injuries, and racing. The PT helped me work on biomechanical issues and gave me daily homework. The exercises were simple stretching and strength exercises that took no more than 10 or 20 minutes per day. Being consistent every day is key to really seeing improvement over a couple months, just like training for swim, bike, and run.

In addition to Pilates and my daily stretching and strength training, I also lifted weights. I focused on squats, lunges, and other lower-body weight training. I have done this type of strength training for many years, performing more in the off-season and tapering the strength training during the race season. It's difficult to keep up with strength training during race season; however, this year I know it will be just as important as getting in a swim, bike, or run.

Several months into the off-season, I wanted to improve my strength training. I worked with a personal trainer who identified my muscle weaknesses and imbalances after watching me perform a few mobility movements. My main weakness is common in triathletes: weak glute muscles due to tight hip flexors (think about the bike position). When the hip flexors begin to get tight, they acutely shorten at the muscle belly and start to overpower the glutes. When the glutes are overpowered, they gradually begin to atrophy, and the hip flexors become more overpowering. The hip flexors begin to shorten because of the time spent on the bike in a fixed range of motion. The more aggressive position on a time-trial bike puts the hips in a more flexed angle. The great amount of time triathletes spend on the bike causes an imbalance between the hip flexors and glute strength. The hip flexor muscles include the iliopsoas, sartorius, rectus femoris, tensor fasciae latae, and pectineus. These muscles stabilize and flex the knee toward the chest. In addition, I have floppy ankles due to years of swimming and a number of ankle rolls over the years. I am focusing on balance by performing much of my strength training on one leg. This forces me to work on strength and balance and isolate my weak muscles at the same time. Another area I needed to work on was my rib cage and back flexibility. Again, spending so much time on the bike can make this area very tight. This tightness is counterproductive to proper run mechanics and technique, not to mention everyday posture.

The personal strength-training session makes my brain as fatigued as my body. I realized in the past that I was just going through the motions. When performing weighted squats, I was essentially making my stronger muscles stronger and making my weaker muscles weaker! I was almost always completing exercises on both legs, which does not improve balance and equally strengthening both legs. I realize that when I complete every repetition, I have to focus on what I am doing, making sure I am turning on all the muscles required. I have to think about proper form before I can think about adding any weight.

Before starting any specific strength training, I run through a series of warm-up exercises. The dynamic warm-up routine helps activate the body to perform its best.

Before starting a strength program, I highly recommend that you work with someone who can help you with form and technique and find your muscle weaknesses. This will help you stay injury-free and allow you to push your training to the next level by balancing your body. It is hard to know if you are completing an exercise correctly, so that immediate one-on-one feedback is really important. Even if you have a personal trainer work with you only for a couple sessions, you can continue those exercises on your own using what you have learned.

Most triathletes need to work on hip strength and flexibility, hip flexor strength and stability, glute strength, back and core strength, and shoulder flexibility. Every athlete is different, and it's important to have an evaluation based on prior injuries and muscle imbalances.

Developing Glute Strength

The importance of glute strength training for triathletes is primarily for running and cycling strength and speed. Often, a triathlete's hip flexors become tight due to hours on the bike. An athlete with tight hip flexors is unable to use her glutes effectively, leading to a glute dysfunction down the line. By stretching and strengthening the hip flexors and strengthening and teaching the glutes to fire, you will improve your running biomechanics. This will equate to less injury and a more economical running form. After all, the glutes are among the most powerful muscles in the body, so it makes sense to use them.

Single-Leg Wall Squat With Physioball

Start by placing the ball between the midback and the wall. Stand on one leg that is far enough out in front of the body that when the knee is at a 90-degree angle, the knee stays over the heel (figure 2.5). The ball will move up and down the body as you squat up and down. The prime movers are the glutes and quads. The stabilizers are the lower leg muscles and the pelvic muscles that keep the hips square.

FIGURE 2.5   **Single-leg wall squat with physioball.**

Standing Lunge

Start in a split-leg stance with one leg out front and one leg behind. The key is to go straight to the floor, keeping your spine in a straight line and the front knee behind the toes (figure 2.6). This exercise strengthens the glutes while stretching the hip flexors.

FIGURE 2.6   **Standing lunge.**

Side Lunge With Band

You will need a partner. Place a band around one leg and give the other end of the band to your partner. Stand with feet shoulder-width apart and lunge to the side with the band. As you lunge to the side, your partner pulls lightly on the band to provide resistance (figure 2.7). The key is to keep the hips, knees, and ankles stable and under control and not let the band overpower your stability. This works on the adductors and the abductors to stabilize the hips.

FIGURE 2.7 **Side lunge with band.**

Towel Lunge

Stand with feet shoulder-width apart. Place a towel under one foot. Slide the foot with the towel behind you, trying to keep the upper body still (figure 2.8). Keep the front knee over the heel. Slide the foot back to the starting position and repeat. This exercise works on the glutes and quads and stretches the hip flexors at the same time.

FIGURE 2.8 **Towel lunge.**

Overhead Squat With Foam Roller

Place feet shoulder-width apart and hold a foam roller over your head (figure 2.9*a*). Go down to a squat position, trying to keep the foam roller directly above your head (figure 2.9*b*). This exercise works the upper thoracic spine as well as the glutes and quads.

FIGURE 2.9   **Overhead squat with foam roller:** *(a)* starting position; *(b)* squat.

Improving Core Strength

A strong core is very important in all three disciplines of triathlon. For correct swim technique, athletes heavily rely on their core while rotating their hips and arms through the water. On the bike, a strong core is important for efficient breathing and generating power through the hips. In addition, the stronger the core on the bike, the stronger the core will be during the running segment. Once the core fatigues, run form often falls apart. Core strength keeps athletes balanced and fluid while running. The core helps with knee and arm drive as well as powering the body forward. The core is something to strengthen every day of the week!

Single-Foot Plank (Front and Side)

For the front plank, place your elbows under your shoulders and your feet behind you (figure 2.10*a*). Brace yourself using an isometric contraction of the core. Lift one leg off the floor (figure 2.10*b*). Hold for 30 seconds to 2 minutes. The front plank works the core stabilizers; lifting the leg works the glute muscles.

For the side plank, lie on one side and place the elbow under the shoulder. Lift the hips toward the ceiling. Extend the top arm and lift the top foot toward the ceiling so you are in a jumping-jack position. This exercise works the core stabilizers and the hip abductors. This is a great exercise for balance and coordination.

FIGURE 2.10   Single-foot plank: *(a)* plank; *(b)* plank with leg lift.

Hip Flexor–Glute Toe Raise

Start in a kneeling position with one leg in front at 90 degrees and the toes of your back foot pressing down. Place your hands out in front of you, palms facing away from you and fingers pointing together (figure 2.11). Contract the pelvic floor to stabilize the pelvis, and then lift the knee off the ground. Think about lifting the body straight up off the floor with the glute muscles of the leg in front of the body. The quads and hip flexors of the back leg will act as stabilizers to maintain a secure foundation and keep the hips square as you hold the knee off the ground about 1 inch (2.5 centimeters). Hold the position for 10 seconds to start, working up to 2 to 5 minutes as you get stronger. This exercise also strengthens the small extensor muscles in the feet. Both the glute and hip flexors are contracted isometrically to maintain the position.

FIGURE 2.11   **Hip flexor–glute toe raise.**

Bridge

Lie on your back and bring your heels toward your butt. Lift the hips off the ground so you are supported by your heels and shoulders (figure 2.12a). You can progress to lifting and extending one leg at a time (figure 2.12b) and alternating (figure 2.12c). This exercise works the glutes, hamstrings, and lower back while stabilizers in the core work to keep you balanced.

FIGURE 2.12   Bridge: *(a)* basic lift position; *(b)* leg extended; *(c)* leg extended toward ceiling.

Building Hip Flexor Strength and Stability

Hip flexor strength and stability are important in all three triathlon disciplines. In swimming, the hip flexor drives kick momentum. New swimmers often believe that the power from the kick is generated from the quads, but this will lead to a kick that forces the body up and down, not forward! On the bike, hip flexors are important for powering the pedal stroke. Especially in time-trial position on the bike, the hip flexors have a tendency to become shortened due to aerodynamic positioning. Therefore, it is really important to stretch the hip flexors after every long ride. On the run, the hip flexors are the primary muscles that work on hip flexion, which sets athletes up for a powerful push-off. Tight hip flexors limit stride length and the power of each step a runner takes.

I encourage hip flexor stretching and strengthening before and after runs. Before a run, I recommend active stretching. Perform five or six repetitions of hip flexor exercises to wake up the muscles and get them ready to fire while running. After a bike or run, complete more static stretches, holding each stretch for 30 or 60 seconds on each leg. Athletes who work on stretches each day will see a positive translation to their running with a greater stride length.

Lean-Back Hip Flexor and Quad Stretch

Kneel on the ground (figure 2.13a) and lean back (figure 2.13b) while keeping the hips square. This exercise both stretches and strengthens the quads and hip flexors.

FIGURE 2.13   Lean-back hip flexor and quad stretch: *(a)* starting position; *(b)* lean back.

Leg Raise

Lie on your back and lift the legs toward the ceiling (figure 2.14*a*). Try to keep the legs straight. Lift them from the floor to 90 degrees. Slowly lower them toward the floor (figure 2.14*b*). This exercise works the abdomen muscles and hip flexors.

FIGURE 2.14   Leg raise: *(a)* lift feet toward ceiling; *(b)* lower feet toward floor.

Stretching

After a long day of training, stretching can help accelerate recovery. Spend 10 to 15 minutes focusing on breathing and letting the muscles relax. I am always amazed how much better I feel after letting go and unwinding the body and mind. Stretching is often the first thing to go when triathletes are cramming in a tightly packed schedule. I feel it is more beneficial to cut your run by 5 or 10 minutes so that you can stretch rather than get in the car right away and head off to work without a stretch. Plan time accordingly, and don't forget about the little things. After all, focusing on the little things will help you achieve your big goal. Going to a yoga or Pilates class several times a week helps me set specific times each week so I know I won't cut myself short on strength training and stretching.

Conclusion

During race season, it is tough to be consistent with strength training due to extra travel and fatigue from racing. Still, it's great to stick to a routine that you can do anywhere—in a hotel room or even at the airport on a layover. Travel can make you feel sluggish and tight, so it's especially important to stretch while traveling to and from a race.

Remember that everyone is different and needs to focus on what works for her body. For example, if you have broken your collarbone in the past, you may need to focus on more shoulder strengthening and stability in the gym. If you have had Achilles issues, you may need to focus on foot strengthening and stability exercises. Focus on your weaknesses and set up a program that is tailored to your specific needs.

CHAPTER 3

Fueling the Female Triathlete

Stacy T. Sims, PhD

While the participation of women in sport has increased significantly over the last several decades, research on women athletes has lagged behind that on men. Besides the obvious differences, women have a physiology that is different from men's. Until very recently, most of the studies regarding nutrition and training were conducted on men. That's great for the guys, but women have a menstrual cycle that prevents generalizing, that is, concluding that what's good for a man must be good for a woman. To make things even more complicated, our hormone levels fluctuate between low and high during a 28-day cycle until we hit menopause, which changes our bodies' responses to exercise and food yet again!

Why has research on women in sport lagged behind that on men? Primarily, it has been deemed too difficult to include women in research because of hormone fluctuations. Other times, the research that has been done looks at women in the first 14 days of their cycle, when hormone levels are low and women's responses are very close to men's.

As most women know, symptoms that accompany menstrual cycles vary considerably. Some women do not experience any symptoms; others may suffer slight to severe discomfort before or during initial flow. Changes in exercise performance during the menstrual cycle vary as well. Many women report impaired performance, and just as many do not. A number of women have won Olympic medals while menstruating. Some women experience some minor discomfort but merely push themselves forward during participation. Because most variations in performance are due to the high hormone levels, it is helpful to look at how high levels of estrogen and progesterone, both natural and consequent to the use of oral contraceptives, affect women and performance.

Note: Most formulas and units of measure are provided in metric only. It is simple to convert these measurements with any online conversion tool.

Metabolic Changes and Fueling

As women we have different feedback mechanisms for metabolism during exercise, as compared to men, that strongly influences how we recover. Our recovery window is smaller, and we have a predisposition to become overtrained if we perform too much intensity during different parts of our cycles. Why?

Estrogen decreases the reliance on liver glycogen, increases fat utilization, and decreases amino acid breakdown during exercise. These fuel responses have been attributed to a sex difference between catecholamine (a hormone released by the adrenal glands) responses during exercise. Men release a larger amount of catecholamines at a given moderate- to high-intensity exercise load than women who have similar training status. This glycogen-sparing, increased fat use is even greater during the high-hormone phase (luteal phase) of the menstrual cycle when estrogen is at its highest concentration.

How does this translate to everyday practice? Women have a greater capacity for burning fat and sparing glycogen (in both the liver and the muscle) in the high-hormone phase. To maintain the capacity to hit intensities, women should look to stay on top of carbohydrate intake during exercise in this phase; but during the low-hormone phase, a woman can afford to ingest less carbohydrate than her age- and fitness-matched male counterpart (think 45 to 55 grams per hour as opposed to 65 to 70 grams per hour) (Henderson et al. 2008; Enns and Tiidus 2010; Devries et al. 2006).

Does this mean a female triathlete needs to eat more fat? Actually, not necessarily. Researchers have looked at the recovery phase in men and women. Although women metabolize and use more fatty acids during prolonged exercise and we have greater fat stores than men, women have a greater ability to maintain energy substrate stores during exercise and during recovery. Three hours postexercise, men still have higher rates of blood glucose fluctuations and lower glycogen stores, whereas women are relatively close to the preexercise state. This also contributes to the harder-to-get-lean issue that many women face due to a lesser window of elevated metabolic state and fatty acid use at rest (Boisseau 2004).

Protein Use During Exercise

Although there is no reported sex difference in the muscle enzyme that controls muscle breakdown and use of protein during exercise, during the luteal phase of the menstrual cycle, progesterone (or a lower estrogen-to-progesterone ratio) increases the use of protein during exercise. This phase difference is important to note for recovery since amino acids are key to immune function as well as muscle adaptations to stress (Burd et al. 2009; Kriengsinyos et al. 2004).

There are differences in how a woman's body fuels itself for exercise, but how do we apply this information? First, it is important to understand that women have greater fat stores than men and access fat to a greater degree during exercise, thus sparing liver glycogen. Women don't oxidize as many branch-chain amino acids during exercise as men; but in the luteal phase of the menstrual cycle, there is a greater reliance on protein during exercise and at rest. Thus recovery protein intake is critical for muscle synthesis and recovery.

The postexercise recovery phase is different for a woman. Two to 3 hours postexercise, a woman's metabolism is pretty close to her preexercise or baseline levels.

Therefore the 2-hour recovery window after the first of a twice-a-day exercise session needs to be carefully planned in order to restore muscle fuel stores. This quick return to baseline metabolism also contributes to the reduced ability of women to get lean. Again, women need to take advantage of the 2-hour window to promote body composition change and glycogen–fat store recovery.

Hydration During Exercise

Plasma is the watery component of blood that reduces the thickness of the blood and allows blood to flow quickly to working tissues. When we begin to sweat, plasma volume is lost first, as this is the fluid that helps make up the sweat. We sweat to reduce heat. As women, we have an elevation of our resting core temperature in the luteal phase of the natural menstrual cycle, and in the last 15 days of oral contraceptive pill (OCP) use, due to elevated progesterone concentrations. The increased progesterone stimulates the phrenic nerve, increasing respiration. It also acts to increase sweat production later than in the low-hormone phases of the menstrual cycle. Thus, with elevated progesterone, there is a natural resetting of the baseline body temperature by as much as .3 to .5 degrees Celsius. When this is coupled with an increased time to sweating during the luteal phase, it can be seen that athletic performance is compromised due to higher body temperature and lesser ability to get rid of the heat. What's more, high estrogen and progesterone act on the kidney's hormones to reduce plasma volume, a drop of up to 8 percent from ovulation to the midluteal phase. This fluid redistributes, causing the bloating often associated with premenstrual syndrome (PMS). In general, during the luteal phase of the menstrual cycle, women are less able to cope with the heat and have a reduced ability to sweat to remove the heat from deep inside the body.

With elevated estrogen and progesterone, the water in the blood (plasma volume) drops by about 8 percent, reducing the water available for sweating and blood circulation. Elevated progesterone leads to increased total-body sodium losses, predisposing women to hyponatremia. Progesterone is thermogenic, meaning that it increases resting internal (core) temperature by .5 degrees Celsius, reducing heat tolerance and cognition.

For a female triathlete, a nutrition plan for training and racing is critical to race success, just as a specific swim, bike, run training plan gets her fit for the starting line.

▶ What About Peri- and Postmenopausal Women?

There is very limited research on postmenopausal athletes, but there is quite a bit on the changes in body composition and muscle integrity with menopause and the transition into menopause.

A few key points to remember when the hormone flux ceases (i.e., menopause):

■ Blood vessels are less compliant, meaning that blood pressure changes are slower.

■ Core temperature flux tolerance is lower, meaning that the athlete can't handle hot temperatures very well.

■ The athlete sweats later in activity and vasodilates longer as the body tries to get rid of heat by sending more blood to the skin instead of relying on sweating for cooling over a longer period of time.

(continued)

What About Peri- and Postmenopausal Women? *(continued)*

■ Sensitivity to carbohydrate is greater, causing more blood sugar swings and less need for carbohydrate overall.

■ The body uses protein less effectively, so the type and quality of protein eaten and the time it's eaten become very important for building lean mass and holding on to it.

■ The athlete experiences less power production and therefore should train for power, not for endurance, on the bike and in the gym.

Postmenopause, women have issues similar to those of women who still menstruate. The one key thing to remember is muscle function and the quality of the muscle (i.e., integrity). If the athlete doesn't maintain muscle integrity, she can't hit intensities, can't produce power, and will gain body fat around the abdominal region in particular.

Women should still focus on hydration to maintain blood circulation, especially with the increased initial reliance on vasodilation and the lack of heat tolerance. Using a hydration product that is designed for hydration (not calories) will help maintain blood volume and ease some of the thermoregulation challenges. Using a small amount (3 to 5 grams) of branch-chain amino acids (BCAAs) before training will help dampen central nervous system fatigue and help with recovery. The actual recovery window is the most important aspect of all in peri- and postmenopausal women. Trying to maintain muscle integrity and really adapt depend on the ability to have reduced stress hormones and bathing the broken muscle fiber in essential amino acids. Within 30 minutes, consuming 25 to 30 grams of a whey- and casein-based protein source (nonfat Greek yogurt is one of the best recovery foods) will release amino acids into the system over the course of a few hours, extending the time the muscles have for synthesis and reparation. This dose of protein also helps extend insulin sensitivity, so that the carbohydrate consumed with the next meal will go to replenishing glycogen, not stimulating cortisol and belly fat storage.

A note on soy: Soy is not an ideal source of protein for postmenopausal women. It has an amino acid profile that may help stop the breakdown effects of exercise, but it does not have a high enough BCAA profile to trigger muscle synthesis.

Training Nutrition Plan

Training nutrition is part of lifestyle nutrition. What you eat and when can directly affect your body composition, recovery, sleep, and training adaptations. You need a specific plan to ensure you are meeting your body's needs for increased nutrient requirements, as well as to ensure proper recovery. Remember, training adaptations occur during recovery, not during training itself. The increased nutrient requirements depend on your training volumes, frequency, and intensity. Your requirements also vary during the different training phases of the year.

Female athletes must focus on these critical elements:

■ Get quality sleep, at least 7 to 8 hours per day. Fewer than 7 hours is associated with greater cardiovascular and metabolic disease risks and reduces the amount of time your body has to repair. If you have problems sleeping, try kava or valerian tea before bed.

- Frontload calories near the beginning to middle of the day. The body is primed for food and is less sensitive to carbohydrate during the morning to midday time frame. Growth and repair happen during sleep; thus protein is essential in the evening.

- Increase protein and fat intake, reduce hidden sugars, eat more throughout the day, and eat a wide and varied selection of fruits, grains, and vegetables. Think color!

- During recovery, you'll have a 30-minute window for protein with a bit of carbohydrate (25 to 30 grams of protein with 10 to 15 grams of carbohydrate) and up to 90 minutes postexercise to replace glycogen by eating a carbohydrate-rich meal. These two windows are important to separate. The postexercise protein is used to repair and rebuild muscles as well as extend insulin sensitivity. This extended insulin sensitivity gives your body a longer window in which it can take carbohydrate and store it as muscle and liver glycogen. If you do not extend the insulin sensitivity, your ability to restore glycogen diminishes to about 45 minutes postexercise.

- Recent research has shown a direct effect of the gut microbiota on stress and associated cravings; primarily, the chemicals produced by the bacteria affect the host's nervous system (e.g., microbiome–gut–brain axis). Individuals who are stress-prone (anxiety, poor sleep, high heart rate) with salt–fat cravings have been shown to be low in the Lactobacillus strain, in particular *L. casei* and *L. helevticus,* and *Bifidobacterium longum.* Treating the gut with probiotics can decrease the effect on the vagus nerve, reducing stress-related responses and salt–fat cravings.

The Triathlete Diet

There has been a recent upsurge in anti-Western diet philosophy, with a movement toward higher-fat, higher-protein, and lower-carbohydrate intake in which the *kind* of food matters as much as or more than the *macro*nutrient aspect of the diet. This increased interest in the use of nutrition and nutrient timing as a method for improving general health and wellness is a good thing.

But where does this fit in with regard to athletes? There's substantial debate about the efficacy of a lower-carbohydrate, no-grain diet and its relationship to actual athletic performance. You may have heard that low-carbohydrate, high-fat diets are awesome for performance. Well, sort of. Yes, low-carbohydrate diets do increase fatty acid oxidation during exercise and encourage intramuscular fat storage. The body is smart. If there isn't enough primary fuel to support the stress it's under, it'll go for a secondary source, in this case fat, and then store more of it for the next time it encounters that stress. But this does not translate into improved performance, as the ability to maintain high-intensity or prolonged exercise is compromised (Burke 2010). Differences aside, the body needs carbohydrate to exist. And it needs accessible carbohydrate to perform in our cycling–endurance world.

Role of Carbohydrate

First, some basic physiology. The roles of carbohydrate in the body include providing energy for working muscles, providing fuel for the central nervous system, enabling and perpetuating fat metabolism, and preventing the use of protein as a primary energy source. Remember, carbohydrate, specifically glucose, is the preferred source of energy for muscle contraction and biologic work.

Second, glycogen (the storage form of glucose in the muscles and liver) is limited in its storage (about 300 grams of muscle glycogen and 40 to 45 grams of liver glycogen in a nonobese 60-kilogram [132 pound] woman). The glycogen stored in the muscle is used directly by that muscle during exercise. It cannot borrow glycogen from other, resting muscles. Hence, it becomes critical for the endurance athlete to replenish glycogen stores.

Third, the minimum intake of carbohydrate necessary for survival is 130 grams per day to support the central nervous system, red blood cell production, the immune system, and tissues dependent on glucose. But this 130 grams does not support additional physical activity.

When we examine the effects of aerobic exercise on muscle glycogen utilization, intensity and duration of the exercise directly affect the amount of glycogen used. It's common knowledge that low-intensity exercise (e.g., 20 to 30 percent $\dot{V}O_2$max) uses minimal glycogen. But when the intensity approaches 75 percent of $\dot{V}O_2$max, muscle glycogen is almost completely depleted after 2 hours of cycling. It is interesting to note, on intensity, that the rate of glycogenolysis is higher in type IIa and IIb muscle fibers at intensities greater than 75 percent $\dot{V}O_2$max (usually type I fibers deplete first); thus in a race situation when it's "Go" from the gun, the actual rate of total-muscle glycogen depletion will be faster, increasing the probability of early fatigue. It appears that glycogen availability is the primary limiting factor with respect to sustaining intensity during prolonged exercise, with the initial amount of glycogen stored in the muscle directly proportional to the athlete's ability to sustain work rates greater than 70 percent $\dot{V}O_2$max over time. With dietary carbohydrate a significant contributor to muscle glycogen stores and thus performance, how does an athlete maximize her stores on a lower-carbohydrate, no-grain diet? The best answer is to use your body's natural windows of glycogen replenishment and specific types of carbohydrate to maximize glycogen stores.

Muscle glycogen synthesis is more rapid if carbohydrate is consumed directly after exercise as opposed to several hours later. Several pro athletes I've worked with had the idea that if they delayed food postexercise, they would maintain fat burning and lose weight more effectively. In fact, it did the opposite. It put them in a catabolic (breakdown) state that perpetuated weight gain and led to inadequate recovery. The difference between eating within 30 to 60 minutes postexercise and 2 to 2.5 hours later is a 50 percent reduction in glycogen synthesis. As those minutes tick away, insulin sensitivity declines, resulting in a slower rate of muscle glucose uptake and overall glycogen storage. Eating immediately after exercise delays this decline in insulin sensitivity; thus you can extend the ability to rapidly store glycogen by up to 8 hours with a hit of carbohydrate every couple of hours.

Perhaps you've heard that you need to mix protein and carbohydrate postexercise. There are three key reasons for this. First, protein intake within 30 minutes of exercise shifts the body from the catabolic state of exercise into the anabolic (muscle repair and synthesis) state. Carbohydrate helps this by increasing muscle insulin sensitivity. Second, the ingestion of carbohydrate and protein postexercise can reduce inflammation and positively affect the immune system. The third, and most interesting, reason is that carbohydrate and protein work synergistically to increase glycogen storage rates.

In a comparison of glycogen storage rates in the first 40 minutes following exhaustive cycling (3 hours at greater than 75 percent $\dot{V}O_2$max), glycogen storage was four times faster after carbohydrate–protein supplementation (2:1 carbohydrate to protein; 80 grams carbohydrate, 40 grams protein, 6 grams fat) than after an isocarbohydrate supplement (80 grams carbohydrate, 6 grams fat) and twice as fast as with an isocaloric treatment (120 grams carbohydrate, 6 grams fat). The take-home message is that if you are eating a lower-carbohydrate diet, maximize your glycogen resynthesis by eating protein with carbohydrate within the first 30 to 40 minutes postexercise. Then top up with another hit of protein and carbohydrate 2 hours later.

Carbohydrate Sources

Many people believe that the best sources of postexercise carbohydrate are grain based (e.g., oatmeal, pasta, bread, cereals), but this isn't exactly true. The best sources of carbohydrate are those that have a greater composition of glucose or are high on the glycemic index. For example, starchy veggies such as sweet potatoes and yams, winter squash like butternut, and root veggies like parsnips are good options as they are moderate to high on the glycemic index and in carbohydrate content. Raw cassava has 78 grams carbohydrate per cup; mashed plantains have 62 grams per cup; and mashed sweet potatoes have 58 grams per cup. Compare this to cooked oatmeal at 27 grams per cup, quinoa at 39 grams per cup, and the ever-popular cooked pasta at 43 grams per cup.

What about fruit, since it can be high on the glycemic index? The critical difference between starchy veggies and fruit is the type of carbohydrate in each. The veggies are composed of longer chains of glucose, whereas fruit is primarily fructose. Glucose is more efficient at muscle glycogen resynthesis, as fructose is preferentially used by the liver.

What's the bottom line? The metabolic window of opportunity is the time after exercise in which the muscle is highly capable of responding to the anabolic effects of insulin with the ingestion of carbohydrate and protein. Without any nutrient intake, this window begins to close 45 minutes postexercise. By taking advantage of this postexercise window and extending insulin sensitivity with the ingestion of specific carbohydrates with protein, individuals who adhere to a lower-carbohydrate, no-grain diet can maximize glycogen storage.

Lifestyle Nutrition Plan

Food has many connections to us aside from serving as fuel for our bodies. The psychological connection of taste, smell, and texture far supersedes the conscious voice that says "This food is better for me so I should have it." The concept behind the lifestyle nutrition plan is to encourage the selection of nutritious foods that enhance liver and muscle glycogen storage and body fat loss, as well as expanding your overall choices for greater micronutrient intake.

Body composition changes are facilitated with the types of carbohydrate consumed and when (see table 3.1 for 20-gram portions of carbohydrate). The body is primed for a carbohydrate load first thing in the morning and toward midday in an attempt

TABLE 3.1

A 20-Gram Portion of Carbohydrate

Food type	Serving
Bread and baked products	2 slices thin whole-wheat bread 1 slice thick whole-grain bread 1/2 bagel 1/2 large tortilla 1 small pita bread 1 crumpet or English muffin 2 thin pancakes 1/2 muffin (fruit)
Breakfast cereals and grains	1 cup cooked oatmeal 0.6 cup cooked oat bran 1 cup cornflakes, bran flakes, Rice Krispies 3/4 cup Kashi Go Lean 1 cup Nature's Path Optimum flax cereal 1/3 to 1/2 cup low-fat, low-sugar granola 1/2 cup rice 2 cups plain popped corn 1/2 cup cooked quinoa
Fruits and vegetables	1 medium banana 1 large apple, pear, orange, or peach 2 large apricots, grapefruit, or kiwifruit 20 cherries or grapes 12 fresh strawberries 1 cup fresh blueberries 1 cup edamame (soybeans) 1 cup broad beans 0.6 cup garbanzo, kidney, or black beans 2 medium artichokes 3/4 cup sweet yellow corn, raw 1 thick pineapple slice 6 dates or figs, fresh 3 dates or figs, dried 8 dried apricot halves 2 Tbsp. raisins
Dairy products	2 cups nonfat milk 0.8 cup rice milk, plain 1 cup nonfat, low-sugar fruit yogurt 6 oz. kefir
Confections and drinks	1 1/2 Tbsp. jam, honey, maple syrup 1 oz. hot chocolate mix 1.2 oz. chocolate chips

to boost blood glucose levels for the brain, heart, lungs, kidneys, and other organ systems to exist and function. The body becomes more adept at using protein during the midafternoon toward bedtime. (See table 3.2 for 15-gram portions of protein.) Protein is key to many cellular processes and muscular repair, which happens in the hour or

TABLE 3.2

A 15-Gram Portion of Protein

Food type	Serving
Lean meat	2 oz. lean beef, cooked 3 oz. lean hamburger, cooked 2 oz. lean pork or lamb chop, cooked
Poultry and eggs	2 large eggs 1/3 cup chopped chicken or turkey breast, cooked
Fish	1 small baked fillet 1/3 cup canned salmon or 1/4 cup canned tuna 7 oysters 1/2 cup mussels
Dairy products	10 oz. nonfat milk 1 1/4 cups nonfat yogurt 6 oz. nonfat or low-fat Greek yogurt 2 1/2 oz. hard cheese 1/2 cup nonfat cottage cheese 10 oz. kefir
Beans, lentils, and chickpeas	1 cup kidney or baked beans 1 1/2 cups lentils, garbanzo, or black beans 1/2 cup hummus 3 oz. Quorn (nonsoy meat substitute)
Nuts and seeds*	1/2 cup almonds or cashews 1 cup Brazil nuts 1 1/2 cups walnuts or hazelnuts 3 Tbsp. pumpkin seeds 8 Tbsp. sunflower seeds
Breads and cereals**	3 cups cooked rice or pasta (Barilla Plus pasta is a good option) 2 cups cooked quinoa 1 cup low-fat granola with fruit and nuts

*High in good fat content.
**Use minimally as protein sources.

two after exercise and most effectively while you sleep. The key to general eating is to plan several small meals throughout the day, with greater emphasis on complex carbohydrate in the morning and toward midday and a greater emphasis on quality protein midafternoon through evening.

You want to incorporate fat into your diet not only for physiologic functions of the body but also for satiation. (Remember, eating fat does not make you fat; a diet of highly refined food and stress do!) Choose more nuts, seeds, nut butters, avocados, olives, and flaxseed and rice bran oil with minimal trans and hydrogenated fats (fats that are solid at room temperature, including margarine and palm oils).

Choosing foods that are moderate to low on the glycemic index will help curb blood sugar fluctuation throughout the day. One way to moderate the effect of simple sugar or carbohydrate is to add protein; thus protein becomes an important asset to your plan.

The emphasis here is not on weight change, but on improving overall body composition and power-to-weight ratio. For health and performance, focus on eating at regular intervals throughout the day and on recovery nutrition. By fueling the body when it needs fuel, you will recover faster and become stronger.

These are your goals per day:

Carbohydrate: 4 to 5 grams per kilogram of body weight per day

Fat: 80 to 90 grams per day (this may change based on total caloric intake; aim for about 25 to 29 percent of total caloric intake from high-quality fats)

Protein: 1.8 to 2.0 grams per kilogram of body weight per day

This works out to about 45 percent carbohydrate, 30 percent fat, and 25 percent protein. This intake is a baseline intake. The lower number in the range is for rest–recovery days that span a week; the upper end is for long training days. These goals do not include training food; training food is in addition to this baseline intake.

Your carbohydrate choices are essential. Reduce simple processed sugars and choose more complex ones. Think of eating low on the food chain; the more fruit, vegetables, and cold-water fish, the better.

Here is a sample eating plan based on a 140-pound (67.6-kilogram) woman who has a morning and an afternoon training session.

Wake Up 5:30 a.m.

Pretraining, have 6 ounces (170 grams) nonfat Greek yogurt thinned with 4 ounces (118 milliliters) almond or rice milk (vanilla is great!). This provides 130 calories with 16 grams protein and 8 grams carbohydrate. Coffee or tea is fine during pretraining.

Training 6:00 a.m. to 7:15 a.m.

Drink 8 to 10 milliliters per kilogram body weight, per hour, of a low carbohydrate, electrolyte water (when in doubt, a quick fix is 1/8 teaspoon iodized table salt plus 1 teaspoon maple syrup per 20 ounce bottle of water). Due to the pretraining drink, food isn't needed. The postexercise recovery is important.

Breakfast 7:30 a.m. (Within 30 Minutes of Finishing the Training Session)

Choose one option:

- 1 1/2 cups high-protein, lower-sugar cereal (Nature's Path) or 1/2 cup oatmeal that has been soaked in 1/2 cup almond milk overnight. To either, add 1/2 orange or 1 small banana and 1 scoop (10 to 15 grams) protein powder.
- Omelet (4 egg whites plus 2 yolks) with 1/2 cup mixed veggies on 1 piece buttered Ezekiel sprouted-grain toast

Morning Snack 10:00 a.m.

Choose one option:

- 1 low-fat Polly-O string cheese and 20 almonds
- 1 small whole-wheat tortilla spread with 1/2 tablespoon almond–flax butter and 1/2 tablespoon nut spread, topped with 1/4 cup nonfat cottage cheese and 4 crushed strawberries
- 1 slice sprouted-grain toast with 3 ounces (35 grams) low-fat cheddar or Colby cheese, 1/2 tomato, sliced, and 1/4 avocado

Lunch 12:30 p.m.

Choose one option:

- 8 pieces of sushi with edamame, small mixed greens salad
- One 6-inch whole-grain pita filled with 1/3 cup hummus, unlimited vegetables (spinach or kale, cucumbers, tomatoes, and so on), and 1/2 cup low-fat cottage cheese or 1/2 cup grilled lean protein; 1 piece of fruit such as apple, orange, kiwi, or grapefruit
- 1 palm-sized serving of lean protein in a mixed green salad (spinach with berries or apples, walnuts, flaxseeds, peppers, cucumbers, artichokes, or other vegetables)
- Medium tortilla burrito made with quinoa and beans and low-fat cheddar cheese or 1/2 cup low-fat cottage cheese, topped with salsa
- Modified peanut butter and jelly sandwich made with a medium whole-wheat tortilla spread with 2 tablespoons organic almond–flax butter, topped with 1/2 cup nonfat cottage cheese and 4 crushed strawberries; handful of mixed carrots and snow peas

Afternoon Snack 3:30 p.m. to 4:00 p.m. (Pretraining)

Choose one option:

- 2 hard-boiled eggs and 1 small piece of fresh fruit
- 113 grams low-fat Greek yogurt thinned with vanilla almond milk

Training 5:00 p.m. to 6:30 p.m.

Drink 8 to 10 milliliters of fluid per kilogram of body weight per hour. If you have eaten within the last 2 hours, you can afford to just hydrate during this 90-minute session. For intensity sessions, you will want to use a few jelly beans or glucose tablets to help fuel the last few intensity repetitions.

Posttraining 6:45 p.m. (Within 30 Minutes of Finishing the Training Session)

Choose one option:

- 10-ounce (296 milliliters) homemade smoothie made with 8 ounces (237 milliliters) almond milk or other milk alternative, 15 grams protein powder, 1/2 banana, and 1 tablespoon nut butter
- 6 ounces (170 grams) low-fat or nonfat plain Greek yogurt with 1 tablespoon maple syrup or honey

Dinner 8:00 p.m.

Choose one option:

- 1 cup cooked quinoa; 2 cups cooked stir-fry vegetables; 5 ounces (142 grams) lean protein (bison, chicken) or cold-water fish (salmon, cod); 1 tablespoon cashews or almonds; mixed spinach–arugula salad with berries, walnuts, orange, beans, and carrots
- 1 cup broth-based soup (miso, vegetable, chicken); 1 palm-sized serving of protein (lean beef, chicken, or fish); 1 heaping cup of broccoli cooked with 1 teaspoon olive oil; 1 small sweet potato; 2 kiwifruit sliced and sprinkled with 1 tablespoon toasted unsweetened coconut; mixed spinach–arugula salad with berries, walnuts, orange, beans, and carrots

During training, practice for race day fueling. Drink 8 to 10 milliliters per kilogram of body weight per hour of a functional hydration drink (avoid liquid calories) with food. Start food after 45 minutes if on a bike ride lasting 90 minutes or more. Eat nut butter sandwich bites, a handful (about five) of small new potatoes (cooked and salted), three or four rice balls (basmati rice with honey, tamari, or soy sauce), or an engineered nutrition bar with protein, fat, and carbohydrate. Avoid fructose. Your goal is 3 to 3.5 food calories per kilogram of body weight per hour.

Within 30 minutes after training, consume about 25 to 30 grams of protein (whey and casein) and about 50 to 70 grams of carbohydrate. Try a 16-ounce (473-milliliter) smoothie made with 1 small frozen banana, 1/2 cup milk alternative, 1 scoop (20 grams) protein powder, and 1/2 cup low-fat unsweetened yogurt. Get into the habit of having something in the fridge to eat as you are decompressing from your training session.

Training and Racing Nutrition

Training and racing nutrition should be the same. The adage about not trying something new on race day is absolutely true when it comes to endurance racing. The goals of nutrition in these situations should be to

- slow the rate of body water loss (dehydration),
- prevent the depletion of glycogen and energy stores and maintain blood glucose,
- maintain electrolyte balance (and avoid hyponatremia), and
- prevent gastrointestinal upset.

Let's address these goals in depth. There are two critical factors in fatigue: a drop in body water and low energy stores. You can come back from low energy in a few minutes by eating something, but it takes hours to come back from dehydration. Technically dehydration is a loss of body water leading to a drop in blood volume. (Blood volume is based on the water, cells, electrolytes, and other components that make up your blood.)

The idea behind fluid absorption is to slow the rate at which you lose the water component of your blood volume. When you exercise, your muscles and skin compete for blood. The muscles need fuel and also require waste and heat removal. Skin is where the heat is offloaded for convective and evaporative cooling. As you sweat, you lose body water; thus your blood becomes a bit thicker, and the competition between blood demand by the muscles and blood demand by the skin becomes critical. Usually the skin wins out because heat needs to leave the body. By keeping blood volume up, you have a longer time to fatigue, which means greater power throughout your training and racing sessions.

Within the hydration realm, the focus should not be on trying to replace sodium or other electrolytes, and fluid intake should be based on body weight. Two issues are involved in considering what to drink: Is this fluid actually going to be absorbed rapidly? Is the sodium and potassium content high enough to promote fluid absorption (not replace sweat losses), as sodium and potassium work with the body's physiology to help pull fluid into the water spaces of the body?

The body has plenty of sodium stores. Yes, we do lose some in sweat, but the concept of using a sports drink with higher sodium to replace sweat sodium losses is misleading. In the human body, fluid is composed of water and electrolytes. The key electrolyte that allows fluid to move freely is sodium. For maximal fluid absorption, a drink should contain sodium and two sugars, sucrose and glucose, in a 3.5 to 4 percent solution, keeping calories separate. Remember, the goal with exercise hydration is to keep blood volume high so that you can keep blood circulating to the skin and the muscles. If you consume 90 percent of sweat fluid losses and only 50 percent of sweat sodium losses, you will maintain an equilibrium of water and sodium to promote blood volume retention.

How should you fuel if you aren't drinking calories from a bottle? Real food. The calorie in a bottle approach is focused to get a high amount of carbohydrate into the body per hour, but this one-size-fits-all approach is suboptimal; intensity, duration, training history, environmental conditions, and the menstrual cycle phase all dictate what kind of fueling should be used. For high-intensity, short-duration exercise, carbohydrate-focused food such as jelly beans or quick hits of sugar like glucose tablets are ideal; for a longer, slower session, mixed macronutrient food is best. The body is not linear in that metabolism and exercise process change under stress and the affected feedback mechanisms. A hit of carbohydrate fuels the muscles quickly but is not sustainable for longer tempo and threshold-type intensity. Mixed macronutrient foods such as sandwich bites, salted sweet potato bites, or, if you need to go with engineered nutrition, non–soy-based protein bars provide a more even energy level, sustaining fueling for the long duration. Remember, what you eat and drink on the bike directly affects your run. If you overload the system on straight carbohydrate, your body does not have any reserves to draw on for the run, and the chances of gastrointestinal (GI) distress with a triathlon shuffle increase significantly. Aiming for 3 to 3.5 food calories per kilogram of body weight per hour on the bike and 2.5 to 3 food calories per kilogram of body weight per hour on the run will set you up for a strong finish. If you need quick hits of sugar to maintain pace in the last few kilometers of the run, use glucose tablets or jelly beans as in your high-intensity, short-duration exercise sessions. Either of these will minimally affect digestion and allow blood sugar to come up quickly.

Separating Hydration From Fueling

When we consider the biggest issues faced by female endurance athletes, the balance between nutrition and fluid intake to successfully fuel activity and delay fatigue—without causing GI distress—rates right up there with training properly and staying injury-free. Different upper and lower GI symptoms occur in 45 to 50 percent of endurance athletes. The symptoms may be related to more than one cause. The physiology is complex, so the fuel (carbohydrate choices primarily) and fluid you put into your system may compound the problem.

When exercise is intense or when dehydration causes hypovolemia (decreased blood volume), exercise induces changes in blood flow by shunting blood from the gut to the working muscles. This blood shunt effectively causes a bit of hypoxia in the GI tract and increases neural activity of the submucosa (connective tissue) of the gut. This change in the GI tract increases the secretion of certain hormones and decreases absorption through the intestinal cells. This combination induces diarrhea, intestinal cramping, and delayed gastric emptying (extra pressure in the stomach or the slosh factor); and it may lead to some bleeding of the stomach and colon, which is why some people experience blood in the urine and stool. Anti-inflammatory drugs (nonsteroidal anti-inflammatory drugs [NSAIDs], aspirin) aggravate bleeding and interfere with fluid balance in the kidneys, perpetuating dehydration. Anxiety tends to induce lower GI symptoms, and there tends to be a sex difference in symptoms as well. Women have a five times increased risk of diarrhea, intestinal cramping, and side aches as compared to men. Most of this increased lower GI symptom risk is attributed to the fluctuation of estrogen and progesterone, with a greater incidence of lower GI issues during the five to seven days preceding menstruation (the luteal phase of the menstrual cycle). Ingestion of fructose also contributes to women's GI distress and dehydration, as this is one sugar that is poorly absorbed by women.

For fueling, aim for 3-3.5 food calories per kilogram of body weight per hour. For longer, less intense training sessions, try sandwich bites, low-fat brownies, or other real food. For higher intensities, look to use kids' fruit chews, energy chews, jelly beans, or other sucrose-based chewy candy. For efforts that require short bursts of intensity or the last few kilometers of a triathlon run, glucose tablets provide quick hits of sugar that do not affect digestion.

Antioxidants and Supplements

In many athletes' kitchen cabinets is the typical sport nutrition cache of electrolyte drinks, bars, and recovery drinks, and often an array of vitamins and supplements purported to maximize workouts, speed recovery, and minimize downtime and the risk of injury. The Food and Drug Administration (FDA) in the United States doesn't tightly regulate supplements, and often the purported effects are exaggerated or lacking in scientific support. Recently the efficacy of vitamin supplementation, particularly with antioxidants, has come under scientific scrutiny (Peternelj and Coombes 2011; Strobel et al. 2011).

The blurred line of understanding what is good for overall health comes from the existing mentality that what is good in small doses must be great in large quantities. For example, good, strong epidemiologic data suggest that a diet rich in foods naturally high in antioxidants is associated with better health outcomes. But with supplements, the data shift; individuals supplementing with high-dose antioxidants actually have worse health outcomes (Peternelj and Coombes 2011).

But doesn't an athlete, whose body experiences a significantly greater exposure to oxidation due to training, need supplementation? After all, no one can eat 10 pounds of kale a day. Let's examine what oxidation in the body actually is. Cellular organelles called mitochondria are the powerhouses of the cells. These are where the body converts food to energy, a process that requires oxygen and thus is called oxidation. Endurance athletes know the importance of oxygen for steady-state power output (aerobic pathways), but the metabolites left over from the conversion of food to fuel have the potential to damage cells in the form of reactive oxygen species (ROS). Cumulative damage from ROS is referred to as oxidative stress and is generally considered to be one of the major factors leading to DNA (deoxyribonucleic acid) damage (Paulsen et al. 2014; Peternelj and Coombes 2011; Strobel et al. 2011). This is where antioxidants come into play. Antioxidants work to eliminate oxidative stress by neutralizing ROS as they develop, preventing cell damage. Here is the key concept: The body has a series of complex systems that produce its own natural antioxidants to neutralize specific ROS—processes that are too critical and intricate to rely solely on the ingestion of antioxidants.

Exercise, especially of long duration or high intensity, and its consequent tissue injuries are known to increase ROS production in mitochondria. To overcome this increased ROS production, the body must experience the stress and boost its antioxidant capacity. Remember, these are complex systems; not just one component increases, but a series of feedback mechanisms comes into play. When an athlete increases her antioxidant intake through supplementation, the body doesn't fully adapt to increase these systems naturally, and the backlash can be more harmful than ambiguous. Reviews of key studies on the effects of antioxidant supplements on exercise-induced muscle damage are telling. Measures of muscle damage in the bloodstream—enzymes such as creatine kinase that indicate cell rupture—offer no strong evidence that supplementation has any meaningful effect on muscle damage (Paulsen et al. 2014; Peternelj and Coombes 2011; Strobel et al. 2011). Even more concerning, some studies suggest that supplements may induce muscle injury and actually delay recovery (Paulsen et al. 2014; Peternelj and Coombes 2011; Strobel et al. 2011).

It's with regard to the acute recovery period that the data are most concerning. Antioxidant supplements seem to be working against the beneficial cardiovascular effects of exercise. Mechanisms include the following:

- Promoting, rather than reducing, oxidative stress. In some cases, supplements appear to raise, rather than reduce, indicators of inflammation (Peternelj and Coombes 2011).

- Reducing the ability to adapt to exercise-induced oxidative stress. Cells naturally adapt to increases in ROS by upregulating their natural enzyme systems. Supplements have been shown to actually inhibit adaptation (Strobel et al. 2011).

- Affecting physiologic processes such as muscle contraction and insulin sensitivity. Supplementation, by affecting the concentration of ROS, may interfere with muscle function and recovery from the effects of exercise. Several recent studies showed that supplementation with vitamins E and C inhibited the usual insulin-sensitizing effects of exercise (Paik et al. 2009; Paulsen et al. 2014). The result: inhibited glycogen recovery and reduced muscle fiber repair.

Does this mean not only that endurance athletes don't need any supplements but that in fact supplements could work against getting fitter and faster? The short answer is yes. In light of what we know about antioxidants and exercise, the trend in the data strongly suggests zero benefit at best, with the real possibility that supplementation may have negative consequences. We aren't as smart as nature is. Our bodies need the chance to understand and overcome stress, which is the whole concept behind training and adaptation. Look to use real food as the functional components of the body's intricate feedback systems and leave the supplements with antioxidants on the shelf.

Putting It Together

This section presents sample schematics for hydration and fueling for both shorter and longer distances.

Hydration and Fuel for Olympic Racing

For Olympic racing, these are your fluid and caloric intake goals:

Fluid intake (bike and run): 8 to 10 milliliters per kilogram of body weight per hour (in the heat, shoot for the upper end)

Food caloric intake (bike): 3 to 3.5 calories per kilogram of body weight per hour (you can eat more on the bike due to lack of impact)

Food caloric intake (run): 2.5 to 3 calories per kilogram of body weight per hour

For solid foods, try protein bites; peanut butter and jelly sandwich bites pinched into balls; small salted potatoes; white flour tortillas with jam and a sprinkle of salt rolled up and cut into bite-sized pieces; low-fat brownie bites; or engineered nutrition. For semisolid foods, try energy chews, kids' fruit chews, or glucose tablets.

Taper Week

Seven days out and continuing through the week, top off minerals by consuming an extra 300 milligrams of potassium, 150 milligrams of magnesium, 500 milligrams of calcium, and 1,000 milligrams of sodium per day, either through food or supplementation. Magnesium-rich foods include pumpkin seeds, avocados, low-fat or nonfat Greek yogurt, mung beans, and dark chocolate. Focus on increasing total carbohydrate intake, especially posttraining. This is effective carbohydrate loading. Aim for 6 to 8 grams of carbohydrate per kilogram of body weight per day.

Five days out, reduce overall dairy consumption. Use dairy products such as low-fat or nonfat Greek yogurt or whey protein with almond milk for recovery only. Focus on eating regularly and eat minimally processed foods.

If you are staying in a hotel, plan to have on hand almonds or other nuts, oatmeal, yogurt, apples, bananas, oranges, potatoes, salt, bread, almond or peanut butter, jam, almond milk, and chocolate milk

Friday Night

Eat a normal meal.

Saturday Night

Eat an early dinner, around 5:00 p.m. Try quinoa mixed with rice (pasta is too carbohydrate heavy, which causes lethargy and bloating and can lead to poor sleep) along with protein and vegetables. Have a snack before bed, for example, 1/2 cup berries with 2 tablespoons nuts or a protein-oriented nutrition bar.

Race Day Breakfast

Eat almond butter and honey on toast or bread, a banana, and water, or try oatmeal with one scoop of protein powder and almond milk. To prevent GI issues, take one Tums Ultra.

Prerace

Consume an electrolyte drink if you want to. To top off your food, eat half a nut bar or half a bagel with jam.

Bike (40 Kilometers)

Consume a functional hydration drink at a rate of 8 to 10 milliliters per kilogram of body weight per hour. As to food, plan for about 225 to 250 food calories for the 40-kilometer ride; choose from sandwich bites, salted sweet potato cubes, or, if you need to, a protein-oriented bar (no energy chews yet). Take one Tums (calcium carbonate; 500 milligrams) in the last 15 kilometers to help with neuromuscular function and cramp prevention.

Transition 2

Grab one or two Tums and glucose tablets or energy chews for your pocket.

Run (10 Kilometers)

On the course, drink water for fluid. Eat bites of pretzels, jelly beans, gels, or energy chews every 3 to 4 kilometers or take one glucose tablet every 10 minutes.

Hydration and Fuel for 70.3 to Ironman Racing

Here are your fluid and caloric intake goals for longer events:

Fluid intake (bike and run): 8 to 10 milliliters per kilogram of body weight per hour (in the heat, shoot for the upper end)

Food caloric intake (bike): 3 to 3.5 calories per kilogram of body weight per hour

Food caloric intake (run): 2.5 to 3 calories per kilogram of body weight per hour

For solid foods, try protein bites; peanut butter and jelly sandwich bites pinched into balls; small salted potatoes; white flour tortillas with jam and a sprinkle of salt rolled up and cut into bite-sized pieces; low-fat brownie bites; or engineered nutrition. For semisolid foods, try energy chews, gels, kids' fruit chews, or glucose tablets.

If you are racing in the luteal phase of your menstrual cycle, you need to be aware of certain physiologic changes. This is the phase during which your baseline core temperature is about 5 degrees Celsius higher and your plasma volume is about 8 percent less (Stachenfeld et al. 2001; Stachenfeld, Keefe, and Palter 2001; Sims et al. 2007, 2008). You will have a harder time accessing glycogen (Devries et al. 2006; Oosthuyse and Bosch 2010), more difficulty recovering (from a muscle repair standpoint) (Boisseau 2004; Burd et al. 2009; Enns and Tiidus 2010; Henderson et al. 2008), and greater total-body sodium losses with a greater predisposition to hyponatremia (Bisson et al. 1992; Myles and Funder 1996). All of this is due to the higher levels of circulating estrogen and progesterone.

You can work with your physiology to mitigate these changes. First, avoid fructose and maltodextrin in your fueling plan. Both of these increase osmotic pressure in the intestines, drawing water into your gut and reducing the body water available for muscle metabolism and thermoregulation. Second, eat small amounts of salted food at regular intervals and consume a functional hydration beverage with at least 160 milligrams of sodium per 8 ounces (237 milliliters) to reduce GI problems as well as to keep your energy constant. Third, use a sodium-based hyperhydration drink with added BCAAs the night before and morning of the race to top up your sodium stores, increase plasma volume, and supply BCAAs to help mitigate central nervous system fatigue.

Mixing what you're consuming on the course and Tums will help minimize the potential for nausea and GI problems. Using a taper week to top up electrolytes and glycogen stores will help keep you on the right side of the tipping point for GI and cramping problems.

Taper Week

During taper weeks (two to three weeks before the event) stick to your usual recovery food after every training session. Even though you are doing low volume with a bit of intensity, stick to the 30-minute protein and 2-hour glycogen windows. Then, 2 to 3 hours postsession, hit it again with another 20 to 25 grams of protein.

Seven days out from the event (continuing through the week), top up on the essential-to-racing electrolytes. Consume an extra 150 milligrams of magnesium, 500 milligrams of calcium, 300 milligrams of potassium, and 1,000 milligrams of sodium per day, via food or supplementation. Increase total carbohydrate intake for effective carbohydrate loading. Aim for 6 to 7 grams of carbohydrate per kilogram of body weight per day.

Five days out, reduce overall dairy consumption. Use dairy such as low-fat or nonfat Greek yogurt or whey protein with almond milk for recovery only. Focus on eating regularly and eat minimally processed foods.

If you are staying in a hotel, plan to have on hand almonds or other nuts, oatmeal, yogurt, apples, bananas, oranges, potatoes, salt, bread, almond or peanut butter, jam, almond milk and chocolate milk.

Friday Night

Eat a normal meal.

Saturday Night

Eat an early dinner, around 5:00 pm. Try quinoa mixed with rice (pasta is too carbohydrate heavy, which causes lethargy and bloating and can lead to poor sleep) along with protein and vegetables. Have a snack before bed—one protein-oriented bar.

Race Day Breakfast

Eat one or two slices of toast or bread with almond butter and honey with 1 cup cooked oatmeal with one scoop of protein powder and almond milk. To prevent GI issues, take one to two Tums.

Prerace

Consume an electrolyte drink if you want to, and finish your hyperhydration drink 20 to 30 minutes before race start. Top off your food by eating half a nut bar or half a bagel with jam.

Transition 1

You've been swimming for about an hour, and glycogen levels and body water will be a bit low. Your two goals at T1 are eating solid food and hydrating before you jump on the bike. At the transition, have a bottle of your functional hydration beverage that has been frozen overnight (if the weather is hot). Swig a few gulps and grab your solid food (bar, protein bites, sandwich bites) to eat within the first 5 kilometers of the ride as you get up to pace. This will frontload you for the second half of the bike.

If it is a hot race, start with frozen bottles on your bike (they will be semisolid by the time you exit the swim). Have a special needs bag for the bike turnaround. In the bag, have two insulated bottles that have been frozen overnight and wrapped in foil. Try to get as much insulation as possible for a hot race. Have a salty sandwich such as olive tapenade spread on white bread or jam sprinkled with salt on white bread.

Bike, First Half

To the halfway point, drink 8 to 10 milliliters per kilogram of body weight per hour. During the first 3 to 5 kilometers as you ramp up to speed, eat a full bar. Consume sandwich bites, potatoes, bars, or other real food (no energy chews yet). Your goal is 3.5 to 4 calories per kilogram of body weight per hour. Estrogen will accelerate your ability to access fat, but you'll be a bit compromised in tapping into glycogen for any surge or intensity. Mixed macronutrient food is going to be golden to help keep even energy and allow access to more glycogen if needed.

In your special needs bag, have a sandwich on white bread (stay away from fiber and fruit; they will hurt you on the run) and emergency bars that are easier to eat.

Bike, Second Half

In the second half of the bike, you have the same fluid and calorie needs. If you need to switch to energy chews, try to hold off until the last hour of the bike. In your pockets, you should always have Tums. Take one Tums every 30 to 40 kilometers on the return. You want the extra calcium to help prevent cramping and prevent any queasiness in the first 3 to 5 miles (4.8 to 8 kilometers) of the run. Shifting blood and pounding on the gut and leg muscles at the start of the run can cause cramping and nausea; the goal is to minimize it, and Tums is key.

Transition 2

At Transition 2, it would be ideal to have another salty sandwich if possible to prep for the run. This can be sea-salted focaccia bread (similar to a dinner roll, but you don't have to worry about its getting smooshed or any refrigeration factors) or soft pretzel bites. Grab, take a couple of bites, and stash the rest in your pocket or ditch it. Put Tums and glucose tablets in your pocket.

Run, First Half

Drink your functional hydration drink from the bottle you have with you. Take one or two Tums every hour. For on-course emergency fluid, have a half-and-half solution of electrolytes and water. For food, have pretzel bites, salted jam sandwich bites, or protein bites. Hold off on chews until the second half of the run, if possible. If not, then alternate pretzel bites with chews or sport beans.

Run, Second Half

Follow the same fluid plan as in the first half. For food, you can move to chews or sport beans. For the last 10 to 12 kilometers, consume one glucose tablet every 5 to 7 minutes. Take two to four Tums per hour. If you choose to use caffeine, soda is fine, but avoid caffeine tablets.

Conclusion

Research on women and athletic performance is lagging, but information is available to maximize training for performance. Knowing that the high levels of estrogen and progesterone associated with the luteal phase and OCP use affect metabolism, blood flow, thermoregulation, and overall performance can allow women to alter their racing schedule to maximize performance. Moreover, although OCP use is decreasing, many women athletes use the pill to alter their cycles. It is not uncommon for female athletes who regularly compete in hot environments to alter their cycles to compete two or three days post-bleed and achieve excellent performances. This can be attributed to controlled low levels of estrogen and progesterone leading to increased aerobic and anaerobic capacity, lower core temperature, greater plasma volume, and a greater ability to sweat as compared to what is seen in the later stages of their cycles.

It is impossible to alter the training and racing cycles to maximize the benefits of low hormones. However, you can schedule your training and nutrition to maximize a session in accordance with the phase of your menstrual cycle. For example, schedule your high-intensity sessions during the low-hormone phases while scheduling longer recovery and steady-state (low to moderate intensity) weeks during the high-hormone phases of your cycle.

From a nutritional standpoint, focus on recovery especially in the high-hormone phase. To counteract the catabolic effects of progesterone (Tarnopolsky et al. 1997), eat a protein-rich snack within 30 minutes of finishing each session, and then use real food to replace glycogen over the next 2 hours. Begin by keeping a training log and monitoring your cycle versus your performance. This will enable you to establish the strongest and best training days and the days to back off—modifying your training schedule through planning for strenuous sessions, peak training, and rest.

CHAPTER 4

Mental Training for the Inner Athlete

Siri Lindley

In all sports, the mental game is just as important as the physical one. I learned this as an athlete and spent a large part of my career working on strengthening that aspect of my game. As a coach, I put as much thought into training my athletes mentally as I do physically. Performance is directly related to the physical effort extended but also to the mental input distributed throughout the athlete's race.

Limiting Negative Thinking

Psychological preparation is every bit as important as physical preparation. These are closely knit and depend heavily on each other. A coach must be able to prevent an athlete's psyche from sabotaging her ability to perform to her potential. The coach begins by making the athlete mentally aware of her thought processes during training and racing. The coach might have the athlete keep a log of the words she used during a great session and those she used during a bad session. For instance if the athlete had an awesome session and remembers focusing purely on technique cues, like, "shoulders back, chest forward, quick feet" and that led them to their best run, the athlete and coach should note that technique cues are a great way to get into the zone, and in a position to have a great session.

The coach should point out how negative thinking and negative self-talk lead to negative feelings and bad performance but that positive thinking and positive and effective self-talk lead to positive feelings and good performance. Soon athletes really start to see this connection and train themselves to be more disciplined in managing their thoughts and self-talk.

The athlete must understand just how powerful negative thinking can be. She must understand how negative thinking can truly hinder performance. In many cases, negative thinking can be so powerful that it leads an athlete to give up under difficult circumstances.

How does a coach get her athletes to limit negative thinking? The most important thing is to teach them to think process-related thoughts rather than outcome-related thoughts. Whether in training or racing, the athlete will be most successful if she stays focused in the moment, on executing the task to the best of her ability. She must concentrate on technique, effort, and attitude. Athletes need to be laser focused on themselves and themselves alone and doing the best they can in every moment.

These are examples of outcome-related goals:

- Will I swim in the front pack?
- Will I bike as strong as everyone else?
- Will I run my fastest run?
- Will I be able to accomplish the task?
- Am I as good as my competitors?
- Will I succeed? Will I fail?
- Will I win? Will I lose?

These outcome-related thoughts do the athlete no good whatsoever. They just lead to distracted focus and loss of power.

The first step for a coach is to educate the athlete on the power of her thoughts and teach her key words or effective methods of transforming negative thoughts into more effective positive ones. Here are some of my favorite key phrases:

- Concentrate on being the best you can in every moment.
- Stay in the moment.
- Keep it simple.
- You have no control over other people or what they do, so keep the focus on you.
- Positive thoughts lead to positive energy. Negative thoughts lead to negative energy and negative feelings.
- Hone in on the process, not the outcome.
- Believe.

I put my athletes into situations that they are likely to encounter in races or competitive training environments. For example, I'll put two athletes of equal ability on the track together to see who will take the lead, how they will handle the pressure of competition in the moment, and how they react when the going gets tough. I'll experiment with how I deliver the session. I'll watch how they react to a big task such as hitting a certain time for an interval instead of just doing the best they can. I observe their reactions to these stimuli and the ways they perform under the various stressors. Some respond more effectively to the pressure. Others do better with a more open approach that isn't loaded with expectation. Then I pinpoint any vulnerability and incorporate things into their training that will help them get comfortable with these stressors and able to deal with them effectively. Perhaps I can even succeed in turning these stressors into motivators instead.

Being Laser Focused

A crucial lesson in psychological training is to remain calm under stressful conditions, which an athlete accomplishes by a laser focus on the moment and the task at hand. Exercises to strengthen this include, but are not limited to, meditating, breathing exercises, and getting comfortable in a training environment fraught with distractions.

Meditation is going into a silent space in which all your thoughts are on only one thing. Sit quietly, zeroing in on that and that alone. While meditating, breathe deeply and relax the body so you are able to sit quietly and concentrate.

Blocking Out Distractions

For example, I had an athlete who had a terrible problem dealing with all the distractions that popped up in races—athletes drafting, someone taking off early on the swim, being hit on the swim, people yelling out, athletes bantering. He became so distracted by everything going on around him that he struggled to attend to only his own race and thus performed way beneath his potential in every race. When an athlete is less focused and easily distracted, this takes away from the power he can put out in a race or, in a practice, the effectiveness of the training session.

My idea was to have this athlete spend 45 minutes every day meditating in the central play area at a very busy aquatic center. The distractions were endless: screaming children, splashing swimmers, adults chatting over coffee, lifeguard whistles, and water aerobics classes going on all at once. The first time, he left angry, saying how ridiculous this exercise was, how impossible it would be to meditate in such a chaotic environment. I stuck to my guns and demanded he go back every day to try to increase the amount of time he meditated. The session continued to be very frustrating for him, but somehow each day he was able to check out from the chaos and get deep into his own thoughts. Finally, after a couple of weeks, he excitedly reported that he had had an incredible 45-minute meditation. He has no idea how, but he was able to tune out all the chaos and focus entirely within. On the basis of this great success, I let him know that tuning out the minor distractions he would face in a race would be easy in comparison.

Thankfully this exercise led to great improvement in his race performances. He was able to tune out other athletes and disturbing distractions. He focused within and was able to race his own race and tap into his full potential. This was an enormous success and a very valuable tool that he could use to boost his performance. He was no longer vulnerable to the negativity of distractions because he had experience in knowing how to tune them out to the best of his ability.

Worrying About the Competition

Another trap athletes fall into is spending way too much time thinking about what other athletes are doing. The most powerful state for an athlete to be in is one in which her thoughts are on herself and on doing the very best she can in every moment. An athlete has absolutely no control over what anyone else does, so why waste time and energy worrying about what someone else is doing? This only weakens the athlete by taking that valuable attention away from what she is physically doing. Athletes must learn to race their own race and keep the focus within. This gives them the ability to tap into their full potential and to pack the most powerful punch. They will enjoy a much more positive experience that will lead to greater self-understanding and self-confidence.

Thinking and Doing

Productive and positive thinking leads to a positive body response. Negative thoughts lead to a negative body response. An athlete who thinks negative thoughts will only feel worse. She will feel weaker, more tired, and unhappy when her self-talk is primarily negative.

Every athlete is faced with a negative thought from time to time. Such thoughts must never be allowed to replace the positive, productive input that could be orchestrating the race. For instance, two athletes who are struggling at the start of the bike may both say to themselves, "I am hurting so bad, and I feel so weak." Athlete 1 starts thinking damage management. She says to herself, "No problem, I will shift into an easier gear, spin a bit quicker, and flush the lactic acid out of my legs. Surely that will make my legs feel better, and I will start to feel strong again." She has found a productive way to deal with a negative feeling. This productive method and positive encouragement will lead her to start feeling better and regaining her strength.

Athlete 2 takes a different path. She says to herself, "My legs are killing me. Oh my gosh, it's only the first part of the race; I have so far to go. Oh no, they are hurting even more. I'm so tired. I'm so weak. I just got passed by another rider. This is terrible." She dives into a negative spiral and suddenly gets slower and hurts more until she truly believes her day is over and she should quit.

When you see how detrimental negative thinking can be and how powerful positive thinking can be, you understand just how important it is to train the athlete's ability to manage these thoughts. I teach my athletes how to deal with negative situations. I teach them about productive thoughts, to concentrate on form and technique, to reconnect with the basics, relax, breathe, focus, and find some key empowering words that will help catapult them back into a positive frame of mind. In doing this, they find a way to be productive and positive regardless of the circumstances, which helps them to turn the situation around for the better. This then allows them to achieve the success they are working toward. Be relentless in practicing these mental exercises, and make sure to put them to use in races or stressful training situations.

Earning Confidence

An athlete's confidence needs to be well-earned confidence based on truth, not empty words. I make sure that my athletes gain confidence by laying out a plan for them and having them successfully tick off the training each day. The first step is to do the work! As they continue to follow the plan and do the work, they inevitably start seeing great progress. I have them log their sessions so they can see their improvement. They can look back at all the great work they have done, reminding themselves of how ready they are to take on the challenge of a race.

I live by the principle of leaving no stone unturned. We work on every aspect of performance: physical training, mental training, proper nutrition, proper hydration, recovery strategy, and reducing stress. We aim to do everything we can to be fully prepared for every challenge we may encounter in a race.

Another aspect of being prepared is to know the race course and what to expect. An athlete should know the course, the conditions, the rules, the setup, and perhaps even her competitors. Having all this knowledge, the athlete will feel more confident going into the race.

As a coach, I feel responsible for ensuring that my athletes have the honest confidence they need in order to go into a race and perform to their potential. I encourage them to take extra nutrition along in case they accidentally drop some during the race, to be ready for a flat by having tubes or CO_2, and to be ready for anything that could possibly happen in the race.

Visualizing Success

I am a big fan of visualization before a hard session or race. It is important for the athlete to see herself executing properly and racing strong, fast, and confidently. I have athletes go through the whole race from start to finish so as to be mentally prepared and able to visualize doing everything right.

The other thing I do—and it's something that is often neglected—is to have my athletes visualize things going wrong. They visualize having their goggles knocked off or getting a flat on the bike and then dealing with the problem successfully. They see themselves remaining calm and composed and dealing effectively with the situation, forging forward, and ultimately achieving success. This is a very important part of the athlete's preparation going into the race.

Conclusion

All these things I have mentioned help the athlete prepare both mentally and physically, which develops the honest, all-important confidence necessary to achieve a powerful state of mind and thus ultimately success.

The coach can help set the mental stage for athletes going into a race by understanding their emotional stability, mindset, and motivation as well as any sensitivities. The coach must present to athletes, in a clear and powerful way, her ideas on the way they should approach each race. Every athlete is different, so coaches need to be prepared to deliver different words of wisdom depending on the needs of each individual.

One thing every athlete should know is that an athlete can struggle many times in one race. Very few races are perfect. A common misconception is that if an athlete blows up, her race is over. This is untrue. An athlete who does blow up needs to back off for a few moments, regain her composure, and then throw herself back into the game with renewed vigor and positive energy. She must be relentless.

When I won the ITU (International Triathlon Union) Triathlon World Championship in 2001, I exited the swim nearly last. I could have given up right then, assuming my race was over. Instead, I put my head down and went as hard as I possibly could to make it the best race possible from that point forward. I persevered; I was relentless in doing the very best I could in every single moment. I never, ever gave up, inspired to do the best that I could with what I had. I became a world champion that day!

Every athlete must spend a large amount of time training her mental skills. This is nearly as important as training physically. As a coach, my goal is to train athletes to be confident and relentless, and most importantly, laser focused. Coaches must train athletes to be positive and productive while focusing within, and most of all, to never, ever give up.

CHAPTER 5

Alternative Exercises for Triathletes

Sage Rountree, PhD

Training for triathlon is time-intensive. Not only are you executing workouts in three sports, you're also managing equipment, washing laundry, and feeding yourself before, during, and after workouts. All of this comes on top of the regular work and household duties that take up your time. It can be tempting to focus exclusively on your swim, bike, and run workouts, perhaps including a perfunctory weight session at the gym. This busy schedule can sacrifice attention to complementary alternative practices such as Pilates, yoga, barre classes, and the like. But including these modalities for cross-training will have a direct positive effect on your sport performance, as they build core strength and hip flexibility while sharpening your focus and breath awareness.

Pilates and yoga use body weight to cultivate a healthy balance between strength and flexibility. This balance is the key to injury prevention. When your body is out of balance, whether balance in space or balance within the body, front to back, side to side, or top to bottom, you're risking injury. By including alternative exercises to complement your swim, bike, run, and strength training, you'll make your body more injury-proof while developing focus that will help you bear down in your next hard workout or race.

Including Alternative Exercises

While yoga is millennia old, many of the yoga poses we practice today were introduced in the last century. This shift has in part been influenced by bodybuilding and gymnastics, and it has developed in symbiosis with other movement modalities such as Joseph Pilates' system of core exercises. The yoga asanas, or poses, were originally seated postures designed to hold the body still for meditation. Each seated position required, as the Yoga Sutras tells us, elements of *sthira* and of *sukha*—that is, elements of strength, especially in the core to hold the spine long, and of flexibility, especially in the hips to keep the lower body relaxed and still. Obviously, this approach helps shore up the body for active movement as well. But don't discount the psychological and spiritual benefits of the practice. Just like triathlon, yoga and Pilates give us a forum for connection among body, breath, and mind, as well as fertile ground for exploring our understanding of what it means to be alive and in our bodies.

Women, especially those with a history of dance or a current yoga practice, may tend more toward flexibility than strength. But as a triathlete, you need just enough flexibility to move fluidly through your stroke and stride and no more. At some point, flexibility can adversely affect your triathlon performance, as it can make you floppy and inefficient and directly inhibit your power production.

In your yoga practice and core strength and flexibility training, aim to garner freedom of movement and to balance your flexibility with integrated strength. This may mean that you consciously stay away from end-range expressions of stretches, instead keeping your body within the limits of a comfortable stretch and no more. If some poses don't feel intense, that's fine. Not every pose or exercise will directly address your personal imbalances or tightnesses, and this is a good thing. Focus on precise alignment and refined execution of the exercises, valuing integration over taking exercises to the extreme.

To develop just enough flexibility through your body and to balance it with integrated strength, consider the ways you move as you swim, bike, and run. For the swim, you need to have a good reach as your arms move out of and into the water, and enough range of motion through the core that you can rotate along the central axis. Your hips need enough flexibility to allow you to balance in the water, and your ankles need to be open enough that you can kick with a smooth whip of the leg. For the bike you need to move smoothly through the pedal stroke without a hitch in your hip, knee, or ankle, as these hitches can contribute to overuse injuries. For the run you need flexibility in the front of the hips and strength in the back of the hips and thighs so you can push off with your glutes and hamstrings. The exercises outlined in this chapter are specially chosen to help strengthen, stretch, and balance your body for injury prevention and better performance in triathlon.

Yoga and Pilates Exercises

If you have the time, take regular classes with an experienced instructor. Having a teacher observe your form and offer individual feedback, either verbally or with a hands-on assist, helps you develop healthy habits and stay safe in your practice. When you execute the majority of your other workouts solo, it's also nice to practice in a group setting for camaraderie.

While having a regular yoga or Pilates routine can do wonders for your training and well-being, an overenthusiastic practice—too hard, too hot, or too frequent—can adversely affect your performance. Be sure that the highest intensity and volume of your exercise is in inverse proportion to the intensity and volume of your training. The off-season is the time to first investigate these practices. As you grow closer and closer to your peak competition, the physical intensity of your practice should become increasingly more mellow. This is the time for gentle and restorative practices and for a focus on meditation and breath awareness.

The following poses and exercises are derived from yoga and Pilates. You can execute them at home to balance strength and flexibility in the core and hips for better, injury-free performance in triathlon. For more on yoga philosophy and physiology and for ways to fit yoga into your training plan, please see my books, including *The Athlete's Guide to Yoga* (2008), *The Athlete's Guide to Recovery* (2011), and *The Runner's Guide to Yoga* (2012).

Include this routine three times a week in your base period, twice weekly in your build period, and once weekly in your peak period. Follow the poses in the order listed here, and complete enough repetitions or hold for enough breaths that you feel the effects, but don't overdo it. Practiced mindfully, these exercises will have powerful benefits for your swim, bike, and run, as well as your general well-being.

Crescent Lunge

The crescent lunge is a critical exercise both for strength and for flexibility through the hips. It approximates the movement your legs make as you swim, bike, and run. The more balanced and fluid you are in a lunge, the more efficient your movement will be and the more you'll be able to ward off injury.

For the crescent lunge, start by standing tall. Step your right foot back a few feet, and check that it is not directly behind the left foot but still at hip width, a few inches to the right. Keep your left knee directly over the top of the left ankle, but let it bend as much as feels good (figure 5.1). You'll feel a release in the front of the right hip, especially if you push back through the right heel and lift the right thigh toward the ceiling. Your hands can rest on your hips, come to prayer position, or lift overhead, together, parallel, or in a Y position, as your chest stretches. Hold for 10 breaths, then repeat on the other side.

FIGURE 5.1   **Crescent lunge.**

Warrior III

Warrior III asks you to hold the lines of plank pose while standing on one leg. Thus it builds core strength in addition to stability in the hip and lower leg.

Stand tall, then shift your weight into the left foot and lift your right leg behind you as you lean your pelvis and torso forward (figure 5.2). Aim to hold a long line from your foot through your hips and shoulders. Hands can be on the hips, in prayer, or extended off or in front of the shoulders for more challenge. Hold for 10 breaths on each side, and if that's easy, repeat two or three times.

For a quick dynamic warm-up or strength-building two-pose flow, move back and forth between crescent lunge and warrior III. Try to make the transitions refined, deliberate, and smooth. Taking 10 breaths or more while flowing between the two poses will get your hip muscles firing, wake up your lower legs, and build your focus and balance before your workout.

FIGURE 5.2   **Warrior III.**

Front Plank With Leg Lift

Holding strong up the central line of the body is critical for efficiency in the swim, bike, and run; plank is the ideal exercise to build strength up the center. Hold your pelvis neutral and your spine long. Letting the hips sag or lifting the bottom too high will add strain to your back, so find a neutral alignment. Plank (figure 5.3a) can be done on the hands or on the forearms, palms together or parallel. Either keep your knees to the floor several inches behind your hips, or lift to the balls of the feet with the heels pressing back. Hold for three to five rounds of 5 to 20 breaths each.

For more work, try slowly lifting and lowering one leg (figure 5.3b), then the other. This mimics the movement of kicking, pedaling, and running, all of which require that you hold the core steady while the legs alternate movement. To find further challenge, try lifting one arm (figure

5.3c), then the other, which builds strength for the swim stroke and helps you hold a steady line on the bike while you reach for your water bottle. For even more challenge, lift opposing legs and feet simultaneously while holding the central channel of the body long (figure 5.3d). This can be done from any version of plank, whether on the knees, feet, hands, or forearms.

FIGURE 5.3 **Plank variations: *(a)* basic front plank; *(b)* front plank with leg lift; *(c)* front plank with arm lift; *(d)* front plank with opposite arm and leg lift.**

Side Plank

Changing your plank's relationship to gravity will change the challenge. When you rotate your plank to the side (figure 5.4), you'll build strength through the shoulder girdle, the obliques, and the hips. As with the downward-facing plank, side plank can be modified to suit your needs. Try it from the forearm or from the palm, with the knees bent or the legs straight. If your legs are straight, step the top foot in front of the bottom one, or stack the feet, or lift the top foot.

FIGURE 5.4   **Side plank.**

Clamshell

Perform this exercise with as much precision as you can, and you'll soon get to know the gluteus medius, the second layer of gluteal muscles that work to stabilize your hip in a single-leg stance. Staying strong in your glutes relieves pressure from both your deeper hip rotators, such as the piriformis, and your iliotibial band, running along the outside of each leg. This helps keep you injury-free.

Start from your side, head in your hand or resting on your biceps, hips stacked perpendicular to the ground, knees bent, inner edges of the feet together. Inhale and open your top knee to the ceiling while keeping your core in line and your feet touching (figure 5.5a); exhale and clamp the top knee against the bottom knee (figure 5.5b). Complete at least 20 repetitions per side, or as many as you can with good form.

FIGURE 5.5   Clamshell: *(a)* Lift top knee toward ceiling; *(b)* clamp top knee against bottom knee.

Downward-Facing Dog With Leg Lift and Core Plank

Downward-facing dog stretches and strengthens the upper body while it stretches the back of each leg. Adding a leg lift with external hip rotation both twists the spine and releases the outer and front lines of the raised leg while stretching deeper into the hamstrings of the base leg.

Start in an inverted V, hands shoulder-width apart, fingers spread wide (figure 5.6a). Lift your hips while letting your heels sink—they need not hit the ground. Keeping your shoulders squared, lift your left leg and bend the left knee (figure 5.6b). Stay for 5 to 10 breaths.

To add further core challenge to the pose, alternate leg lifts in downward-facing dog with a three-legged core plank. Inhale in the leg lift, then exhale and shift your shoulders over your wrists while you pull the left knee toward the left elbow (figure 5.6c). Swing back and forth 5 to 10 times. To add challenge, hover in core plank for several breaths.

FIGURE 5.6   Downward-facing dog with leg lift and core plank: *(a)* downward-facing dog; *(b)* lift leg; *(c)* lower into core plank.

Bicycle

This classic core move strengthens your obliques and challenges you to hold your core steady while you alternate leg and arm movements. Start from your back, hands behind the head, knees bent. Inhale and lift your head and neck; exhale and drop your left elbow to the floor as you pull the left knee toward the right elbow (figure 5.7). Inhale through center; exhale to the other side. As you cycle, keep your chest open and your spine long. For more work, straighten the leg that's not pulling in. Complete two or three sets of 15 to 20 pulses.

FIGURE 5.7　　**Bicycle.**

Bow

Follow your bicycle crunches with several breaths of bow pose to release the hip flexors and abs while strengthening the back. Roll to your belly and bend your knees, reaching your hands to your feet. If they won't reach, instead choose locust pose, an unconnected form of bow pose. Kick your feet into your hands and lift your shoulders, chest, and thighs off the floor (figure 5.8). Keep your neck relaxed and hold your lift for 2 or 3 sets of 5 to 10 breaths, resting on your belly in between. For more stretch, try holding the ankles or the inner edges of the feet.

FIGURE 5.8   **Bow.**

Bridge With Leg Lift

To strengthen the back of your body from the hamstrings through the glutes and up the spine, take bridge pose and add a series of leg exercises. For bridge, start on your back, knees bent, feet hip-distance apart. In the yoga version of this pose, you will tuck your shoulder blades toward your spine to stretch your chest open. For the leg lifts, however, keep your shoulders in neutral position. Push your feet firmly and evenly into the floor as you raise your hips toward the ceiling (figure 5.9*a*).

After a few breaths in bridge pose, shift the weight into one foot and lift the other toward the ceiling (figure 5.9*b*). If this is tough, do it with your knee bent. If this is easy, alternate your breath: Inhale as your foot reaches toward the ceiling, then exhale and lower your lifted knee alongside your base-leg knee. Complete 10 rounds of leg lifts. For extra challenge, hold your leg in a diagonal line for several breaths. For even more, point your foot toward the ceiling and draw 5 to 10 basketball-sized circles in one direction, then the other. Don't let your hips drop!

Repeat on the second side. Don't be surprised to find this much more challenging for one hip than for the other. You're building critical glute strength that will help keep you injury-free.

FIGURE 5.9   Bridge with leg lift: *(a)* bridge with shoulders in neutral; *(b)* lift one leg toward the ceiling.

Camel With Side Bend

Camel pose is similar to bridge pose, but it uses gravity to pull you into a backbend while releasing the chest and hip flexors. Kneel on both knees, adding padding underneath them if they are sensitive. Keep your pelvis forward, hips over knees. Take your left hand to your left hip and stretch your right arm into the space over the left shoulder for a side bend (figure 5.10). If you have room to go farther, drop your left hand to your left heel for the backbend. (Turning the toes under lifts the heel higher toward you.) Take 10 breaths on this side, then lift slowly and move to the other side.

FIGURE 5.10   **Camel with side bend.**

Squat With Twist

The squat releases your lower legs, shins, thighs, hips, and low back. Adding a twist will help stretch the muscles along the spine, as well as your chest and shoulders. Take a wide squat, knees and toes facing 45 degrees off the midline (figure 5.11a). Drop your hips low, but don't worry if your heels lift. After a few breaths in the squat, lower your left hand to the floor and either take your right hand to your right knee or lift the right hand toward the ceiling (figure 5.11b). Stay 5 to 10 breaths, then repeat on the other side.

FIGURE 5.11   Squat with twist: *(a)* wide squat; *(b)* lower hand to floor and twist.

Revolved Head-to-Knee

The revolved version of head-to-knee pose is a good multitasker, working the hamstrings and inner thighs while opening the chest and adding a side bend that stretches the obliques and the quadratus lumborum, a thick muscle that connects the pelvis and the hips.

Start on the floor, left leg extended, right knee bent and resting on the ground, sole of the right foot near or on the left inner thigh. Lay the back of your left hand against your inner left leg, and open the right arm up and away from the left leg (figure 5.12a).

Stay here or add a side bend, leaning the torso over the extended left leg (figure 5.12b). Your right arm can continue to reach away from the left leg or lift toward the space over the left leg.

FIGURE 5.12   Revolved head-to-knee: *(a)* Lift right arm up and away from left leg; *(b)* add a side bend.

Pinwheel Pigeon

Yoga's pigeon pose delivers a deep stretch to the iliotibial band, glutes, and hip rotators. It can, however, put a strain on the knee if your hip muscles are tight or if your setup is aggressive. The pinwheel version alleviates this pressure while building flexibility safely.

Sit on your right hip with your right knee bent. Bend the left knee and slide it toward the sole of the right foot. Lean your sternum forward over the right knee until you feel a pleasant stretch in the right hip (figure 5.13). Hold 15 breaths, then repeat on the other side.

FIGURE 5.13   **Pinwheel pigeon.**

Reclining Twist

An easy reclining twist releases the hips, wrings out the spine and organs, and can further stretch your chest and arms. Lie on your back, knees bent, right knee on top of the left. Drop both knees to the left, stacking the right hip over the left (figure 5.14). If your right shoulder has lifted, wiggle your elbow to the left so that it can sink toward the floor. Turn your head away from your legs, and stay for 15 breaths or more. Unwind and repeat on the other side.

FIGURE 5.14   **Reclining twist.**

Corpse

End your session with several breaths of rest in corpse pose, lying on your back with your legs extended (figure 5.15). Relax your arms and your neck, close your eyes, and just breathe. It can be tempting to shortchange this period of rest, especially when you are practicing at home where distractions can tempt you to jump off the mat and back into fulfilling obligations. But for maximum adaptation, you need to find a healthy balance between work and rest. Spending 3 to 10 minutes just resting still can do wonders for your body, as well as your mind. Don't shortchange yourself.

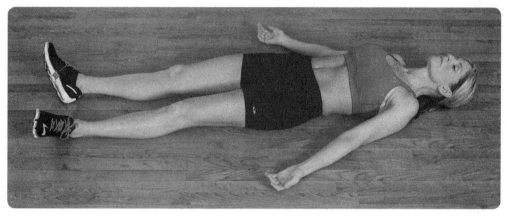

FIGURE 5.15   Corpse pose.

Conclusion

In the context of your full schedule, exercises like those described in this chapter can seem like too much work. But without balance in your body, you're heading toward an injury that can derail your training. Spending time to observe and address imbalances in your body—and to simply rest in stillness with no agenda—will make you more injury-proof and able to enjoy triathlon for many years to come.

CHAPTER 6

Streamlining Your Swim

Sara McLarty

Triathlon is the fastest-growing sport in the United States. Almost a million people participate in one or more events each year. More Americans than ever before are being introduced to triathlon by family, friends, and colleagues. No matter what reason or inspiration has brought your attention to this challenging multisport, you can become a triathlete!

The largest percentage of new participants are in the 35 to 50 age group, with middle-aged men and women looking for an exciting way to increase their fitness. Many beginner triathletes have not participated in organized sport since their high school years. Also, most have never learned how to swim beyond survival skills for casual water recreation. As a result, the swim is usually the most intimidating leg of the triathlon.

Many parts of a triathlon swim cause anxiety and fear among nonswimmers. Most triathlons take place in open water such as a lake, ocean, or river, but you also can find small races that use the local pool for the first leg of the race. In open water, swimmers must be aware that there will be limited visibility in murky water, no lane ropes or pool edges to hold on to, and no solid bottom to stand up on—and that the weather might whip up a few ripples on the surface.

Triathlon races start with waves of people. All the participants in your category (for example, women over 40 or women 30 to 39) start together, and this causes a few minutes of disorder as everyone tries to find some open space and get into a stroke rhythm. Areas near the turn buoys also can become crowded as multiple waves of people converge to take the shortest distance around the course.

These are just some of the reasons why learning to swim and being comfortable in the water are very important before starting a triathlon. There is a big difference between splashing in the waves at the beach and swimming a quarter-mile beyond the breakers. The first step is to get in the water and practice. Time spent in the pool will improve your swim stroke, and time spent in open water will help with the psychological preparation for race day.

Breathing

Before you can swim fast, you must learn to control your breathing so that easy swimming does not leave you gasping after one lap. Imagine how you inhale and exhale while cycling and running: take a short but steady inhale followed by a short and steady exhale with no pausing, no holding your breath, and no gasping for air. That is exactly how we breathe while swimming.

Start by jumping in the water and holding on to the edge of the pool. Perform a couple of slow bobs during which you inhale through your mouth when your head is above water and then exhale out your nose underwater. As soon as your face goes under, start a steady and continuous exhalation as you slowly count to three. Lift your head back out of the water, take a quick inhale, and return under the water for another exhalation. If you are having trouble with the exhalation, try humming under the water.

The feeling of being out of breath, or gasping, is caused by holding your breath and letting the carbon dioxide build up in your lungs. This feeling rarely occurs on dry land because we are never forced to hold our breath. Don't change how you breathe just because you are swimming. Inhale when your face is out of the water and exhale while your face is in the water.

After bobbing at the edge of the pool, swim a lap using the same breathing technique. Try to find a good rhythm by inhaling during every third stroke. This breathing pattern is optimum because you will breathe on both sides of your body. Bilateral breathing also results in a balanced stroke that will be straight and even.

As you become more comfortable and relaxed with a steady inhale and exhale, you will be able to complete more laps of the pool without stopping to catch your breath. This is a critical element of open-water swimming and triathlons because there are very few places to stop during the race. If you do start gasping, roll onto your back to take a few deep breaths and regain your composure, then roll onto your stomach and continue swimming.

Body Position

Being efficient in the water is more important than just working hard and trying to go fast. An efficient swimmer uses less energy, is more relaxed, glides through the water, and has an easier transition to the bike. The best swimmers in the world, in the pool and in open water, use their bodies to work with the water rather than fight against it. Learning how to swim smoothly and efficiently is important to becoming a great swimmer.

The first step is to learn to float on your stomach. Take a deep breath, hold it in your lungs, and calmly lie facedown in the water. Can you float on the surface, or do your feet sink to the bottom of the pool? Think about what your body is doing and try to relax. Do not try to hold yourself on top of the water. Let your arms and legs relax into the water.

How is your head position? Look straight down at the bottom of the pool and let the water line cut your head in half (half underwater, half above). The key to floating is to arch your back a little bit and push your stomach and pelvis toward the bottom of the pool. This will allow your lower body (hips, legs, and feet) to rise up to the surface. Do not push your butt up; the exact opposite will happen and your legs will sink.

The horizontal body position of floating is exactly how we swim freestyle. Everything should be in line directly behind your head so that you are moving through one hole in the water. This is also called a *streamline position.* You should be in streamline position when you push off the wall: palm of one hand on top of the other hand, arms straight overhead, and chin tucked into chest (figure 6.1). Squeeze your ears against your head with your biceps. Kick gently four to six times before starting to take strokes. When you start swimming with a horizontal body position, you will see immediate improvement in your times and speed.

When you start to swim, remember to keep your face pointing down and a slight arch in your back. If your hips and legs are in line with your spine, you will feel your feet breaking the surface of the water with each kick. Practice this with a kickboard: Make short and shallow movements with your legs (go only 8 to 10 inches [20-25 centimeters] underwater). Make quick and fast kicks for a high cadence. Feel the tops of your feet slapping down onto the surface of the water and making a splash.

The second step to becoming a more efficient swimmer is to learn to glide through the water. A good way to practice gliding is with the catch-up drill.

FIGURE 6.1   **Streamline position.**

Catch-Up Drill

In a streamline position on the surface of the water, take one complete stroke with your right arm. Keep your left arm extended overhead. When the right arm completes a full stroke, tap the left hand. Now take a complete stroke with your left arm while the right arm remains extended. Continue this drill the length of the pool. Count the number of strokes you take across the pool with the catch-up drill and compare that number to your regular swim stroke. Which method has more glide and is therefore more efficient?

Swimming slowly and smoothly is the best way to improve efficiency in the water. Focus on technique, gliding, relaxing, and body position during the warm-up, cool-down, and drill sets. Only when the set calls for fast swimming or descending times should you be concerned with times. Place most of your focus on good technique during your first months of swimming to develop fewer bad habits. Each stroke you take in the pool is creating muscle memory in your body, so make sure those muscles have good memories!

Four Parts of the Stroke

The freestyle stroke can be divided into four parts: catch, pull, finish, and recovery. Focus on one part of the stroke at a time to keep things simple. A swimming drill is included here for each part of the stroke. The drills will help you improve technique and master each part of the stroke.

Catch

The *catch* is a term for the very beginning of each stroke. After your arm drops into the water above your head, stretch it straight out from your shoulder toward the opposite end of the pool (figure 6.2*a*). This will put your body in a long and streamlined position. When you start to take a stroke, drop your fingertips toward the bottom of the pool, keep your wrist straight, and let your elbow pop up (figure 6.2*b*). The whole action takes only a fraction of a second but is critical to a powerful stroke.

FIGURE 6.2   The catch: *(a)* arm stretched out from the shoulder; *(b)* beginning of the stroke.

Fist Drill

The fist drill is a perfect way to emphasize a good catch. Swim a lap of freestyle with your hands balled up into fists to feel the water pressure on your forearms during each stroke. Never bend your wrist or let your elbow drop when you are swimming.

Pull

A strong catch will set you up for a powerful pull. Each underwater pull should trace the shape of a question mark (?). During the pull, your hand sweeps slightly away from your body (figure 6.3*a*), then sweeps back in near the hips, and finishes straight back along the thigh (figure 6.3*b*). Keep your fingertips pointing down to the bottom of the pool and do not let any part of your arm sweep across the center line of your body.

Much of a successful and strong underwater pull comes from correct body rotation. Your arm is grabbing the water, but your large core and upper back muscles are doing a majority of the work. Your torso should be rotated 30 to 45 degrees as you catch the water. Rotate your torso to the other side during each pull to engage the pecs, lats, obliques, and abs.

FIGURE 6.3   **The pull:** *(a)* **Arm sweeps back near hips;** *(b)* **arm moves to side of thigh.**

Single-Arm Drill

The single-arm drill is good for trying to develop a strong pull. Keep one arm at your side or extended above your head. Swim one lap of the pool using only your other arm. This will allow you to focus on each underwater pull. Watch your arm under the water and look for good and poor aspects that you can improve. Switch arms and practice both sides evenly.

Finish

The finish is the last push before the end of each stroke. It is very similar to a triceps push-down in the gym and uses the same muscles. By extending your arm and hand all the way to the middle of your thigh, you can add a little more length to each stroke. Do not pull your hand out of the water next to your hip.

Shark Drill

The shark drill is a fun and challenging drill that helps develop the finish phase. Hold a pull buoy or kickboard between your thighs. As you swim a lap of the pool, reach back and tap the top of the buoy at the completion of each stroke. This will encourage you to finish each stroke as well as engage your core stability to prevent overrotating during the drill.

Recovery

Finally, the recovery refers to lifting your arm out of the water, swinging it forward, and dropping it in the water above your head. This phase of the freestyle stroke is aptly named because it is an effortless and relaxed movement. The priority of the recovery is to quickly and efficiently return the arm to a streamlined and hydrodynamic position in front of the body. After the finish, lift the elbow and swing it forward. Without pausing or slowing down, let your hand, arm, and elbow splash into the water with a plopping noise. Do not keep your hand near your body during the recovery. Instead, let it swing out wide and away from your body to prevent any shoulder impingements or injuries.

Finger Drag Drill

The finger drag drill will put your arm in a good high-elbow position during the recovery. As your hand exits the water, keep your fingertips in the water and drag them forward along the surface. Keep your elbow high and fingertips low until you reach the top of the stroke and drop your entire arm into the water.

Swim Equipment and Training Tools

Lots of toys, tools, and equipment are involved in swim training. Some items, such as the kickboard and fins, help with technique. Some, such as the pull buoy and paddles, are for building strength and endurance. Many pools have kickboards and pull buoys available to the users, but you might have to make a purchase if you want to try some of the other common items. Invest in a durable mesh bag to easily carry and store all your personal equipment.

Kickboard

A kickboard is the most basic swimming tool. Almost every pool in the world has a couple of kickboards available for use. The simplest use is to hold it in front of your body and use only your legs for forward propulsion. This builds leg strength and improves kicking technique. A kickboard has various other uses; for example, you can use it as a makeshift pull buoy when one is not available.

Pull Buoy

A pull buoy is probably the second most popular piece of training equipment. Usually it is a piece of shaped Styrofoam or two pieces hooked together by a strap. A swimmer holds the buoy between her upper thighs to keep her hips and legs floating at the surface without kicking. Using a pull buoy allows you to use just your upper body for propulsion and to build strength.

Fins

Swim fins are a controversial piece of equipment. Some say that triathletes do not need to kick, that fins are cheating, or that they cause calf cramps. However, fins are a great tool for any level of triathlete or swimmer because they provide free speed, strengthen your legs, and encourage good technique. Using full-length, pliable rubber fins will teach your legs to move in the proper kicking movement. You cannot flex your foot when wearing full-length rubber fins! For weaker kickers, fins are the perfect way to strengthen specific leg and hip muscles to improve overall swim speed.

Fins also provide free speed when you are trying to master a new technique drill. Many of the common swimming drills are difficult to execute at slow speeds. If you feel as though you are sinking in the water, try using a pair of fins. Without much effort from your legs, you can move faster through the water and focus on executing the drills correctly. Just as with any exercise, build up to your fin usage. If you do too much too soon, you might suffer from sore feet and cramping calves.

Hand Paddles

Paddles are as varied as are people in the pool. Different shapes, sizes, and brands are designed to help build upper-body strength by creating a larger surface to pull through the water. When purchasing your first paddles, look for ones that are slightly larger than the span of your hand. To start, use the paddles for only a small percentage of your pulling sets. Increase the total distance slowly to allow your shoulders to acclimate to the added surface area.

Swimming Snorkel

Unlike a recreational snorkel, front-mounted swimming snorkels do not get in the way of freestyle strokes or fill with water. Elite swimmers use snorkels to improve lung capacity and their ability to deal with excess carbon dioxide in their lungs. Swimmers of any level can use a snorkel to focus more on stroke technique.

Ankle Band

You can purchase a comfortable Velcro band from various swim manufacturers or fashion your own from an old bike tube. Cut the tube into thirds. Take one-third and tie it into a loop. The band goes around your ankles to limit your kicking ability. Use a band with a pull buoy to prevent your lower legs from kicking, or use it without a buoy to improve body position and increase stroke tempo.

Tempo Trainer

A waterproof tempo trainer is a great addition to any speed-focused swim practice. Set the metronome to beep at a regular stroke rate, and then increase the tempo when doing fast or sprint training sets.

During a long swim, you can set the metronome to beep at a goal pace. For example, if you want to swim 2,000 yards holding 1:30 minutes per 100 yards, set the beep interval at 90 seconds and you will be able to judge your pace while swimming without needing to look at a clock.

Training for Open Water

A large percentage of swim training takes place in a pool. There are a few exceptions for the lucky people who live in warm climates and have easy access to open water. With the right tools, drills, and preparation, training in a pool can properly prepare anyone for open-water swimming and triathlons.

All triathletes must be aware of the challenges that open-water swimming presents. There are no walls to hold on to, no lane lines to separate people, no solid bottom to stand on, and no black line to follow, in addition the water is murky. In a pool, no matter how quickly you turn at each wall, you are still getting a moment of rest every 25 yards. To prepare for the nonstop swimming that is required in a triathlon, do a long swim once a week during which you turn at the T. Instead of turning at the wall, flip or turn when you swim over the black T before the wall. This will replicate the fatigued feeling you might get during open-water swimming.

At triathlon events, large, brightly-colored buoys are in the water to mark the swimming course. It is your responsibility to understand the course, know which buoys designate a turn, and know which direction to go. Once you are in the race, you will use a method of sighting, or lifting your face out of the water, to see where you are going. Practice sighting in the pool with the Tarzan drill.

Tarzan Drill

Swim half the pool with your head out of the water, looking toward the opposite wall. This might make your neck very tired at first, but with practice, it will strengthen important sighting muscles.

Lifting your head out of the water will help you with direction, but it will also affect your swimming technique. Counterbalance to prevent your legs from sinking by arching your back to keep your feet near the surface.

The crowds of people in the water can be the most daunting part of triathlon swimming. Another competitor may accidently swim over you or push you under the water. It's a good idea to be prepared for these situations before the race starts. Bumping, touching, and other forms of friendly and unfriendly contact are common in a triathlon swim. Use your teammates and friends to help you get comfortable swimming close to other people. Start with one other person in the same lane. Push off the wall next to each other and swim one length to experience the choppy water and splash you will feel when swimming next to another swimmer.

Next, try swimming three wide. Add a third person to your lane, push off at the same time, and swim one length. It will be a little crowded, with lots of bumping and jostling. After each length, swap places and let a different person try swimming in the middle.

Before your first open-water competition, I highly recommend at least one swim in open water. The best option is swimming at the race site a week or a month before the event. If that option is not feasible or permitted, find somewhere close by that is open and safe. Bring other people, a safety boat, and brightly colored swimming caps. Don't rush into the water and immediately start to swim. Instead, spend a few minutes playing in the water with friends and teammates. This will create an enjoyable atmosphere, give you a positive attitude, and help to bury your fears.

Before you know it, you will be swimming in open water and enjoying the new experience. Bring the same positive and fun attitude on race day. This will help keep your energy high and create a successful race experience. I want everyone to have a fantastic swim. Now, get in the water!

Prerace

Scout the swim course before the start of the race. Many events open the course for practice a day before the race. Use this time to get to know the water, currents, bottom conditions, course design, number and location of buoys, sun direction, and finish area. With limited time on race morning, the details picked up during a practice swim can provide good data for during the race.

Talk with the locals and question the lifeguards. Get details about currents, potential rips, tide times, wave and wind conditions, and so on. Check the bottom surface at the start and finish areas and make note of the degree of slope from shore. Practice run-ins and count the number of steps from the starting line into knee-deep water and the number of dolphin dives to waist-deep water. Use these numbers during the race as a general guide when the visual conditions are not perfect.

Every athlete should know the shape and direction of the swim course. The total number of buoys and the color and shape of the turn buoys should also be memorized. This is especially important when multiple race courses are marked at the same time. Pick out high landmarks that can be sighted during the race. When you are surrounded by other swimmers or in choppy and wavy conditions, the buoys and finish chute are not always visible. Find something like a building, tree, or radio antenna that is directly in line with the course. Use these landmarks for general sighting to stay on course.

Start

The shortest line from the starting line to the first buoy is a straight line (see line A in figure 6.4). In this example, the turn buoy is 400 meters away from the left side of the beach. Many athletes crowd into this position assuming that it is the fastest path to get to the first turn buoy. If the starting line (line B in figure 6.4) is 50 meters wide, a simple calculation shows that line C, the furthest line to the turn buoy, is only 403

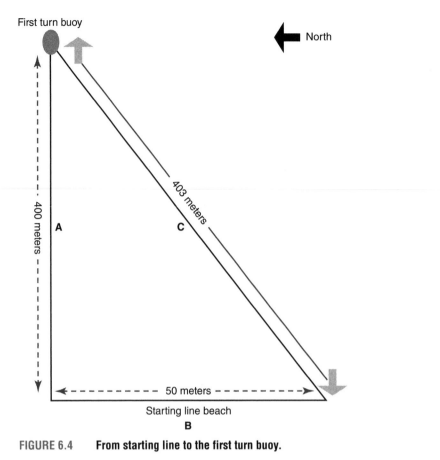

First turn buoy

North

400 meters

403 meters

A

C

50 meters

Starting line beach

B

FIGURE 6.4   **From starting line to the first turn buoy.**

meters. The time it takes to cover a distance of 3 meters in open water is insignificant when you consider the hazards avoided by starting away from the crowd.

While an outside starting position has advantages, weaker swimmers benefit from it less. The shortest line usually will provide a strong drafting area created by the large crowd of swimmers racing to the buoy. However, novice athletes and others not comfortable with the high-contact zones should start to the outside for a more pleasant experience.

Dolphin Diving

The original dolphin dives were developed and used by ocean lifeguards to quickly get through breaking waves and rescue struggling swimmers. Today, triathletes have adopted dolphin diving as a quick and efficient method to move through shallow water and waves at the start of a race.

The rule of thumb is to run through the water until it is midthigh depth, dolphin dive until it is navel depth, and then start swimming. In the ocean, continue dolphin diving under the waves until you are past the breakers. Here is how to execute a dolphin dive:

1. Dive forward into the water with your arms outstretched. Tuck your chin to your chest and keep your hands in front to block any underwater obstacles.
2. When your hands touch the bottom, dig your fingers into the sand and pull your body through your arms. As your head passes your arms, start lifting your chin and looking toward the surface.
3. Plant your feet on the bottom and push yourself forward and out of the water.
4. When your body comes out of the water, swing your arms around as in a butterfly stroke and keep your chin close to the surface.

Sighting

You will spend hours practicing perfect stroke technique in the pool, getting stronger in the gym, and purchasing all the latest suits that promise faster swim splits. But on race day, the most important issue is following the buoys and staying on course. *Sighting* is a term given to the action of lifting your head to look for markers located above the water. This is a skill that needs to be practiced and perfected before race day.

Lift your head only as high as necessary. In calm water, as in a lake or a river, lift just your eyes out of the water. In wavy conditions, as in the ocean, time your sighting to occur on the top of a wave for the best view of the course. Feel your body rise and fall on the swells and plan accordingly. When conditions are choppy and unpredictable, lift your head extra high but try to minimize the total number of times you sight during the race. Use landmarks and other swimmers visible when you breathe to the side.

Do not breathe while looking forward. Separate the two actions by sighting forward and then immediately rolling your head to take a breath to the side. As you prepare to sight, press down with your hand and arm during the catch phase of your stroke. This will slightly lift your upper body and make it easier to raise your head. Arch your back while lifting your head. This will allow your legs and feet to stay near the surface, minimizing drag under the water. Kick extra hard for a moment while you are sighting. This will help maintain forward speed and also keep your feet from dropping.

Sight two or three times in a row, during every other stroke. Use the first sight to locate the buoy, the second sight to adjust your angle, and the third to verify your direction. Swim straight for 10 to 20 seconds before repeating the sighting system.

Safety Stroke

The safety stroke is anything that you are comfortable doing in open water when you are feeling tired or panicked or just need to adjust your goggles. The main purpose of a safety stroke is to allow you to catch your breath and lower your heart rate during an open-water swim. Knowing another stroke can make your race experience more enjoyable and relaxed. The goal is to become so comfortable that your automatic reaction when stressed in the water is to immediately switch to your safety stroke.

Practice safety strokes during regular swim workouts to get comfortable and proficient. Breaststroke, backstroke, and sidestroke are just some examples. Add these strokes during warm-up and cool-down or substitute rest on the wall with an easy lap of your safety stroke.

Backstroke, or kicking on your back, is a great way to take a break to catch your breath. With your face up toward the sky, you can breathe uninhibited and as often as necessary. Goggles can easily be adjusted and emptied of water from this position. Breaststroke with your head out of the water is a good way to lower your heart rate and relax. It is also a great way to find the course buoys if you are disoriented or off course.

It is not uncommon to become tired during the first leg of a triathlon. Prepare for the unexpected by knowing more than just the freestyle stroke before you start a race.

Edit Your Stroke

Open-water swimming is never like pool swimming. There are always natural factors such as wind, currents, and waves that you never experience during pool training. No matter how hard you work in the pool to develop a perfect and flawless stroke technique, it will be tested when the race starts. These are a few ways to change your stroke technique for common open-water situations:

- **Quick cadence.** Increase your stroke tempo when you are in crowds of people at the start or around buoys. This is not efficient for long periods of time but will help you maintain your speed when you are pressed for space.

- **High hand recovery.** Lift your hand high above the surface of the water during recovery in wavy and choppy conditions. This will prevent you from slamming your hand into a rogue wave during the recovery phase.

- **Single-side breathing.** Breathe to one side in open water when the wind and waves are buffeting you on the other side. Take note that you are more likely to swim crooked but you will not take in as much unwanted water.

- **Armpit breathing.** In choppy and wavy conditions, turn your face toward your armpit when you breathe. Your head, shoulder, back, and recovering arm will block most of the spray and create a cove of air for a clean inhale.

Conclusion

Training harder is not the only way to become a faster and more successful swimmer or triathlete. Focusing on technique, developing good muscle memory, learning from your own mistakes, watching experienced athletes, and using a few commonsense tips can help make your next race an enjoyable and successful experience.

As Vince Lombardi said, "Practice doesn't make perfect. *Perfect* practice makes perfect." Focus on one part of the freestyle stroke each day at practice. Swim drill sets slowly and correctly. Don't rush through the workout. Take your time and learn good technique for the rest of your swimming career.

Open-water swimming and triathlons can be daunting, but things get easier and more fun the more you practice and participate. Approach every day as a challenge and take it head on!

CHAPTER 7

Biking Strong

Lindsay Hyman

There is no secret to training, no matter what you might read or hear. When one of my athletes tells me she wants to improve her bike split for next season, this is what I have to say: The only way to get faster is to train, and the only way to make the middle leg of your triathlon faster is to ride. A triathlete who is looking to improve in one aspect of triathlon needs to become great, not just good, within this segment of the race. As for becoming a strong cyclist, the first place I turn is to a single-sport athlete, the cyclist. I ask one simple question: What is this athlete doing with her training to improve power and efficiency?

In this chapter I'll cover a few ways to maximize performance on the bike, the middle leg. This includes a comprehensive understanding of physiological adaptations as well as cycling-specific training and how these riding skills can best prepare each athlete for an optimal ride after the swim. I'll also discuss how to get the most out of the run off the bike.

Principles of Training

An understanding of human physiological adaptations is crucial for effective training, and I believe that coaches and athletes have to understand the physical effects of training in order to make the greatest improvements. Learning the general framework of exercise physiology and sport nutrition, as well as the components of training and proper periodization, is important because it gives the athlete the ability to recognize and interpret the three main principles of training: overload, recovery, and adaptation.

In order to gain positive training adaptations, you must overload an energy system. In general we have three energy systems: the aerobic (foundation and endurance training), the threshold (maximal steady-state training), and the glycolytic ($\dot{V}O_2$max training). The overload principle applies to individual training sessions as well as entire cycles within training. For instance, a lactate threshold interval training session requires a stimulus of intensity with the proper duration to stress the threshold energy system in order to achieve a positive response of increased power on the bike. The total time spent at threshold or $\dot{V}O_2$max and the number of interval sessions per week are also important because it may take more than one training session to induce adequate overload to lead to a positive training response. As long as you properly overload an energy system in the body and allow it time to recover properly, the energy system will grow stronger and be ready to handle the same stress that was applied in training to future training and racing.

In order to benefit from overloading an energy system, you have to give that system time to rest. When you are on the bike throwing down in the middle of a high-intensity interval set, you are not improving fitness but rather applying a large amount of stress. Later, when you are home relaxing and enjoying a posttraining recovery drink, you are improving your fitness. Gains are made when you allow enough time for your body to recover and adapt to the stresses you have applied. Athletes tend to have little to no problem overloading their bodies and energy systems; they have more trouble allowing for proper recovery. Recovery is part of training and, in fact, is one of the most important aspects of training.

Organizing training into structured cycles or training blocks has been one of the cornerstones of success for many endurance athletes. Within cycling, countless studies prove that the structure of macro-, meso-, and microcycles works. A macrocycle refers to the overall training period; this is more commonly known as an annual training plan based on one or more years of training foresight. A mesocycle is the transition period, a block of training that generally is three to four weeks in length. Last but not least, a microcycle focuses on one week of training at a time. The goal of breaking training periodization into these three categories allows you to better plan your training and racing schedule throughout the year. Proper periodization of applied overload, training adaptation, and sufficient recovery allows athletes to train consistently while training right. They are able to train and race without injuries or setbacks, even decreasing the time off between seasons. All these components allow for the greatest improvements during a single season and also over years.

A pure cyclist is able to ride without having to establish the delicate balance of overload, adaptation, and recovery in three sports. This may allow cyclists to tap into their inner single-sport athlete and be able to produce more consistent progression of increased power and efficiency. However increased oxygen consumption and better efficiency can help can help produce better long-term development of athletes competing in all levels and all sports.

Training With Power

The biggest advantage of measuring power on the bike is that, compared to speed and heart rate, it provides both a direct and an immediate answer to the question "How hard am I really working?" Power can be defined as the amount of work done during a given period of time and is measured in watts (W). A watt is produced by multiplying torque (force applied at the crank arm), by angular velocity, which can be measured through rotation such as cadence in revolutions per minute (rpm) or the circular motion of the rear wheel; therefore, W = force × angular velocity. Power data collected over the course of multiple training sessions and races are fundamental in determining trends in overall performance due to changes in equipment, aerodynamic positioning, and training methodology. Power output has become an indispensable tool in cycling for assessing, quantifying, and prescribing training.

Training with power provides many benefits. Power can eliminate the guessing game of estimating intensity. Power provides the coach and athlete feedback and data of actual work performed despite environmental conditions such as wind, altitude, humidity, temperature, and gradient. A watt is a watt!

Race data give a clear picture of the total energy demand needed for a particular course. The athlete will be able to establish proper pacing and power ranges during nondrafting races and also understand the power demands needed for a breakaway. Additionally she will have the ability to bridge a gap during a draft legal race. Ultimately, once the demands are known, training programs can be created based on the needs of each athlete to perform at her best.

Power meters and their monitoring tools allow the demands of training and racing to be quantified on a daily, weekly, monthly, and yearly scale. For a better understanding of this, a power meter captures every second of training. There are many parameters we could review; however, we can gather the most useful information by looking at watts, heart rate (collected by a heart rate monitor), cadence, calories burned (kilojoules), speed, distance, time, and even altitude. By collecting these data during training and racing events, we are able to see multiple pieces of the puzzle all at once, and when put together, they create a clear picture of the achievements and even limitations of that particular day's results. Furthermore, athletes and coaches can determine fatigue using interpretive tools such as normalized power and quadrant analysis, which are covered in great detail in the book *Training and Racing with a Power Meter* by Hunter Allen and Andrew Coggan (2010).

Using a power meter will help you maximize training time in a time-crunched schedule and ensure appropriate overload with a training plan of 20 hours or more per week. With the use of power you are able to determine how much work has been accomplished. The unit of measure used for this is kilojoules (kJ). The National Heart Foundation defines a kilojoule as a unit of energy; it refers to the energy value of food and the amount of energy our bodies burn. The more common term is *calorie*.

By reviewing the data, you will be able to better structure your training sessions, to make the most of each training day on the bike through daily assessment. For example, if you have a training session full of intervals and are unable to reach or maintain a designated power range, this is a good indication that you have achieved your overload for the day. It is time to go home to rest and to recover before you attempt the same or a similar training session in the days that follow.

Additionally, when training with power you have the opportunity to fine-tune your training and racing while making the most of every effort. Power (in watts) is given as an absolute number, unlike heart rate. Heart rate is the result of the work you just performed; watts provide real-time second-to-second feedback. For example, with respect to heart rate, if you were to stand up out of your chair right now and sprint across the room, your heart rate would rise with every step and even continue to climb after you reached the other side of the room. With respect to power, if you were to do the same sprint across the room you would be able to view the actual work done every step of the way from point A to point B. One of the biggest advantages to using power is that you are no longer training within the gray zone; either you can perform the work or you cannot. Ultimately, the biggest advantage of training with a power meter is to use this tool to increase power output, ranging from seconds to hours, through an all-inclusive feedback loop of information and data while on the bike.

Cycling-Specific Training

Most triathletes train with other triathletes. This is great in that it perpetuates the social interaction and fun nature of community within the sport. However, if your goal is to improve your cycling power or efficiency, it may be in your best interest to train with pure cyclists.

An excellent way to begin is to find a local group ride that attracts mainly cyclists. In most cities you can find A or B group rides through your local cycling shop. In Colorado Springs, our local group ride is known as the Weekend World Championship; Tucson has the Shootout, and you'd better not show up with a triathlon bike! The benefit of training with roadies goes beyond putting in fast and furious miles. These challenging group rides naturally force you to learn to ride better, stronger, and faster. During these fast-paced rides if you happen to miss a cue such as a gearshift or have a moment of insecurity, you will be off the back before you can blink. Through these aggressive group rides, you will begin to establish proficient handling skills, learning to ride the bike in unpredictable conditions by reading the body positions of those around you, as well as anticipating smooth gearing changes during riding through to the subtle energy changes the group carries through corners and turns.

Group Rides

The dynamics between a triathlon group ride and a roadie group ride vary greatly. The main difference is that a triathlon group ride tends to be at a more steady or even pace, whereas a cycling group ride may start easy but then progressively becomes more challenging and includes many high-paced and high-powered accelerations. The size of the group varies as well. On average, most triathlon group rides are no more than 10 to 15 people, while a typical cycling group ride can be from 30 riders up to 100. Furthermore, the overall dynamics of the two groups vary. The pulls on the front of a road ride are short and intense; you may have to fight for position and get on your wheel of choice. The accelerations are hard, and typically no one waits for anyone who has dropped off the back. This may sound intimidating, but most riders offer advice when someone is doing something incorrectly and aid in direction as the ride becomes more challenging. If someone is off the back or dropped, others will be, too. In this case, everyone works together in an organized fashion to chase the group and get back on the pain train.

Group rides are my secret weapon. Triathletes gravitate toward triathlon not only because it involves a great group of athletes, but also because they excel at endurance events. Some believe the longer, the better! The biggest benefit of group riding for a strong and steadier ride comes from the countless unplanned and irregular accelerations. For many the challenge of a group ride does not come from the average power and speed of the ride, but rather the vindictive accelerations over and over. These accelerations go far beyond the power demands needed for a time trial in a triathlon race, but if the upper limit of your capacity to do work is limiting your threshold, then group rides will begin to raise your top-end power output.

A power file from a group ride may look similar to figure 7.1, whereas a triathlon or time-trial intervals would look more similar to figure 7.2. The horizontal line represents a particular athlete's 20-minute threshold power; the rings are an example of the high power demand that is necessary to stay with the group. In figure 7.1, the accelerations are well above this athlete's threshold, and the most challenging efforts are focused in the middle of the ride, although they occur through the entire training session. While working on the top-end power, in this case the numerous accelerations, the athlete is working on her weakness. The goal over time for this athlete, as she concentrates on her weakness on the bike, is to begin to improve her overall cycling capability. A rising tide raises all ships; in essence, by increasing the top end of your power output, you ultimately will be able to improve your aerobic and threshold energy systems as well.

To better explain, let's consider an athlete whose 20-minute threshold is 85 percent of her $\dot{V}O_2max$ (maximum rate of oxygen consumption). Over a year, she improves her 20-minute threshold to 89 percent, yet her maximum capacity ($\dot{V}O_2max$) has remained the same. After one year of complete training, this athlete can now ride longer and can produce more watts at a maximal steady-state, threshold effort, but more importantly she can ride with less fatigue at her previous 85 percent level of intensity. This is the overall goal of training—to ride with more power and better efficiency. As a result, the limiting factor in a group ride, on a hilly course, in a training race, or in a draft legal race is the same—accelerations and higher power demands. Therefore, the goal of improving maximal capacity to do more work (watts) allows for a greater improvement in race-specific power.

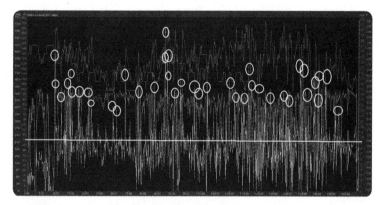

FIGURE 7.1   **Power profile from a group ride.**

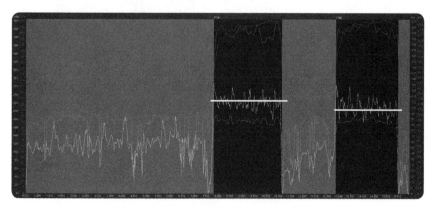

FIGURE 7.2   **Power profile from a triathlon race or time trial.**

Furthermore, the dynamics of the group ride greatly aid in an improved feel for the bike. Being able to anticipate when the intensity increases based on the body position, cadence, and rhythm of others and listening to shifting saves crucial seconds when gaps of inches can become a mile to make up. Riding more frequently out on the open road and with others may help you develop a sixth sense, an overall heightened awareness on the bike. This enhanced feel and confidence on the bike will improve the distribution of power to the bike. You will ride more relaxed. The less you have to think about what is happening, the more effectively you can react and the better you can ride without distraction.

Riding on Dirt

A comparison of triathletes, track cyclists, road racers, and mountain bikers shows that the most efficient pedal stroke is performed by the mountain biker. This may be no surprise to those who already ride on dirt and gravel roads. Think about what you have to do to keep traction between the rear wheel of the bike and the dirt—maintain a smooth pedal stroke, even weight distribution between the front and rear wheel, and a relaxed upper body.

Riding on dirt is my second secret weapon in training design. To be the most efficient on a bike, the goal is to have a smooth pedaling stroke that eliminates the peaks and valleys of power distribution. Think of a fast pedal drill (110 or more rpm)—what exactly are you trying to accomplish? You are pedaling fast in a smooth circle, but you are actually trying to unweight the leg on the upstroke so the leg on the downstroke has little to no resistance. Complete a fast pedal and listen to the rotation of the wheel. If you hear an undulating sound, you may be working against yourself. If you hear a more steady sound, you are heading in the right direction, toward a smooth and efficient pedal stroke.

Fast Pedal Drill

The goal of the fast pedal drill is better and more efficient pedaling mechanics through high-speed pedaling.

This workout should be performed on a relatively flat section of road. The gearing should be light with low pedal resistance. Begin to slowly increase your pedal speed, starting at around 15 or 16 pedal revolutions per 10-second count. This is a cadence of about 90 to 96 rpm. While staying in the saddle, increase your rpm, keeping your hips smooth with no rocking. Concentrate on pulling through the bottom of the pedal stroke and over the top. After this initial ramp-up period, you should be maintaining 18 to 20 16-pedal revolutions per 10-second count, or a cadence of 110 to 120 rpm for the entire amount of time prescribed for the workout. Your heart rate may climb while you are doing this drill, but don't use it to judge the overall intensity. It is important that you try to ride the entire length of the fast pedal drill with as few interruptions as possible.

Complete some cycling training on a mountain or cyclocross bike to help increase pedal efficiency and also stress the top end through natural accelerations. A power profile from a mountain bike session would be filled with peaks and valleys (similar to what is seen in figure 7.1), with constant high-powered and lower-powered outputs. This constant fluctuation in power stresses the weakness of most triathletes. The aerobic engine is stressed by the top-end, high-power efforts, helping the athlete become more accustomed to going hard and recovering, then going hard again. Training on a mountain or cyclocross bike helps most athletes become more efficient cyclists through better pedaling mechanics while still being sport specific and providing the necessary saddle time.

The more time you can spend in the saddle without losing fitness gained in swimming and running, the more power on the bike you will develop. The more confident and comfortable you are on the bike, the better you will be able to handle cycling form in unpredictable conditions, ultimately making it possible to ride faster.

Training Versus Racing

Does your training match your race performance? For most athletes the answer is no. During most training rides, you spend roughly 15 percent of the total ride coasting, between 0 and 10 watts; during a race (sprint, Olympic, Half Ironman, and Ironman), the typical time spent coasting is closer to 2 to 5 percent of total ride time. Over the course of a 2 1/2-hour race, this becomes a significant difference. How do the numbers add up? Well, 2 percent of coasting time is 3 minutes over 2 1/2 hours, compared to 15 percent, which is 22 minutes during a 2 1/2 hour ride. That is a 19-minute difference. This won't correlate exactly to a 19-minute improvement in your race day bike split, but becoming aware of the demands of your race and implementing this into your training will allow for a more efficient bike leg as well as an increased capability to run faster off the bike.

Through the technology of power meters, it is easy to categorize how much time is spent coasting and at which specific power outputs. For instance, as shown in figure 7.3, in a 70.3 Ironman Boulder race, the athlete spent 2.6 percent of the race coasting, or 3 1/2 minutes. A race-specific training profile (figure 7.4) shows that she spent 11 percent of her training session coasting, for a total of 19 minutes. This means the next

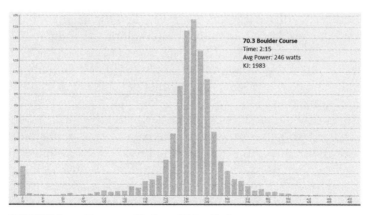

FIGURE 7.3   **Power profile for a 70.3-mile Ironman race.**

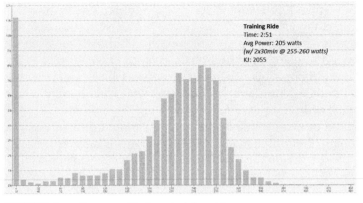

Training Ride
Time: 2:51
Avg Power: 205 watts
(w/ 2x30min @ 255-260 watts)
KJ: 2055

FIGURE 7.4   **Power profile for a training ride.**

time this athlete heads out for a similar training session, the goal will be to concentrate on maintaining a more consistent power output throughout the session to better match the demands she will encounter on race day. In order to achieve this desired response on the bike, be more aware of pedaling during the slight downhills and with forceful tailwinds. Be mindful of recovery during subthreshold intervals and improve your position to be more comfortable in order to sustain a more consistent power output.

During a nondrafting race when you are pedaling 10 percent more than in an equivalent-demand training session, you will be able to generate a higher average power. Within a time-trial format, the highest average power will correlate to a faster speed. However, there is always a cost in asking your body to do more work. By pedaling more, you may run the risk of accumulating more fatigue and thus expending more total energy (kilojoules) during the bike leg of your triathlon. In order to be prepared for these demands, a straightforward approach would be to match the kilojoules for a race within a training session. As you can see from figures 7.3 and 7.4, the training session is about 35 minutes longer, with the overall goal of working toward a 2,000-kilojoule expenditure to match the energy demands for race day.

During a race, pedaling more often leads to a higher energy and caloric expenditure. You may need to reevaluate and modify your nutrition and hydration plan by consuming an additional 50 to 100 calories per hour based on the length and intensity of the race. This value may seem low, but the increased caloric expenditure will accumulate rather quickly over the course of 26.2 to 112 miles (42 to 180 kilometers). Preparing your body with all the tools you can during training will ultimately lead to more consistent results and guide you to your potential of achieving personal bests in your race-day performance.

Matching the energy demands is essential to what you want to accomplish during your training in order to better prepare for the expected demands on race day. The best way to accomplish this is to plan ahead and map out a few longer rides that will have few to no interruptions due to traffic and have terrain more similar to what you will tackle on race day. Training on an indoor trainer is a good starting place, but I encourage you to get outside to best prepare for the rolling hills, turns, wind, and temperatures that you will experience on the course on race day.

Racing to Your Strength

As you roll out of transition, begin to think "breathe, relax, drink, steady effort." Even if you are a power-hungry cyclist who is looking forward to the bike leg, keep in mind that everything you do during the swim and bike will affect your run, and a great run often has a larger impact on your overall race than a brilliant bike does. Build into your power over the first half-mile, steadily and patiently working toward your goal power or effort level. Begin to increase your cadence and then shift into a more challenging gear. This is when you need to be mindful of the accelerations, but rather focus on riding at your highest sustainable average power. The best power and effort for the bike leg depend on many factors. Generally the level of intensity will be closer to your lactate energy system or maximum sustainable power for sprint-distance races and progressively become slower as the distance gets longer. You should be slightly under a threshold effort for an Olympic distance; for a Half Ironman, you're going to want to ride at a subthreshold effort, and for an Ironman the pace will be even less, almost conversational.

During the race there will be subtle changes in power due to passing and avoiding draft zones, headwinds, and hills. As you approach a hill, focus on your cadence. Avoid major fluctuations. Ideally you want to maintain your cadence plus or minus 5 rpm. When your speed begins to drop below 15 miles (24 kilometers) per hour, come out of an aero position (you are no longer gaining an aerodynamic advantage). This less-aggressive position will make your chest and hip angle more open, which is more powerful and will aid you in pushing through the tops of hills. If your speed really begins to decrease, get out of the saddle and use your body weight to aid you through each pedal stroke. Often it is best to shift into a harder gear before standing to maintain your momentum during your transition from sitting to standing. Just don't forget to shift again when you sit down!

The difficulty of the course conditions may also determine whether you are down in the drops and racing in an aerodynamic position. While riding into a headwind, it is best to stay as low as possible without compromising your power output. The increase in speed and opposing headwind will compound one another and an exponential curve of added resistance will begin to work against you. Counterintuitively, when you have a tailwind, you also want to stay low and aero to take full advantage of a fast and smooth streamline position. The best way to think about staying low and aero is to imagine that when you are on your bike your body is punching a hole through the air; the smaller the hole, the faster you can go! This means that even with a tailwind, you want to maintain a low profile to take advantage of an aerodynamic position.

Optimizing your best aerodynamic position is often a matter of balancing wind resistance, power output, and comfort on the bike. The more you enhance one aspect, the more likely it is you are going to take away from the other two. Ideally you want to find the perfect balance that allows you to produce the most power with the lowest amount of drag, and then be able to tolerate that position throughout the race. For a sprint-distance race, you may work toward a more aggressive position (less drag and neutral power output but less comfortable), but as you work toward an Ironman-distance event, you may compromise drag for comfort to ensure that you have the capacity to produce power and run well off the bike. It takes practice to be able to adapt to an aerodynamic position on the bike, so incorporate riding in the aerobars or drops frequently during training at a wide range of intensities, and practice eating, drinking, and cornering to maximize your aerodynamic advantage.

When you are having a great race, you should feel as if you are in the zone. Obey the rules and avoid drafting and blocking penalties while cruising down the road. When you encounter an opportunity to pass a fellow competitor, evaluate the cost of the pass. Chances are you will need to increase your power during this 10- to 30-second window. Be mindful of your power accelerations during a pass, and remember to carry your momentum through smooth efficient shifting and pedaling while taking advantage of a low aerodynamic drag.

During the final few miles, or about 10 to 15 minutes to go on the bike leg, concentrate on riding smooth and steady. Maintain a consistent cadence while continuing to hydrate and eat before heading into transition. Your power and effort level on the bike should not change. Do not increase or decrease it. Remember, the goal is the highest average power to gain the fastest bike split. By focusing on your cadence, you will be able to ride a consistent effort into the finish.

In most races the approach into transition often includes a handful of turns and awkward corners. Take this as an opportunity to keep your legs spinning with less force to mentally prepare for the run off the bike. And remember, a fast transition is free time for the run. Be organized and efficient.

Conclusion

Remember, there are no shortcuts to riding fast. You will need to put in the time on the saddle and the hard work of getting out of your comfort zone to be able to enhance your skills and confidence on the bike. Allow the middle leg of your triathlon to become your favorite aspect of racing by using the tools and including the training necessary for you to ride fast.

CHAPTER 8

Running Smart

Margie Shapiro

The concept of running smart seems simple: Follow the basics of traditional run training, and you'll be ready for a triathlon run. When you break it down more completely, however, the idea of running smart, particularly as a female triathlete, morphs into something larger and slightly more complicated. Being a smart runner comprises mental and physical aspects related to safety, movement awareness, and reasonable training.

A smart runner considers safety at all times, understands her body's biomechanics and the ways to affect them (movement awareness for proper technique), and chooses to train for optimal athletic performance following proven physiological principles leading to reasonable training. I have had the good fortune of working with some of triathlon's greatest gurus on these aspects of smart running, and I hope to use the lessons they've taught me and what I've learned from my own coaching and training experience to provide a succinct handbook for your journey to excellence in triathlon running.

Safe Training

As women runners, we must always keep our safety at the forefront of our minds. Follow these guidelines to be a safe runner:

- Run with other people when possible.
- Be aware of your surroundings at all times. Keep your eyes and ears open!
- Run familiar routes.
- Let someone know where you're going and when you'll be back.
- Wear bright, reflective clothing that is weather appropriate.
- Wear the proper footwear for your body's needs to avoid injury.

We can extend the concept of safety beyond its most obvious implications and into the realm of training. First, practicing proper technique not only makes us run faster and more efficiently, but it also provides safety by preventing injury through balanced and healthy movement patterns. Further, preparing and executing a smart training plan gives us a measure of psychological and emotional safety (i.e., confidence) beyond the physiological gains it creates, and at the same time sets up an environment in which we can take risks, pushing ourselves to new limits with trust in our overall preparation.

Learning and Practicing Movement Awareness

Get to know your body and how it works mechanically. A complicated system of pulleys makes up the body's musculoskeletal system, and nearly all of them connect to the trunk (the core). A foundation of a strong and stable core (all the muscles between the lower ribs, front and back, and the upper thighs, front and back) allows us to generate power in and through the limbs. Muscles work in opposing pairs to move our bones: The gluteus muscles (hip extensors) flex while the hip flexors in front (iliopsoas and others) relax; the quadriceps flex while the hamstrings relax; the muscles on the backs of the lower legs flex when those on the front relax, and so forth. We aim for optimal balance between opposing muscle groups so that they can enhance each other's motions, working in concert instead of limiting each other. When one muscle gets too tight, it limits the function on the opposite side. Similarly, when one muscle gets overly fatigued, a muscle on the opposite side may respond by overworking.

We extend this concept of the parts of the body working in concert when comparing the upper body and lower body. Movement above the waist can affect the lower body, and movement below it can affect the upper body. For example, when a runner excessively crosses her arms over her torso, the legs respond to the torsion with their own twisting, leading to potential hip, knee, or ankle problems. If the arms swing too far in front of the body, the legs may respond by opening too far in front of the body as well. When the arms are too tight and do not swing enough behind the body, the legs will struggle to cover enough ground with each step, lacking the assistance of the arms and the core's cross-sling muscles (which connect each shoulder to the opposite-side hip, both front and back), thus causing overwork and potential injury to the muscles of the lower body.

Becoming aware of the relationships among muscle groups, we can run more mindfully and adapt our body's movements when we notice subtle characteristics or flaws within our own form. For example, because of an old shoulder injury, I tend to hug my right arm close to my ribs and swing it minimally. This tendency leads to limited hip function on the opposite side (my left), and therefore overworking my right lower body.

If we can get very good at movement awareness, understanding how our bodies move, we can improve movement patterns for greater efficiency. For some people, body awareness comes naturally. For others, it requires quite a bit of attention (focus) and intention (deliberate movements). I recommend using video analysis whenever possible. Getting a visual picture of what we're actually doing, which is often far different from what we think we're doing, helps tremendously when trying to make changes to run technique. Also, I urge you to run mindfully. Develop clear communication between body and mind. Runners who listen to their bodies anticipate and prevent problems more easily. And runners whose bodies listen to their minds get more out of themselves. In both cases, the stronger the mind–body connection, the more effective we can be.

Engaging the core muscles adequately makes all the difference in practicing proper movements during running. A strong core allows for greater overall endurance as well. Make sure to include regular functional core strength work all year long to optimize your run technique. Instead of doing a series of sit-ups, practice core exercises that put you in running-related positions. Even the simple front plank (see chapter 5) allows you to practice good posture for running (straight back, engaged abdominal and back muscles).

From a biomechanical standpoint, I break down run technique into four main objectives:

1. Engage in proper posture and balance.
2. Set up and attain the ideal foot strike.
3. Achieve efficient cadence or foot speed.
4. Use the arms effectively for balance and propulsion.

Posture

As runners whose goal is to move forward efficiently, we want to use the musculoskeletal system effectively and take advantage of gravitational forces, but often we do just the opposite (see table 8.1). When a runner fights gravity by leaning back at the waist, extending the lead foot far in front of her body, she must use her hamstrings to pull the lead leg back underneath her before propelling herself forward and cannot use the gluteus muscles as much for propulsion. By contrast, when a runner uses gravity's assistance by leaning forward from the ankles, planting the foot directly under the hips, she can engage the gluteus muscles fully to stabilize the planted foot and leg.

Foot Strike

With good posture, we are able to fall forward with gravity's assistance, then engage the core properly to swing the leg from the hip instead of from the knee, and then plant the foot in the ideal location, under our center of mass. An efficient foot strike (table 8.2) results from correct movements at the hip, knee, and ankle joints.

TABLE 8.1

Goals and Common Mistakes: Posture

Postural goals	Postural mistakes
Stand tall with a straight spine	Curving the spine too far back
Lean forward from the ankles	Leaning forward from the neck or waist
Engage the core muscles to stabilize the pelvis	Allowing the pelvis to tilt forward with an arched back
Balance the use of the hip flexors and extensors	"Sitting down" or leaning back while running, causing excessive hip flexion and minimal extension

TABLE 8.2

Goals and Common Mistakes: Leg Swing and Foot Strike

Leg swing and foot strike goals	Leg swing and foot strike mistakes
Keep knee angle tight when in front of body	Reaching foot in front of knee
Plant foot on ground directly beneath hips	Planting foot on ground in front of hips
Extend leg behind body with glute flexion	Kicking leg behind body using hamstrings
Plant with unweighted heel, dorsiflexing the foot	Striking heel first with toe pointed up or striking toe first in front of hips

Cadence

Setting up the proper foot strike requires good posture but can be assisted with extra focus on cadence (steps per minute). While I believe no single optimal cadence number exists across the board, individualized optimal cadence does.

Most runners find greatest efficiency in the range of 180 or more steps per minute. To test your own cadence, go out for an easy run, count your steps for 1 minute a few times throughout the run, and average the results. If you find yourself significantly below 180 steps per minute, I recommend using a metronome to practice running with quicker steps. (You can download free apps for your smartphone or purchase a handheld or clip-on cadence monitor.)

Start by using proper cadence (table 8.3) during drill sessions, but be conservative and gradual in increasing your cadence during regular runs. Some runners find that improvement comes best with small bursts of cadence focus within a run (e.g., for 30 to 60 seconds, turn on the metronome and match 180 beats per minute; then turn it off, resume your normal rhythm, and repeat every 5 minutes). Another approach is to increase your cadence goal by two to four steps per minute for three to five runs before increasing it again. In either case, you expose your body to the higher cadence incrementally to avoid injury or frustration.

Arm Movement

Sometimes posture, foot strike, and cadence all come more easily with greater focus on arm movement (table 8.4). I encourage runners to practice their arm swing in front of a mirror, often with the assistance of the metronome set at goal cadence.

TABLE 8.3

Goals and Common Mistakes: Cadence

Cadence goals	Cadence mistakes
Run at a cadence that allows proper foot strike and minimal contact time	Running with a cadence that creates too much contact time
Run at a sustainably high cadence	Forcing a cadence that is too high and minimizes stride length

TABLE 8.4

Goals and Common Mistakes: Arm Swing

Arm swing goals	Arm swing mistakes
Swing arm from a relaxed shoulder	Swinging arm primarily from elbow
Allow a rear-pulling arm swing	Swinging arms excessively in front
Find lateral balance with minimal twisting	Crossing the midline with the arm swing
Keep the hands relaxed for fluid movement	Clenching the hands tightly

One of the best ways to implement good running technique is through the neuromuscular practice you get from technique drills. I'd bet that former track runners (high school or college) remember some drills from their practice days. The list of running drills for technique (increasing activation, mobility, and neuromuscular control) goes on and on. I will not attempt to list or describe them all here, though we'll discuss a few shortly. Use drills regularly in your training, both before and after workouts or easy runs, to encourage proper technique and balance and improve the body's neuromuscular coordination and speed.

Smart Training

Once we have a handle on the mind–body connection that allows for excellent movement awareness, we can let the subconscious mind continue to work on proper technique while focusing the conscious mind on executing reasonable training for success.

While I believe that various training philosophies can be effective, most coaches apply their own time-tested training philosophy to all of their athletes. Mine is to develop all of the energy systems with great attention, giving the athlete every possible tool in the box, but to focus primarily on those most pertinent to the priority races at hand (following the principle of specificity) and to prioritize life–athletics balance along the way.

While athletes at the highest level need to be single-minded in their focus (and therefore, arguably, *unbalanced*), most of us find our attention divided among a multitude of worthy beneficiaries including family, work, friends, and health, and we get the greatest fulfillment in an environment that strives for balance and reason when it comes to athletic pursuits. Considering the reality of our world in addition to simple logic, I think we thrive when we do the least amount of training (work) for the greatest gain (reward). Doesn't it make more sense to arrive at the starting line 5 to 10 percent less trained but minimally stressed and fully motivated than 100 percent trained but stressed out, sleep deprived, and lacking deep competitive motivation because the preparation was too strenuous?

Whether you hire a coach, use a plan from a book or magazine, or design your own program, I encourage you to be smart with your training.

- Identify weaknesses and make them priorities.
- Identify strengths and give them some attention as well. (Confidence is everything!)
- Stick to the plan, unless the body tells you to stop sooner.
- Focus on the positives. What did you learn from the workout? How can you grow from failure? What will you change for next time?

Identify Weaknesses

Identify the areas needing the most work and prioritize those. In his popular book *The Triathlete's Training Bible,* exercise physiologist, author, and coach Joe Friel (2004) used the term *limiter* in explaining race-related challenges an athlete may face. His distinction between weakness and limiter is useful in leveling the playing field: Even the greatest swimmers, cyclists, runners, or triathletes in the world will be challenged by elements of the particular race, both physical (hills, wind, and so on) and physiological (muscular endurance, power, and so on). Everyone can work on limiters. Figure out race elements that will be a challenge to you and focus on improving yourself in those areas. Build workouts into your training plan that examine these challenges and provide practice opportunities to improve your ability to face them.

If you are training for a short-distance triathlon such as a super-sprint or sprint, you will need to focus on a combination of endurance and speed, not to mention the course's unique challenges (rough surf, cold water, course terrain, and so on) and the technical focus of making your transitions very fast. In contrast, if you are training for a longer-distance race such as Olympic distance or a long-distance triathlon, your main objective should be increased endurance (both aerobic and muscular), but you can use speed workouts to enhance technique and efficiency and to provide you the tool of anaerobic efficiency so you can access that energy system when you need it, as at the top of a long hill climb or during a sprint to the finish.

Identify Strengths

Give your strengths attention as well. If you come from a swimming background and know you'll be strong in the water, use this ability to your advantage without ignoring it in training. Swim workouts for you may be less difficult than for a newer swimmer, so treat many of them as recovery days or lighter workouts, putting more time and energy into the bike and run. If you come from a running background, of course you should spend more time working on the swim and the ride; but you should continue your run training, although it should be lighter than if running were your single sport. First, you may not run as well off the bike as you expect, and second, you will run better at the end of the race not having neglected the training. A typical training week for someone with a single-sport background may seem more lopsided toward the other two sports, but should still include a nice mix of all three sports, as well as functional strength training.

Know When to Stop

Acknowledging the logical end point and sticking to it perhaps constitutes the most difficult ability a triathlete must develop. If a workout is going really well, it can be hard to resist the urge to keep going and going until it gets too hard. For example, a runner may tell me she felt so great during her long run on the treadmill that she just kept increasing the speed, minute by minute, until she was running, believe it or not, 10K pace! I have to resist the urge to share her excitement in achieving such a speed and instead urge her to stick within the bounds of the workout's purpose, which was not to run 10K pace but to run 2-hour pace. On the other hand, if a workout is going very poorly due to injury or illness, a smart runner would pull the plug, rest up, and revise the plan in order to execute the workout on a better day.

In a similar way but on a larger scale, if a series of training weeks seem to yield great progress, an athlete may resist stepping back for a recovery week even if it's exactly what she needs. My own case in point: Going into a race feeling overly fresh and coming out of it not feeling as sore as I'd expected, I've wanted to go right into another big training week. I've had to be told to respect my body's recovery needs even if, in the moment, I want to ignore them. Planning ahead and anticipating these moments of unwillingness to stop will become increasingly important as you step up your training demands or raise the level of your goals.

Be humble in your training. Accept and embrace the fact that sometimes you're going to feel great but need to stop, and other times you're going to want to stop but will need to keep on going. The body responds to cumulative workloads followed by recovery time to repair and rebuild stronger than before. We must do the work, no doubt, but also we must allow ample recovery time for adaptation to occur. Be smart with your design and implementation of work and rest, allowing no more than three consecutive weeks of building volume and intensity before giving yourself some recovery time.

Another key time to honor your body's need to stop may present itself with pesky and persistent aches or pains. Occasionally we experience acute injuries that happen suddenly from a single false move or misstep, but more often we develop chronic injuries over time as a result of repeated stress to an area not prepared to take it. When injury occurs, regardless of the type, we must react by admitting and addressing the problem. I may be the most blatant offender of this rule, having tried to deny injury after injury over the course of my career. But I've enjoyed the longest periods of success when I listened to my body, backed off when appropriate, sought the best therapy possible for the situation, and built back up after proper recovery time. Listen to the pain signals your body gives you. Are they self-preserving signals ("Please stop now because this is uncomfortable and I need more air"), or are they flashing red lights ("You must stop now or this stress reaction will become a fracture")? Sometimes it's hard to know, but over time, with proper mind–body connection, you'll learn to identify your body's messages and respond appropriately.

Analyze Workouts and Races

Learn from your training sessions and races by analyzing them, applying lessons to future plans. If you found a particular type of workout to be quite difficult, perhaps that means you should do more of it; you may have identified one of your body's limiters. If you made a split-second decision in a race and later regretted it, you may want to build a psychological plan to avoid the same mistake next time around. Be kind to yourself by taking note of the things you've done well and the ways you've improved or progressed, but also be honest with yourself to identify ways you might do better next time. The beauty of triathlon, with its many parts and infinite opportunities to improve, is that there is always something to change next time!

Running Well Off the Bike

All triathletes strive to run well off the bike. It's a daunting task with subtle nuances not present in running as a stand-alone sport. We benefit from focusing on the following areas for improvement:

- Technique: The position we use for riding compromises our running muscles and requires a reset of sorts.
- Pacing: The perception of effort and instinct for proper pacing can be even more challenging after swimming and riding than when running only.
- Endurance: Any race more than a few minutes long requires aerobic and muscular efficiency over a longer period, but running off the bike requires even more.

Run Technique

In training, we can work on run technique off the bike in a number of ways. First work on run technique in general. The better you can make your regular run technique, the better it will be off the bike. Developing your neuromuscular pathways through frequent, repeated drill sessions will help your brain tell your body how to function properly whether running before or after any other activity. I cannot emphasize enough the value of regular drill sessions!

Drills

Do drills immediately after you get off the bike, even if you don't plan to run that day. Let's say I get off my bike after an hour-long ride. I stand up to run, my hip flexors are tight, my quads are fatigued, my shoulders have been hunched, my posture is slumped. I could pick a few drills to target these problems right away.

Standing Postural Practice

Stand upright with open shoulders but a straight spine. Gently draw the belly button toward the spine and lean from the ankles to roll forward. Concentrate body weight in the front half of your shoes, then onto the forefoot, then go back to flatfoot, and repeat. This drill sets up proper posture and loosens the ankles and lower legs, which have been fixed to the bike shoes and pedals.

Walking Lunge

Walking lunges can loosen up the hip flexors and engage the glutes for running. Take a giant step forward. Dip the hips and flex the glutes so that the rear knee meets the ground. Drive off the planted heel using the glutes. Move the rear leg to in front of the body, then plant it and repeat on the other side.

Butt Kicks

Butt kicks, or heel flicks, can improve posture while simultaneously loosening the front leg muscles and activating the backside. With a subtle forward lean, take short, quick jogging steps forward, kicking your heels to your rear end with each step.

Practice

Frequently, practice running immediately after riding (even two or three times per week), but keep the duration very short (no need for more than 5 to 10 minutes in most cases). You can even do some workouts (limited to once per week at most, if not less frequently) that involve running fast off the bike.

Short Pace Progression Run Off the Bike

Ride for a predetermined duration at a predetermined level of effort. (I recommend keeping it all easy at first until you've got a good base.) Immediately transition to a short run starting at the lower end of race pace. Give yourself a 10 to 20 second per mile range and get faster as you go.

Brick Intervals

Ride for a short duration, transition to a short run at a fast speed, then jog or ride easy to recover and repeat. For example, you could try one of my favorite workouts:

After a good warm-up including some easy riding and running and some short pickup efforts in each (to race intensity for 15 to 60 seconds), repeat the following sequence two to six times:

- Ride 4 minutes as 2 minutes moderate, 2 minutes very hard.
- Transition very quickly to running shoes.
- Run 3 minutes at race pace.
- Jog 2 minutes very easy and transition back to the bike.
- Ride 1 minute very easy.

Build Strength

Strengthen your core so that it can be more versatile in movement. As I've mentioned already, core strength should be a key focus of every triathlete's training program! If you were to omit one workout per week in favor of another, I would say omit a run workout in favor of a core workout. The stronger you can be through your core, the better form you will be able to maintain while running, both off the bike and not.

Develop Speed

Include speed work in your training; Even very short bursts of speed only slightly faster than race pace count. It's easy to get caught up in logging miles, but a little speed work each week enhances your neuromuscular system, improving technique, and also improves your body's ability to produce anaerobic energy. A very simple speed session might include a warm-up, a series of drills, and then a short fartlek of 30 seconds of acceleration followed by 90 seconds of recovery for anywhere from 8 to 20 minutes. Follow the fartlek with a short cool-down of at least 5 minutes. You don't need to be at a track or a steep hill to practice running with good speed.

Pacing

In addition to running off the bike well from a technical standpoint, we need to practice racing off the bike in a pre-fatigued state. A key challenge many triathletes face involves pacing properly to get through the entire run. While our instinct or adrenaline sometimes can lead us to start the run full throttle and gradually fade as we cover more ground, we can be more successful by starting under great control and, as the race goes on, increasing effort (also getting faster in pace). Ideally this approach leads to a negative-split, where the second half of your race is faster than the first. To train yourself for proper pacing, you can employ some of the following methods:

- Do progressive run workouts during which you start very easy and gradually increase effort (and get faster) as the run continues, so that the last mile is the fastest mile.
- Make sure speed workouts include plenty of cut-down intervals; each one gets faster than the one preceding.

- Use a heart rate monitor to keep track of effort. Set heart rate goals for the beginning, middle, and end of runs that allow a gradual increase in effort.
- Enter running races to practice pacing in a run-only environment, taking mile splits and focusing on getting faster and faster.
- Use the treadmill to run off the bike once a week. Set the pace to start slowly and allow a slight increase in speed every 1 to 3 minutes for the duration of the run.

Good technique and proper pacing will help tremendously, but to run well off the bike, we also need to develop excellent endurance.

Endurance Training

Technique and pacing most certainly make a huge difference in how well we may run off the bike. Endurance training comprises the third key ingredient. In order to run well in any event longer than a couple of minutes, an athlete requires well-developed aerobic, muscular, and anaerobic endurance. Applying this principle to triathlon, we can design training sessions that target the key areas most challenged by the demands of a run following a strenuous swim and bike ride.

Use Swim and Ride Strength

Develop your swim and ride fitness so that they affect your run less. A well-rounded triathlete is a happy one. It's great to have a full-blown strength in one particular area, but the triathlete who has a strong swim is set up to be able to relax more on the bike. Similarly, the triathlete who has been able to relax more on the bike will be set up to run stronger. In an ideal world, we'd all be great at all three (most world champions are); but in the practical world, if we had to focus on one sport to improve the run, I'd say it should be the bike. If you can develop your riding tremendously, you will decrease its energy demands and have more left for the run. Was it Lance Armstrong who said, "It's not about the bike"? Well, in this case, I like the quote "It's ALL about the bike!" Ride frequently and use the bike and swim for the vast majority of your intensity (hard efforts), as your body recovers more quickly from those two sports than from run training.

Run Frequently

Assuming that appropriate work is being done to improve your bike fitness, the next factor in improving run endurance may be to increase weekly running frequency. Contrary to popular running belief, a higher run volume does not need to be achieved with a plethora of extra-long runs! In fact, most people increase injury resistance (durability) by running shorter but more frequently. In other words, if you're shooting for 20 miles per week, four runs of 5 miles may be far better than two runs of 10 miles.

Include Long Workouts

Improve overall endurance with one or two long workouts weekly. The meaning of the term *long* changes based on the athlete's key events. Consider your goal time for the event you're prioritizing; then build to the point that you can make your long workout roughly the same duration as your goal event (or even slightly longer). If you think your sprint triathlon will take two hours, you could plan to work in a weekly workout (eventually, after many weeks of base training) that equals or slightly exceeds that duration. It may be a long ride or a long brick workout combining ride and run, or even a more complete brick workout that involves first swimming, then riding, and then running.

Margie's Favorite Long Workouts

Classic Long Run

After a period of weeks building up, run up to 1 1/2 times race duration at an easy, comfortable pace, not to exceed 2 1/2 hours. This workout can be quite taxing even though it's performed at an easy pace, so make sure to fuel and hydrate properly and practice good recovery afterward.

Long Easy Brick

Ride up to two times the duration of your event's bike course mostly at an easy pace, but include two or three 10- to 15-minute up-tempo (moderate) efforts with at least 5 minutes easy after each. After riding, transition very quickly to running shoes, then run 15 minutes with the first 5 up-tempo, the last 10 very easy. This workout develops aerobic endurance and allows you to practice running off the bike in a fatigued state after a long ride.

Use Proper Intensity

Stay in the appropriate training zone for each training session. Ideally you have a plan laying out your training intensity targets within each workout. For example, "Run 30 minutes easy at zone 1-2" means keep your effort, heart rate, and rate of perceived exertion low. You can define your intensities more accurately through testing in a lab or with field testing, as described in chapter 3. Avoid looking at your watch and worrying about pace too much during an easy run. If you get too focused on running a certain pace, you may creep out of the intended effort zone and lose the ability to focus on proper technique. Endurance development takes time and patience, and you can achieve it best at the lower intensities.

Conclusion

In summary, training smart for the triathlon run requires a balanced approach to address weaknesses and strengths. You can improve your ability to run well off the bike with plenty of endurance work (both in running and in the other sports) but also with great attention to technique and pacing. Be patient as you learn your body's tendencies and ways to improve them. With proper planning, patience, and mindfulness, the body does amazing things. You will astound yourself with what you can do, provided the right opportunity. Running smart, listening to your body, making improvements to your movement patterns, and following a sensible training plan, you'll be bound for success on the triathlon run!

CHAPTER 9

Progressing From Sprint to Half Ironman

Melissa Mantak, MA

Writing this chapter, sharing my knowledge and experience with you, is the result of many, many years of training, racing, and coaching. When I started racing in the mid-1980s, triathlon was such a new sport that there just wasn't much information on how to prepare for a race. In those days, I was gathering information from as many sources as I could find. I achieved great success as an athlete, but these experiences left me thirsting for more knowledge and understanding of how to do things better. So, I became a coach. One of my personal goals as a coach is to be the coach to others that I never had personally. (Triathlon coaches were very rare in those days.)

In this chapter, I present three training plan samples, one for each distance, aimed at novice- and intermediate-level triathletes, along with information on how to customize these plans to meet your specific needs and circumstances. Everyone comes to the triathlon table with varying backgrounds and experience in sport. Throughout, you will find information on how to implement these plans in your daily routine. Refer to these notes often to get the most out of this chapter. My intention is to keep it simple and user-friendly, yet robust. Although these plans are no substitute for a great coach, they will get you well on your way to enjoying and succeeding at all three race distances.

Following the Plans

At the end of this chapter, I include three 12-week sample templates each for sprint (figures 9.1 to 9.3), Olympic (figures 9.4 to 9.6), and Half Ironman (figures 9.7 to 9.9) distances. There is a progression through each one, so you could follow it from day one in a sprint and continue on to the Half Ironman distance. Each plan is geared toward the novice- or intermediate-level triathlete. The Half Ironman program will allow you to comfortably complete the distance feeling strong and capable. At this level you may feel like a novice when doing your first one, but, let's face it, if you can train for and compete at this distance, you are at least at an intermediate level of fitness and capability.

Don't neglect the rest days! Your body needs the stress of exercise to adapt to greater fitness levels, but it's the recovery from exercise that makes you fitter. After recovery, you adapt to greater strength and speed. Rest allows you to recover from the stresses of life and training. Sleep is a powerful training tool that rejuvenates the body and the mind. Also consider getting a massage. It may seem like an indulgence, but it is an important tool to keep you healthy and able to make positive fitness gains as the training gets harder.

Rest can mean no exercise or light exercise. Either will aid recovery from the stresses of training and daily living. Experiment to discover which of these helps you recover better.

Good nutrition nourishes your body and helps you meet your training demands. Fruits and vegetables provide vitamins, minerals, and water to your body.

General Terminology

Triathlon training has its own lingo. I have kept the terminology basic and focused on terms that are commonly used.

Aerobic means in the presence of oxygen, an easy effort you could maintain potentially for many hours. From a physiological perspective, triathlon, even at the supersprint distance, is primarily an aerobic event.

Tempo means adding an anaerobic component (without the presence of oxygen). This is a moderate effort that can be sustained intermittently or steadily with training.

Threshold refers to the lactate threshold at which blood lactate levels begin to build. It causes that burning feeling in your muscles. This is a hard effort.

$\dot{V}O_2max$ is above threshold, a very hard effort. It is sustainable for minutes.

Periodization

Each plan follows the concept of periodization, building phases progressively in time (volume) and intensity over the course of 12 weeks. Each is based on three weeks on and one week for recovery. I have not included specific down weeks but provide notes on how to approach this at the end of each phase. The variables manipulated in any training plan are volume, intensity, volume of intensity, and frequency. Each phase builds on the previous one. In order to reap the greatest benefits, no shortcuts, please! These are the phases I use:

- Base: Building your aerobic base of fitness. Think of this as analogous to the foundation of a house. It is the key to holding the structure built on top of it in place. I have included only one week in base phase for each plan. Simply increase your weekly volume by 10 to 20 percent each week, keeping it all aerobic.
- Preparation: A time to increase intensity to improve fitness.
- Race specific: A period in which race-specific skills and physiological needs are emphasized.

Swim

Swim in a pool measured in either yards or meters; most of us swim in pools measured in yards. The programs in this chapter can be used in either yards or meters, but it is important to know the distance of the pool you are swimming in if you want to track your times accurately.

Freestyle is the fastest and the preferred stroke in triathlon racing, but you are welcome to add other strokes if you have a strong swimming background.

For equipment, you will need a swimsuit, goggles, and swim cap. Pull buoys, kickboards, fins, snorkels, and paddles are good to own, but some pools supply at least buoys and boards.

Swimming is the most technically challenging of the three disciplines. Joining a local masters group, taking group swim lessons, or getting one-on-one coaching in the swim can be very helpful if you struggle in this discipline.

I mention stroke drills in the swim workouts. These are best assigned by a coach or swim instructor to meet your individual needs.

Open-water swimming at least once is key to improving your comfort level and success on race day. It is not the same as swimming in the pool. Get out to the open water as much as you can before your event!

Intervals are the way of pool swimming. Intermittent bouts of work and rest break down the distances and specific skills of swimming—for example, 5 × 100 (yards or meters) as 25 sprint/25 easy on 15 seconds rest. Do a 100 (four lengths of the pool) as one length fast/one length easy/one fast/one easy. Then rest 15 seconds and repeat.

To pull means to use a buoy (a foam floatie that sits between your thighs) to emphasize specific upper-body strength for swimming.

For kick workouts, you can use a kickboard or not. These emphasize the leg action of swimming.

Bike

The most basic need here is to have a bike. The kind of bike you use is entirely up to you and your circumstances. If you are just giving the local sprint a try and your goal is to simply participate and enjoy your first triathlon, a borrowed bike or $100 special will suffice because bike split time to simply complete is quite different from bike split time to be competitive. At the other end of the spectrum, if you have the funds and the desire to be competitive, you will want a triathlon time trial (TT) bike. A TT bike or triathlon specific bike will put you in an aerodynamic position to help you go faster and lower your bike split. Your bike can fit anywhere within this spectrum. The main thing is to find one that fits you properly and that you know how to operate safely in many conditions (hills, wind, rough roads, and so on). Be sure you are equipped with a good helmet, gloves, flat-tire changing tools (most bike shops offer classes on simple bike maintenance), a good pair of shorts, sunglasses, and shoes. A professional bike fit goes a long way toward improving performance and comfort on your bike. The bike is the biggest investment in triathlon; make sure it is a bike that will work for you, not against you.

If you are new to cycling, a spin class is a great way to improve cycling-specific fitness. Also consider riding with friends. Training with others improves your ability to meet your goals and makes the time go by faster.

Do you have any hills in your area? If so, take some hill rides during training. Riding hills makes you stronger. Also don't avoid windy days. Riding in the wind improves strength, and the feel of a tailwind is awesome.

Run

The run requires the least amount of equipment, but investing in a good pair of shoes is a must. We need to take care of our feet, as they carry us everywhere we want to go.

Fartlek means intermittent work that alternates easy and hard continuously. A hill fartlek workout is accomplished on rolling hill terrain and can be simulated on a treadmill.

If you are new to running or concerned about injury, the intermittent run/walk system is the way to go. For example, by alternating running 10 minutes with walking 1 minute, you can build your volume more easily and with less stress on your body. This is key to building that all-important aerobic base.

I like to think of strides as small building blocks of speed. These are short, intense building efforts that rev up your engine and muscles for harder training to come either the same day or in the future. They are measured in seconds with easy walking or jogging in between.

Transition training takes place on two levels. First, perform brick workouts during which you do a run right after a ride (T2) or a ride right after a swim (T1). It is generally more difficult to run off the bike, so it is most important to practice this activity. Second, as you improve and want to go faster, fast transitions will shave minutes off your overall time. To do these, set up a mock transition zone in your backyard, basement, living room, or a local park. Start with 10 push-ups, jump up, run to your bike, get into your helmet, put on your glasses, and jump on your bike as quickly as you can. Ride a short distance, then hop off your bike, take your helmet off, rack your bike, put on your running shoes and number belt, and run a short distance. Practice for 15 to 45 minutes, one to three times per week, depending on your goals.

Strength

Strength is an integral part of your training regimen. As women, we frequently need to work to maintain and improve our upper-body strength, and regular strength training helps to keep us injury-free. The best approach is to have a program that is tailored to you. Having an assessment by a physical therapist or personal trainer or coach who is familiar with the demands of triathlon training is an ideal way to get the right strength training plan for you. Yoga, Pilates, or other group strength training classes can work as well.

Measuring Intensity

The ability to measure your training intensity, easy or hard, is key to achieving your performance and participation goals. Many devices can measure intensity: heart rate monitors, GPS (Global Positioning System) devices, and power meters. These are all great training tools, and at some point in your training career you may want to use one. But one of the simplest methods of measuring intensity is to use the rating of perceived exertion (RPE). I prefer the modified Borg scale from 1 to 10. A rating of 1 would be sitting down; 10 of 10 is a 100 percent, all-out effort (see table 9.1). I use this scale throughout the training plans.

TABLE 9.1

Training Intensity Guidelines

Rating of perceived exertion	Heart rate and power zones	Description of effort	Time in zones
1	No training effect	Sitting on the couch Passive recovery	Most of day
2	Zone 1	Active recovery Very light activity	30 to 90 min
3	Zone 2	Aerobic endurance Build aerobic capacity	30 min to 5 h
4	Zone 2	Aerobic endurance Build aerobic capacity	30 min to 5 h
5	Zone 2 to 3	Tempo, marathon; half marathon pace Add anaerobic component with aerobic	5 to 120 min
6	Zone 3 to 4	Tempo Add anaerobic component with aerobic	5 to 120 min
7	Zone 4	Threshold Lactate threshold	1 to 60 min
8	Zone 5	$\dot{V}O_2$max Anaerobic capacity	1 to 6 min
9	Zone 6	Sprint and power Speed and power	30 s to 2 min
10	Zone 6	Sprint and power Speed and power	8 to 12 s

The next option would be to use a heart rate monitor and calculate training zones. I have also included training zones throughout the sample training plans. Here is how to calculate your heart rate training zones:

1. Take your resting heart rate first thing in the morning. Lie down comfortably, put on your heart rate monitor strap, relax, and read the lowest number on the watch.

2. Calculate your max heart rate with this formula: $217 - (age \times .85)$.

3. Calculate your heart rate reserve (HRR) with this formula: max HR − resting HR.

4. Calculate the percent of effort required for the target zone (see table 9.2) with this formula: HRR × percent effort = Z.

5. Add Z to your resting heart rate to get your final value.

TABLE 9.2

Percent Effort According to Training Zone

Training zone	Percent effort
Zone 1	40 to 50
Zone 2	50 to 60
Zone 3	60 to 70
Zone 4	70 to 80
Zone 5	80 to 90

For example, let's consider a 35-year-old triathlete whose resting heart rate is 60:

217 − (35 [age] × .85) = 187.25 (max HR)

187.25 (max HR) − 60 (resting HR) = 127.25 (HRR)

127.25 × 70 percent (zone 4) = 89.075 (Z)

60 (resting HR) + 89.075 (Z) = 149.075 (HR training zone for zone 4)

Calculate your values for all the training zones.

Customizing the Plans

These plans are meant to be guides to help you on your journey to triathlon race success, but they are generalized. We all come to this sport with different strengths and weaknesses in each discipline. In order to better individualize these plans, the simple rule of thumb is to increase or decrease overall volume (time per session) by 10 to 30 percent, more if you can handle more, less if you need a slower progression. We all have our own individual rates of adaptation. Be willing to challenge yourself, but pay attention to overstress and overtraining, which may lead to illness or injury. You can also use the same 10 to 30 percent rule to add to or subtract from the volume of intensity, again more or less to fit your level of fitness and ability in a particular sport.

Choosing a Race and Race Strategy

When choosing a race, consider the time of year you want to race, whether a local or destination race is right for you, and both the terrain and weather conditions. If you live in a cold climate, it's best to pick a race that is later in the season, say July or August. This gives you ample outdoor warm-weather training time to prepare.

For first-time racers, I recommend a local race to get started. The environment and terrain are familiar, and you have the support of friends and family on race weekend. There are some amazing choices of destination races around the country and around the world. Visit www.usatriathlon.org/events to find a race near you. Traveling does involve more challenges and unknowns. For example, traveling with your bike is costly.

You'll need to consider terrain and climate when making a choice about where to race. Do you live in a flat state but want to race in a hilly state? Make sure you do a thorough investigation about the race course before making a decision. To the best of your ability, tailor your training to that specific terrain and those conditions.

When putting together a race strategy, terrain and weather conditions are a primary consideration. Is it going to be hot? Cold? Rainy? Will you be prepared to face any conditions on race day? Preparation is key. For example, don't avoid riding on windy days in training, as you could easily encounter strong winds on race day.

Once you choose a race, spend some time training on the course. The day before or day of the race, familiarize yourself with the flow of the transition area. Where will you rack your bike and set up your gear? Strategy must also be based on your abilities, fitness level, and confidence. For example, if you are new to swimming and open-water swim races, be sure to first train in the open water and then line up near the back or to the side on your wave start.

There is a bit of a learning curve with regard to pacing. Include race pace or race effort training (as in the template examples) once you are four to six weeks out from your race. For races that are going to take more than an hour, race day nutrition is a key component to success. Train your digestive system to handle sport nutrition during your training sessions so you can avoid stomach upset on race day.

Conclusion

The training plans in this chapter are intended to help the novice and intermediate triathlete progress from the sprint to Half Ironman distance triathlon and to be prepared for both training and race challenges. The plans and information provide a broad, robust overview of the preparation required to participate, compete, and achieve your goals. Take all of this information and make it your own. Make it work in your life and adapt it to your individual circumstances as an athlete. You now know a lot more about the language of triathlon training and racing. Enjoy your journey along the triathlon pathway. May it be a life-affirming and life-changing experience.

Sprint Distance, Base Training Phase

	Swim	Bike	Run	Strength
WEEK 1				
Monday	Rest day			
Tuesday		30 to 40 min aerobic, HR zone 1 or 2, RPE 2 to 4 of 10.		30 to 60 min
Wednesday	20 min continuous swimming, RPE 3 to 5 of 10. How far can you swim? This will provide a good comparison in weeks to come.		Run/walk: Walk 3 to 5 min, run or jog 8 min, walk 1 min. Repeat 2 or 3 times. Finish with 3 to 5 min walk. HR zone 1 or 2, RPE 3 to 5 of 10.	
Thursday	Rest day			
Friday	30 min. Work on technique and breathing. Focus on exhaling with face in water, finish exhale as mouth clears surface. Take a quick inhale, gulping as much air as fast as possible.	30 to 40 min aerobic, HR zone 1 or 2, RPE 2 to 4 of 10. Continuous steady effort.		
Saturday			Run/walk: Walk 3 to 5 min, run or jog 8 min, walk 1 min. Repeat 2 or 3 times. Finish with 3 to 5 min walk. HR zone 1 or 2, RPE 3 to 5 of 10.	30 to 60 min
Sunday	20 to 40 min continuous swimming, RPE 3 to 5 of 10. Focus on good technique.	30 to 40 min aerobic, HR zone 1 or 2, RPE 2 to 4 of 10. Continuous steady effort.		
WEEKS 2 AND 3				
Follow the same pattern for the next two weeks. Increase your volume by 10 to 20 percent, depending on your time available and rate of adaptation. In base training phase, the goal is to steadily increase volume (time) at an easy level to build your aerobic engine.				
WEEK 4				
This is a recovery week. Go back to what you did the first week or decrease the volume of week 3 by 20 to 30 percent, depending on fatigue levels, adaptation rate, and time available.				

FIGURE 9.1   **Sample program for a novice triathlete, sprint distance, base-level training.**

Sprint Distance, Preparation Training Phase

	Swim	Bike	Run	Strength
WEEK 1				
Monday	Rest day			
Tuesday		40 to 60 min aerobic, HR zone 1 or 2, RPE 2 to 4 of 10.		30 to 60 min
Wednesday	Warm-up: 100 swim, 4 × 25 alternate stroke drill, 25 swim, rest 15 s. Kick with kickboard: 4 × 75, rest 15 s. Swim 6 × 25, rest 15 s. Swim 100 to 200 non-stop. Total: 850 to 950		Run/walk: Walk 3 to 5 min, run or jog 10 min, walk 1 min. Repeat 2 or 3 times. Finish with 3 to 5 min walk. HR zone 1 or 2, RPE 3 to 5 of 10.	
Thursday	Rest day		Optional run or walk: Walk 3 to 5 min, run or jog 10 min, walk 1 min. Repeat 2 or 3 times. Finish with 3 to 5 min walk. HR zone 1 or 2, RPE 3 to 5 of 10.	Rest day
Friday	Warm-up: 100 swim, 4 × 25 alternate stroke drill, 25 swim, rest 15 s. Kick with kickboard: 4 × 75, rest 15 s. Swim 6 × 25, rest 15 s. Swim 100 to 200 non-stop. Total: 850 to 950	40 to 60 min aerobic, HR zone 1 or 2, RPE 2 to 4 of 10. Check your gear; make sure everything is in good working order.		
Saturday		Bike/run brick: Bike 45 min aerobic, HR zone 1 or 2, RPE 2 to 4 of 10. Right after the bike, run 15 min. OK to run/walk. Have your run gear ready so you can move quickly to the run after the bike.		30 to 60 min
Sunday	Warm-up: 100 swim, 4 × 25 alternate stroke drill, 25 swim, rest 15 s. Kick with kickboard: 4 × 75, rest 15 s. Swim 6 × 25, rest 15 s. Swim 100 to 200 non-stop. Total: 850 to 950	40 to 60 min aerobic, HR zone 1 or 2, RPE 2 to 4 of 10. Continuous steady effort.		

FIGURE 9.2   **Sample program for a novice triathlete, sprint distance, preparation-level training.**

WEEK 2				
	Swim	**Bike**	**Run**	**Strength**
Monday	Rest day			
Tuesday		50 to 70 min aerobic, HR zone 1 or 2, RPE 2 to 4 of 10. Work to improve your endurance and go a little farther each week.		30 to 60 min
Wednesday	Warm-up: 100 swim, 4 × 25 alternate stroke drill, 25 swim, rest 15 s. Pull (use pull buoy or just don't kick): 4 × 50, rest 15 s. Swim 4 × 50, rest 15 s. Kick: 6 × 25, rest 15 s. Swim 300 nonstop. Total: 1,150		Run/walk: Walk 3 to 5 min, run or jog 10 min, walk 1 min. Repeat 3 or 4 times. Finish with 3 to 5 min walk. HR zone 1 or 2, RPE 3 to 5 of 10.	
Thursday	Rest day		Optional run/walk: Walk 3 to 5 min, run or jog 10 min, walk 1 min. Repeat 3 or 4 times. Finish with 3 to 5 min walk. HR zone 1 or 2, RPE 3 to 5 of 10.	Rest day
Friday	Warm-up: 100 swim, 4 × 25 alternate stroke drill, 25 swim, rest 15 s. Pull (use pull buoy or just don't kick): 4 × 50, rest 15 s. Swim 4 × 50, rest 15 s. Kick: 6 × 25, rest 15 s. Swim 300 nonstop. Total: 1,150	50 to 70 min aerobic, HR zone 1 or 2, RPE 2 to 4 of 10.		
Saturday		Bike/run brick: Bike 45 min aerobic, HR zone 1 or 2, RPE 2 to 4 of 10. Right after the bike, run 20 min. OK to run/walk. Have your run gear ready so you can move quickly to the run after the bike.		30 to 60 min
Sunday	Warm-up: 100 swim, 4 × 25 alternate stroke drill, 25 swim, rest 15 s. Pull (use pull buoy or just don't kick): 4 × 50, rest 15 s. Swim 4 × 50, rest 15 s. Kick: 6 × 25, rest 15 s. Swim 300 nonstop. Total: 1,150	50 to 70 min aerobic, HR zone 1 or 2, RPE 2 to 4 of 10. Continuous steady effort.		

FIGURE 9.2 **Sample program for a novice triathlete, sprint distance, preparation-level training** *(continued).*

WEEK 3				
	Swim	**Bike**	**Run**	**Strength**
Monday	Rest day			
Tuesday		50 to 90 min aerobic, HR zone 1 or 2, RPE 2 to 4 of 10. If possible, include some hills.		30 to 60 min
Wednesday	Warm-up: 100 swim, 4 × 25 alternate stroke drill, 25 swim, rest 15 s. Swim 300 nonstop. Kick: 4 × 75, rest 15 s. Swim 500 nonstop. Total: 1,400		Run/walk: Walk 3 to 5 min, run or jog 10 min, walk 1 min. Repeat 3 to 5 times. Finish with 3 to 5 min walk. HR zone 1 or 2, RPE 3 to 5 of 10.	
Thursday	Rest day		Optional run/walk: Walk 3 to 5 min, run or jog 10 min, walk 1 min. Repeat 3 to 5 times. Finish with 3 to 5 min walk. HR zone 1 or 2, RPE 3 to 5 of 10.	Rest day
Friday	Warm-up: 100 swim, 4 × 25 alternate stroke drill, 25 swim, rest 15 s. Swim 300 nonstop. Kick: 4 × 75, rest 15 s. Swim 500 nonstop. Total: 1,400	50 to 90 min aerobic, HR zone 1 or 2, RPE 2 to 4 of 10.		
Saturday		Bike/run brick: Bike 45 min aerobic, HR zone 1 or 2, RPE 2 to 4 of 10. Right after the bike, run 25 to 30 min. OK to run/walk. Have your run gear ready so you can move quickly to the run after the bike.		30 to 60 min
Sunday	Warm-up: 100 swim, 4 × 25 alternate stroke drill, 25 swim, rest 15 s. Swim 300 nonstop. Kick: 4 × 75, rest 15 s. Swim 500 nonstop. Total: 1,400	50 to 90 min aerobic, HR zone 1 or 2, RPE 2 to 4 of 10. Continuous steady effort.		
WEEK 4				
Recovery week: Decrease your volume by 20 to 30 percent. Take two rest days. Get a massage. Keep all workouts easy and relaxed for this week to prepare your body for the next training phase.				

FIGURE 9.2 **Sample program for a novice triathlete, sprint distance, preparation-level training** *(continued).*

Sprint Distance, Race-Specific Training Phase

WEEK 1				
	Swim	**Bike**	**Run**	**Strength**
Monday	Rest day			
Tuesday		60 to 75 min aerobic with tempo intervals, HR zone 1 or 2, RPE 2 to 4 of 10. After 20 min warm-up, ride 3 to 5 × 6 min to HR zone 3, RPE 5 to 6 of 10, 2 min easy between. Finish at aerobic effort and cool down.		30 to 60 min
Wednesday	Warm-up: 100 swim, 4 × 25 stroke drill, 25 swim, rest 15 s. Swim 400 nonstop. Pull: 4 × 75, rest 15 s. Swim 600 nonstop. Total: 1,600		Run/walk: Walk 3 to 5 min, run or jog 15 min, walk 1 min. Repeat 2 or 3 times. Finish with 3 to 5 min walk. HR zone 1 or 2, RPE 3 to 5 of 10.	
Thursday	Rest day		Optional run/walk: Walk 3 to 5 min, run or jog 10 min, walk 1 min. Repeat 3 to 5 times. Finish with 3 to 5 min walk. HR zone 1 or 2, RPE 3 to 5 of 10.	Rest day
Friday	Warm-up: 100 swim, 4 × 25 stroke drill, 25 swim, rest 15 s. Swim 400 nonstop. Pull: 4 × 75, rest 15 s. Swim 600 nonstop. Total: 1,600	60 to 75 min aerobic with tempo intervals, HR zone 1 or 2, RPE 2 to 4 of 10. After 20 min warm-up, ride 3 to 5 × 6 min to HR zone 3, RPE 5 to 6 of 10, 2 min easy between. Finish at aerobic effort and cool down.		
Saturday	Swim/bike brick: If possible, get out to the open water for an open-water swim of 30 min. Bike 60 to 90 min at steady effort. Rolling hills are good, if available. Ride right after swim. If open water is not available, repeat this week's swim workouts. Transition training: Set up a mock transition area in your yard, basement, or a park. With race suit on, run to bike and put on helmet, glasses, and shoes. Run with bike to mount line. Mount bike and take a short ride. Hop off the bike and rack it. Put on running shoes and number belt and do a short run. Complete 3 to 5 times.			30 to 60 min

(continued)

FIGURE 9.3   **Sample program for a novice triathlete, sprint distance, race-specific level training.**

WEEK 1 (continued)				
	Swim	**Bike**	**Run**	**Strength**
Sunday		Bike/run brick: Bike 60 min aerobic, HR zone 1 or 2, RPE 2 to 4 of 10. Right after the bike, run 20 to 35 min. OK to run/walk. Have your run gear ready so you can move quickly to the run after the bike.		
WEEK 2				
	Swim	**Bike**	**Run**	**Strength**
Monday	Rest day			
Tuesday		60 to 75 min aerobic with tempo intervals, HR zone 1 or 2, RPE 2 to 4 of 10. After 20 min warm-up, ride 3 to 5 × 8 min to HR zone 3, RPE 5 to 6 of 10, 2 min easy between. Finish at aerobic effort and cool down.		30 to 60 min
Wednesday	Warm-up: 100 swim, 4 × 25 alternate stroke drill, 25 swim, rest 15 s. Pull (use pull buoy or just don't kick): 4 × 50, rest 15 s. Swim 4 × 50, rest 15 s. Kick: 6 × 25, rest 15 s. Swim 800 nonstop. Total: 1,650		Run/walk: Walk 3 to 5 min, run or jog 15 min, walk 1 min. Repeat 2 to 4 times. Finish with 3 to 5 min walk. HR zone 1 or 2, RPE 3 to 5 of 10.	
Thursday	Rest day		Optional run/walk: Walk 3 to 5 min, run or jog 10 min, walk 1 min. Repeat 3 to 5 times. Finish with 3 to 5 min walk. HR zone 1 or 2, RPE 3 to 5 of 10.	Rest day
Friday	Warm-up: 100 swim, 4 × 25 alternate stroke drill, 25 swim, rest 15 s. Pull (use pull buoy or just don't kick): 4 × 50, rest 15 s. Swim 4 × 50, rest 15 s. Kick: 6 × 25, rest 15 s. Swim 800 nonstop. Total: 1,650	60 to 75 min aerobic with tempo intervals, HR zone 1 or 2, RPE 2 to 4 of 10. After 20 min warm-up, ride 3 to 5 × 8 min to HR zone 3, RPE 5 to 6 of 10, 2 min easy between. Finish at aerobic effort and cool down.		

FIGURE 9.3   **Sample program for a novice triathlete, sprint distance, race-specific level training** (continued).

	Swim	Bike	Run	Strength
Saturday	Swim/bike brick: If possible, get out for an open-water swim of 30 min. Bike 60 to 90 min at steady effort. Rolling hills are good, if available. Ride right after the swim. If open water is not available, repeat this week's swim workouts. Transition training: Set up a mock transition area in your yard, basement, or a park. With race suit on, run to bike and put on helmet, glasses, and shoes. Run with bike to mount line. Mount bike and take a short ride. Hop off the bike and rack it. Put on running shoes and number belt and do a short run. Complete 3 to 5 times.			30 to 60 min
Sunday		Bike/run brick: Bike 60 to 90 min aerobic, HR zone 1 or 2, RPE 2 to 4 of 10. Right after the bike, run 20 to 35 min. OK to run/walk. Have your run gear ready so you can move quickly to the run after the bike.		

WEEK 3				
	Swim	Bike	Run	Strength
Monday	Rest day			
Tuesday		60 to 75 min aerobic with tempo intervals, HR zone 1 or 2, RPE 2 to 4 of 10. After 20 min warm-up, ride 3 to 5 × 10 min to HR zone 3, RPE 5 to 6 of 10, 5 min easy between. Finish at aerobic effort and cool down.		30 to 60 min
Wednesday	Warm-up: 100 swim, 4 × 25 alternate stroke drill, 25 swim, rest 15 s. Pull (use pull buoy or just don't kick): 4 × 50, rest 15 s. Swim 4 × 50, rest 15 s. Kick: 6 × 25, rest 15 s. Swim 800 to 1,000 nonstop. Total: 1,650 to 1,850		Run/walk: Walk 3 to 5 min, run or jog 15 min, walk 1 min. Repeat 2 to 5 times. Finish with 3 to 5 min walk. HR zone 1 or 2, RPE 3 to 5 of 10.	
Thursday	Rest day		Optional run/walk: Walk 3 to 5 min, run or jog 10 min, walk 1 min. Repeat 6 times. Finish with 3 to 5 min walk. HR zone 1 or 2, RPE 3 to 5 of 10.	Rest day

FIGURE 9.3   Sample program for a novice triathlete, sprint distance, race-specific level training *(continued)*.

WEEK 3 *(continued)*				
	Swim	**Bike**	**Run**	**Strength**
Saturday	Swim/bike brick: If possible, get out for an open-water swim of 30 min. Bike 60 to 90 min at steady effort. Rolling hills are good, if available. Ride right after the swim. If open water is not available, repeat this week's swim workouts. Transition training: Set up a mock transition area in your yard, basement or a park. With race suit on, run to bike and put on helmet, glasses, and shoes. Run with bike to mount line. Mount bike and take a short ride. Hop off the bike and rack it. Put on running shoes and number belt and do a short run. Complete 3 to 5 times.			30 to 60 min
Sunday		Bike/run brick: Bike 60 to 90 min aerobic, HR zone 1 or 2, RPE 2 to 4 of 10. Right after the bike, run 20 to 35 min. OK to run/walk. Have your run gear ready so you can move quickly to the run after the bike.		
WEEK 4				
Recovery week: Decrease your volume by 20 to 30 percent. Take two rest days. Get a massage. Keep all workouts easy and relaxed for this week to prepare your body for the next training phase or race.				

FIGURE 9.3 **Sample program for a novice triathlete, sprint distance, race-specific level training** *(continued).*

Olympic Distance, Base Training Phase

WEEK 1				
	Swim	**Bike**	**Run**	**Strength**
Monday			Run/walk: Walk 3 to 5 min, run or jog 10 min, walk 1 min. Repeat 2 to 4 times. Finish with 3 to 5 min walk. HR zone 1 or 2, RPE 3 to 5 of 10. Or run continuously for 30 to 40 min. The intermittent run/walk builds an aerobic base with less stress on your body.	
Tuesday	300 drills and warm-up. 5 × 50 pull and 5 × 50 kick, 10 s rest between. 5 to 10 × 100 swim, 10 s rest between. 10 × 25 sprint, 10 to 20 s rest. 200 easy swim and drills. Total: 2,250	50 to 70 min aerobic, HR zone 1 or 2, RPE 2 to 4 of 10, at continuous steady effort.		

FIGURE 9.4 **Sample program for a novice triathlete, Olympic distance, base-level training.**

	Swim	Bike	Run	Strength
Wednesday		50 to 70 min aerobic, HR zone 1 or 2, RPE 2 to 4 of 10, at continuous steady effort.		30 to 60 min
Thursday	300 drills and warm-up. 5 × 50 pull and 5 × 50 kick with 10 s rest between. 5 to 10 × 100 swim, 10 s rest between. 10 × 25 sprint, 10 to 20 s rest. 200 easy swim and drills. Total: 2,250		Run/walk: Walk 3 to 5 min, run or jog 8 min, walk 1 min. Repeat 2 to 4 times. Finish with 3 to 5 min walk. HR zone 1 or 2, RPE 3 to 5 of 10. Or run continuously for 30 to 40 min.	
Friday	Rest day			
Saturday			Run/walk: Walk 3 to 5 min, run or jog 8 min, walk 1 min. Repeat 3 to 6 times. Finish with 3 to 5 min walk. HR zone 1 or 2, RPE 3 to 5 of 10. Or run continuously for 30 to 40 min.	30 to 60 min
Sunday	300 drills and warm-up. 5 × 50 pull and 5 × 50 kick with 10 s rest between. 5 to 10 × 100 swim, 10 s rest between. 10 × 25 sprint, 10 to 20 s rest. 200 easy swim and drills. Total: 2,250			

WEEKS 2 AND 3

Follow the same pattern for the next two weeks. Increase your volume by 10 to 20 percent, depending on your time available and rate of adaptation. In base training phase, the goal is to steadily increase volume (time) at an easy level to build your aerobic engine.

WEEK 4

This is a recovery week. Go back to what you did the first week or decrease the volume of week 3 by 20 to 30 percent, depending on fatigue levels, adaptation rate, and time available.

FIGURE 9.4   Sample program for a novice triathlete, Olympic distance, base-level training *(continued)*.

Olympic Distance, Preparation Training Phase

	Swim	Bike	Run	Strength
WEEK 1				
Monday			Run hill fartlek: Walk 3 to 5 min, run or jog 10 min, then 4 × 20 step strides, 1 min walk between. On rolling hills, push the uphill to RPE 6, relax on downhills. Perform 10 to 12 min of uphill work. Finish with 3 to 5 min walk. HR zone 1 or 2, RPE 3 to 5 of 10. Total run time: 40 to 45 min.	
Tuesday	400 drills and warm-up. 300 pull, 300 kick, 10 s rest between. 3 × 300 swim, 10 to 20 s rest between with 1 and 3 at race effort. 400 swim. 200 easy swim and drills. Total: 2,500	60 to 90 min aerobic with tempo intervals, HR zone 1 or 2, RPE 2 to 4 of 10. After 20 min warm-up, ride 3 to 5 × 10 min to HR zone 3, RPE 5 or 6 of 10, 5 min easy between. Finish at aerobic effort and cool down.		
Wednesday		50 to 70 min aerobic, HR zone 1 or 2, RPE 2 to 4 of 10, continuous steady effort.		30 to 60 min
Thursday	400 drills and warm-up. 300 pull, 300 kick, 10 s rest between. 3 × 300 swim, 10 to 20 s rest between. 400 swim. 200 easy swim and drills. Total: 2,500		Run/walk: Walk 3 to 5 min, run or jog 10 min, walk 1 min. Repeat 2 to 4 times. Finish with 3 to 5 min walk. HR zone 1 or 2, RPE 3 to 5 of 10. Or run continuously 30 to 40 min.	
Friday	Rest day			
Saturday			Run hill fartlek: Walk 3 to 5 min, run or jog 10 min, then 4 × 20 step strides, 1 min walk between. On rolling hills, push the uphill to RPE 6, relax on downhills. Perform 10 to 12 min of uphill work. Finish with 3 to 5 min walk. HR zone 1 or 2, RPE 3 to 5 of 10. Total run time: 40 to 45 min.	30 to 60 min

FIGURE 9.5 Sample program for a novice triathlete, Olympic distance, preparation-level training.

	Swim	Bike	Run	Strength
Sunday	400 drills and warm-up. 300 pull, 300 kick, 10 s rest between. 3 × 300 swim, 10 to 20 s rest between with 1 and 3 at race effort. 400 swim. 200 easy swim and drills. Total: 2,500	1 1/4 to 1 3/4 h aerobic with tempo intervals, HR zone 1 or 2, RPE 2 to 4 of 10. After 20 min warm-up, ride 3 to 5 × 10 min to HR zone 3, RPE 5 or 6 of 10, 5 min easy between. Finish at aerobic effort and cool down.		

WEEK 2				
	Swim	Bike	Run	Strength
Monday			Run hill fartlek: Walk 3 to 5 min, run or jog 10 min, then 4 × 20 step strides, 1 min walk between. On rolling hills, push the uphill to RPE 6, relax on down-hills. Perform 12 to 15 min of uphill work. Finish with 3 to 5 min walk. HR zone 1 or 2, RPE 3 to 5 of 10. Total run time: 40 to 45 min.	
Tuesday	500 drills and warm-up. 10 × 25 sprint, 10 s rest between. 800 swim, aerobic. 10 × 100 alternate 25 sprint/25 easy, 10 to 20 s rest. 200 easy swim and drills. Total: 2,750	60 to 75 min aerobic with tempo intervals, HR zone 1 or 2, RPE 2 to 4 of 10. After 20 min warm-up, ride 3 or 4 × 15 min to HR zone 3, RPE 5 or 6 of 10, 5 min easy between. Finish at aerobic effort and cool down.		
Wednesday		50 to 70 min aerobic, HR zone 1 or 2, RPE 2 to 4 of 10 at continuous steady effort.		30 to 60 min
Thursday	500 drills and warm-up. 10 × 25 sprint, 10 s rest between. 800 swim, aerobic. 10 × 100 alternate 25 sprint/25 easy, 10 to 20 s rest. 200 easy swim and drills. Total: 2,750		Run/walk: Walk 3 to 5 min, run or jog 8 min, walk 1 min. Repeat 2 to 4 times. Finish with 3 to 5 min walk. HR zone 1 or 2, RPE 3 to 5 of 10. Or run continuously 30 to 40 min.	
Friday	Rest day			

FIGURE 9.5   **Sample program for a novice triathlete, Olympic distance, preparation-level training** *(continued)*.

WEEK 2 (continued)				
	Swim	**Bike**	**Run**	**Strength**
Saturday			Run hill fartlek: Walk 3 to 5 min, run or jog 10 min, then 4 × 20 step strides, 1 min walk between. On rolling hills, push the uphill to RPE 6, relax on downhills. Perform 12 to 15 min of uphill work. Finish with 3 to 5 min walk. HR zone 1 or 2, RPE 3 to 5 of 10. Total run time: 40 to 45 min.	30 to 60 min
Sunday	500 drills and warm-up. 10 × 25 sprint, 10 s rest between. 800 swim, aerobic. 10 × 100 alternate 25 sprint/25 easy, 10 to 20 s rest. 200 easy swim and drills. Total: 2,750	1 1/2 to 2 h aerobic with tempo intervals, HR zone 1 or 2, RPE 2 to 4 of 10. After 20 min warm-up, ride 3 or 4 × 15 min to HR zone 3, RPE 5 or 6 of 10, 5 min easy between. Finish at aerobic effort and cool down.		
WEEK 3				
	Swim	**Bike**	**Run**	**Strength**
Monday			Run tempo: Walk 3 to 5 min, run or jog 10 min easy, then 4 × 16 step strides, 1 min walk between. On flat or slight uphill, run tempo 4 to 6 × 5 min, 2 to 3 min jog between, HR zone 4, RPE 7 of 10. Finish with 3 to 5 min walk. Total run time: 60 to 80 min.	
Tuesday	500 drills and warm-up. 10 × 25 sprint, 10 s rest between. 1,000 swim, aerobic. 5 or 6 × 200 alternate 25 sprint/25 easy, 10 to 20 s rest. 1,200 easy swim and drills. Total: 2,850 to 3,150	Bike threshold: 75 to 90 min aerobic with threshold intervals, HR zone 1 or 2, RPE 2 to 4 of 10. After 20 min warm-up, ride 3 or 4 × 8 min to HR zone 4, RPE 7 of 10, 4 min easy between. Finish at aerobic effort and cool down.		
Wednesday		50 to 70 min aerobic, HR zone 1 or 2, RPE 2 to 4 of 10 at continuous steady effort.		30 to 60 min

FIGURE 9.5   **Sample program for a novice triathlete, Olympic distance, preparation-level training** (continued).

	Swim	Bike	Run	Strength
Thursday	500 drills and warm-up. 10 × 25 sprint, 10 s rest between. 1,000 swim, aerobic. 5 or 6 × 200 alternate 25 sprint/25 easy, 10 to 20 s rest. 1,200 easy swim and drills. Total: 2,850 to 3,150		Run/walk: Walk 3 to 5 min, run or jog 10 min, walk 1 min. Repeat 3 to 6 times. Finish with 3 to 5 min walk. HR zone 1 or 2, RPE 3 to 5 of 10. Or run continuously 40 to 50 min.	
Friday	Rest day			
Saturday			Long, steady run: Walk 3 to 5 min, run steady 60 to 75 min aerobic, HR zone 1 or 2, RPE 4 or 5 of 10. Walk 3 min.	30 to 60 min
Sunday	500 drills and warm-up. 10 × 25 sprint, 10 s rest between. 1,000 swim, aerobic. 5 or 6 × 200 alternate 25 sprint/25 easy, 10 to 20 s rest. 1,200 easy swim and drills. Total: 2,850 to 3,150	Bike threshold: 1 3/4 to 2 1/2 h aerobic with threshold intervals, HR zone 1 or 2, RPE 2 to 4 of 10. After 20 min warm-up, ride 3 or 4 × 8 min to HR zone 4, RPE 7 of 10, 4 min easy between. Finish at aerobic effort and cool down.		
WEEK 4				
Recovery week: Decrease your volume by 20 to 30 percent from week 1. Take two rest days. Get a massage. Keep all workouts easy and relaxed for this week to prepare your body for the next training phase.				

FIGURE 9.5   **Sample program for a novice triathlete, Olympic distance, preparation-level training** *(continued)*.

Olympic Distance, Race-Specific Training Phase

		WEEK 1		
	Swim	**Bike**	**Run**	**Strength**
Monday			Run tempo: Walk 3 to 5 min, run or jog 10 min easy, then 4 × 16 step strides, 1 min walk between. On flat or slight uphill, run tempo 3 to 5 × 8 min, 2 to 3 min jog between. HR zone 4, RPE 7 of 10. Finish with 3 to 5 min walk. Total run time: 60 to 80 min.	
Tuesday	300 drills and warm-up. 4 × 400, 20 s rest, with 1 and 3 at race effort, 2 and 4 at aerobic effort. 4 × 75 as 25 sprint/25 easy/25 sprint, 10 to 20 s rest. 400 easy swim and drills. Total: 2,800	Bike threshold: 75 to 90 min aerobic with threshold intervals, HR zone 1 or 2, RPE 2 to 4 of 10. After 20 min warm-up, ride 3 or 4 × 10 min to HR zone 4, RPE 7 of 10, 5 min easy between. Finish at aerobic effort and cool down. Run off bike for 20 min aerobic pace.		
Wednesday		50 to 70 min aerobic, HR zone 1 or 2, RPE 2 to 4 of 10, at continuous steady effort.		30 to 60 min
Thursday	300 drills and warm-up. 5 × 300 threshold, 20 s rest. 4 × 75 as 25 sprint/25 easy/25 sprint, 10 to 20 s rest. 400 easy swim and drills. Total: 2,600		Run/walk: Walk 3 to 5 min, run or jog 10 min, walk 1 min. Repeat 3 to 6 times. Finish with 3 to 5 min walk. HR zone 1 or 2, RPE 3 to 5 of 10. Or run continuously 40 to 50 min.	
Friday	Rest day			
Saturday	Transition training: Set up mock transition area in your yard, basement, or a park. With race suit on, run to bike and put on helmet, glasses, and shoes. Run with bike to mount line. Mount bike and take a short ride. Hop off the bike and rack it. Put on running shoes and number belt and do a short run. Complete this 3 to 5 times.		Run hill fartlek: Walk 3 to 5 min, run or jog 10 min. On rolling hills, push the uphill to RPE 6, relax on downhills. Perform 15 to 20 min of uphill work. Finish with 3 to 5 min walk. HR zone 1 or 2, RPE 3 to 5 of 10. Total run time: 70 to 85 min.	30 to 60 min

FIGURE 9.6   Sample program for a novice triathlete, Olympic distance, race-specific level training.

	Swim	Bike	Run	Strength
Sunday	500 drills and warm-up. 1,500 nonstop, strong aerobic. 200 easy swim and drills. Total: 2,200 Or open-water swim of 45 to 60 min. If available, open water is the best option. Work on steady aerobic swimming, sighting, and swimming straight.	Bike threshold: Ride right after swim for 1 3/4 to 2 1/2 h at aerobic level with threshold intervals, HR zone 1 or 2, RPE 2 to 4 of 10. After 20 min warm-up, ride 3 or 4 × 8 min to HR zone 4, RPE 7 of 10, 4 min easy between. Finish at aerobic effort and cool down. Run off bike for 20 min at aerobic pace.		

WEEK 2

	Swim	Bike	Run	Strength
Monday			Run at 10K race pace: Walk 3 to 5 min, run or jog 10 min easy, then 4 × 16 step strides, 1 min walk between. On flat or slight uphill, run 3 to 5 × 4 min at 10K race effort, 2 to 4 min jog between. At threshold, HR zone 4 or 5, RPE 7 of 10. Finish with 3 to 5 min walk. Total run time: 60 to 80 min.	
Tuesday	300 drills and warm-up. 4 × 400 aerobic, 20 s rest. 4 × 75 as 25 sprint/25 easy/25 sprint, 10 to 20 s rest. 400 easy swim and drills. Total: 3,200	60 to 90 min aerobic, HR zone 1 or 2, RPE 2 to 4 of 10 at continuous steady effort. Run off bike for 20 min at aerobic pace.		
Wednesday		Bike $\dot{V}O_2$max intervals: 60 to 90 min. Warm-up 20 min, with 5 × 30 s sprint, 1 min easy between. Build effort with each one. Ride 5 min easy. For $\dot{V}O_2$max intervals, ride 3 to 6 × 3 min to HR zone 5, RPE 8 of 10, 3 min easy spin between. Finish at easy aerobic effort and cool down.		30 to 60 min

FIGURE 9.6   **Sample program for a novice triathlete, Olympic distance, race-specific level training** (continued).

	Swim	Bike	Run	Strength
	**WEEK 2** *(continued)*			
	Swim	**Bike**	**Run**	**Strength**
Thursday	300 drills and warm-up. 5 × 300 threshold, 20 s rest. 4 × 75 as 25 sprint/25 easy/25 sprint, 10 to 20 s rest. 400 easy swim and drills. Total: 2,700		Run/walk: Walk 3 to 5 min, run or jog 10 min, walk 1 min. Repeat 3 to 6 times. Finish with 3 to 5 min walk. HR zone 1 or 2, RPE 3 to 5 of 10. Or run continuously for 40 to 50 min.	
Friday	Rest day			
Saturday	Transition training: Set up mock transition area in your yard, basement, or a park. With race suit on, run to bike and put on helmet, glasses, and shoes. Run with bike to mount line. Mount bike and take a short ride. Hop off the bike and rack it. Put on running shoes and number belt and do a short run. Complete this 3 to 5 times.		Long, steady run: Walk 3 to 5 min, steady run 60 to 90 min aerobic, HR zone 1 or 2, RPE 4 to 5 of 10. Walk 3 min.	30 to 60 min
Sunday	500 drills and warm-up. 2,000 nonstop, strong aerobic. 200 easy swim and drills. Total: 2,700 Or open-water swim of 45 to 60 min. If available, open water is the best option. Work on steady aerobic swimming, sighting, and swimming straight.	Bike threshold: Ride right after swim for 1 3/4 to 2 1/2 h at aerobic level with threshold intervals, HR zone 1 or 2, RPE 2 to 4 of 10. After 20 min warm-up, ride 2 × 20 min to HR zone 4, RPE 7 of 10, 5 min easy between. Finish at aerobic effort and cool down. Run off bike for 40 min at aerobic pace.		
	**WEEK 3**			
	Swim	**Bike**	**Run**	**Strength**
Monday			Run 10K race pace: Walk 3 to 5 min, run or jog 10 min easy, then 4 × 16 step strides, 1 min walk between. On flat or slight uphill, run 3 to 5 × 5 min at 10K race effort, 2 to 4 min jog between. At threshold, HR zone 4 or 5, RPE 7 of 10. Finish with 3 to 5 min walk. Total run time: 60 to 80 min.	

FIGURE 9.6   **Sample program for a novice triathlete, Olympic distance, race-specific level training** *(continued).*

	Swim	Bike	Run	Strength
Tuesday	300 drills and warm-up. 4 × 500, 20 s rest, aerobic effort. 4 × 75 as 25 sprint/25 easy/25 sprint, 10 to 20 s rest. 400 easy swim and drills. Total: 3,200	Bike 60 to 90 min aerobic, HR zone 1 or 2, RPE 2 to 4 of 10 at continuous steady effort. Run off bike for 20 min, aerobic.		
Wednesday		Bike $\dot{V}O_2$max intervals: 60 to 90 min. Warm-up 20 min, with 5 × 30 s sprint, 1 min easy between. Build effort with each one. Ride 5 min easy. For $\dot{V}O_2$max intervals, ride 3 to 6 × 4 min to HR zone 5, RPE 8 of 10, 4 min easy spin between. Finish at easy aerobic effort and cool down.		30 to 60 min
Thursday	300 drills and warm-up. 4 × 400, 20 s rest, threshold. 4 × 75 as 25 sprint/25 easy/25 sprint, 10 to 20 s rest. 400 easy swim and drills. Total: 2,700		Run/walk: Walk 3 to 5 min, run or jog 10 min, walk 1 min. Repeat 3 to 6 times. Finish with 3 to 5 min walk. HR zone 1 or 2, RPE 3 to 5 of 10. Or run continuously for 40 to 50 min.	
Friday	Rest day			
Saturday	Transition training: Set up mock transition area in your yard, basement, or a park. With race suit on, run to bike and put on helmet, glasses, and shoes. Run with bike to mount line. Mount bike and take a short ride. Hop off the bike and rack it. Put on running shoes and number belt and do a short run. Complete this 3 to 5 times.		Long, steady run: Walk 3 to 5 min, steady run 60 to 90 min aerobic, HR zone 1 or 2, RPE 4 to 5 of 10. Walk 3 min.	30 to 60 min

FIGURE 9.6 **Sample program for a novice triathlete, Olympic distance, race-specific level training**
(continued).

WEEK 3 *(continued)*				
	Swim	**Bike**	**Run**	**Strength**
Sunday	500 drills and warm-up. 2,000 nonstop, strong aerobic. 200 easy swim and drills. Total: 2,700 Or open-water swim of 45 to 60 min. If available, open water is the best option. Work on steady aerobic swimming, sighting, and swimming straight.	Bike threshold: Ride right after swim for 1 3/4 to 2 1/2 h at aerobic level with threshold intervals, HR zone 1 or 2, RPE 2 to 4 of 10. After 20 min warm-up, ride 2 × 20 min to HR zone 4, RPE 7 of 10, 5 min easy between. Finish at aerobic effort and cool down. Run off bike for 40 min at aerobic pace.		
WEEK 4				
Recovery week: Decrease your volume by 20 to 30 percent. Take two rest days. Get a massage. Keep all workouts easy and relaxed for this week to prepare your body for the next training phase or race.				

FIGURE 9.6 **Sample program for a novice triathlete, Olympic distance, race-specific level training** *(continued).*

Half Ironman Distance, Base Training Phase

WEEK 1				
	Swim	**Bike**	**Run**	**Strength**
Monday	Rest day			
Tuesday	900 choice. 10 × 200 as 1 to 5 pull with 25/20/15/10 s rest descending, 6 to 10 swim on 10 s rest, strong aerobic effort. Total: 2,900	60 to 80 min aerobic, HR zone 1 or 2, RPE 2 to 4 of 10 at continuous steady effort.		
Wednesday			Run/walk: Walk 3 to 5 min, run or jog 10 min, walk 1 min. Repeat 2 to 4 times. Finish with 3 to 5 min walk. HR zone 1 or 2, RPE 3 to 5 of 10. Or run continuously for 30 to 40 min. The intermittent run/walk builds an aerobic base with less stress on your body.	30 to 60 min

FIGURE 9.7 **Sample program for a novice to intermediate triathlete, Half Ironman distance, base-level training.**

	Swim	Bike	Run	Strength
Thursday	500 drills and warm-up. 2 × 800 aerobic, 30 s rest between. 500 easy as 50 drill/50 swim. Total: 2,600	50 to 70 min aerobic, HR zone 1 or 2, RPE 2 to 4 of 10 at continuous steady effort.		
Friday			Run/walk: Walk 3 to 5 min, run or jog 8 min, walk 1 min. Repeat 2 to 4 times. Finish with 3 to 5 min walk. HR zone 1 or 2, RPE 3 to 5 of 10. Or run continuously for 30 to 40 min.	
Saturday	900 choice. 10 × 200 as 1 to 5 pull with 25/20/15/10 s rest descending, 6 to 10 swim on 10 s rest, strong aerobic effort. Total: 2,900	75 to 90 min aerobic, HR zone 1 or 2, RPE 2 to 4 of 10 at continuous steady effort.		30 to 60 min
Sunday			Run/walk: Walk 3 to 5 min, run or jog 8 min, walk 1 min. Repeat 3 to 6 times. Finish with 3 to 5 min walk. HR zone 1 or 2, RPE 3 to 5 of 10. Or run continuously for 60 to 80 min.	
WEEKS 2 AND 3				
Follow the same pattern for the next two weeks. Increase your volume by 10 to 20 percent, depending on your time available and rate of adaptation. In base training phase, the goal is to steadily increase volume (time) at an easy level to build your aerobic engine.				
WEEK 4				
This is a recovery week. Go back to what you did the first week or decrease the volume of week 3 by 20 to 30 percent, depending on fatigue levels, adaptation rate, and time available.				

FIGURE 9.7 **Sample program for a novice to intermediate triathlete, Half Ironman distance, base-level training** *(continued)*.

Half Ironman Distance, Preparation Training Phase

		WEEK 1		
	Swim	**Bike**	**Run**	**Strength**
Monday	Rest day			
Tuesday	400 choice (include drills). 10 × 50 as 25 sprint/25 easy, 10 s rest. 2 × 50/100/150/200/200/150/100/50 free on 10 to 20 s rest; set 1 aerobic, set 2 threshold. 100 cool-down. Total: 3,000	Bike $\dot{V}O_2$max intervals: 60 to 90 min. Warm-up 20 min with 5 × 30 s sprint, 1 min easy between. Build effort with each one. Ride 5 min easy. For $\dot{V}O_2$max intervals, ride 10 to 15 × 1 min to HR zone 5, RPE 8 of 10, 30 s easy spin between. Finish at easy aerobic effort and cool down.		
Wednesday			Run/walk: Walk 3 to 5 min, run or jog 10 min, walk 1 min. Repeat 2 to 4 times. Finish with 3 to 5 min walk. HR zone 1 or 2, RPE 3 to 5 of 10. Or run continuously 30 to 40 min.	30 to 60 min
Thursday	500 drills and warm-up. 2 × 1,000 aerobic, 30 s between. 500 easy as 50 drill/50 swim. Total: 3,000	50 to 70 min aerobic, HR zone 1 or 2, RPE 2 to 4 of 10, at continuous steady effort.		
Friday			Run threshold: Walk 3 to 5 min, run or jog 10 min easy, then 4 × 16 step strides, 1 min walk. On flat or slight uphill, run 3 to 5 × 5 min, 2 to 4 min jog between. At threshold, HR zone 4, RPE 6 of 10. Finish with 3 to 5 min walk. Total run time: 60 to 80 min.	

FIGURE 9.8 Sample program for a novice to intermediate triathlete, Half Ironman distance, preparation-level training.

	Swim	Bike	Run	Strength
Saturday	400 choice (include drills). 10 × 50 as 25 sprint/25 easy, 10 s rest. 2 × 50/100/150/200/200/150/100/50 free on 10 to 20 s rest; set 1 aerobic, set 2 threshold. 100 cool-down. Total: 3,000	40 miles at aerobic pace, HR zone 1 or 2, RPE 2 to 4 of 10, at continuous steady effort. Run off bike for 30 min at aerobic pace.		30 to 60 min
Sunday			Long, steady run: Walk 3 to 5 min, steady run 60 to 90 min aerobic, HR zone 1 or 2, RPE 4 to 5 of 10. Walk 3 min.	
WEEK 2				
	Swim	Bike	Run	Strength
Monday	Rest day			
Tuesday	600 choice. 16 × 50 odds, 25 kick (no board)/25 swim. 2 × 600 as set 1 strong aerobic, 30 s rest, set 2 alternate 50 at threshold, 50 as polo drill (swim with head up, hold good body position, and kick). Total: 2,700	Bike $\dot{V}O_2$max intervals: 60 to 90 min. Warm-up 20 min with 5 × 30 s sprint, 1 min easy between. Build effort with each one. Ride 5 min easy. For $\dot{V}O_2$max intervals, ride 7 to 10 × 3 min to HR zone 5, RPE 8 of 10, 3 min easy spin between. Finish at easy aerobic effort and cool down.		
Wednesday			Run/walk: Walk 3 to 5 min, run or jog 10 min, walk 1 min. Repeat 4 to 6 times. Finish with 3 to 5 min walk. HR zone 1 or 2, RPE 3 to 5 of 10. Or run continuously 40 to 60 min.	30 to 60 min
Thursday	500 drills and warm-up. 1 × 1,500 aerobic. 500 easy as 50 drill/50 swim. Total: 2,500	50 to 70 min aerobic, HR zone 1 or 2, RPE 2 to 4 of 10, at continuous steady effort.		

FIGURE 9.8 **Sample program for a novice to intermediate triathlete, Half Ironman distance, preparation-level training** (continued).

WEEK 2 (continued)				
	Swim	**Bike**	**Run**	**Strength**
Friday			Run threshold: Walk 3 to 5 min, run or jog 10 min easy, then 4 × 16 step strides, 1 min walk. On flat or slight uphill, run 3 to 5 × 8 min, 2 to 4 min jog between. At threshold, HR zone 4, RPE 6 of 10. Finish with 3 to 5 min walk. Total run time: 60 to 80 min.	
Saturday	600 choice. 16 × 50 odds, 25 kick (no board)/25 swim. 2 × 600 as set 1 strong aerobic, 30 s rest, set 2 alternate 50 at threshold, 50 as polo drill (swim with head up, hold good body position, and kick). Total: 2,700	50 miles aerobic, HR zone 1 or 2, RPE 2 to 4 of 10, at continuous steady effort. Run off bike for 30 min at aerobic effort.		30 to 60 min
Sunday			Long, steady run: Walk 3 to 5 min, steady run 7 to 9 miles aerobic, HR zone 1 or 2, RPE 4 to 5 of 10. Walk 3 min.	
WEEK 3				
	Swim	**Bike**	**Run**	**Strength**
Monday	Rest day			
Tuesday	600 choice. 16 × 50 odds, 25 kick (no board)/25 swim. 2 × 600 as set 1 strong aerobic, 30 s rest, set 2 alternate 50 at threshold, 50 as polo drill (swim with head up, hold good body position, and kick). Total: 2,700	Bike $\dot{V}O_2$max intervals: 60 to 90 min. Warm-up 20 min with 5 × 30 s sprint, 1 min easy between. Build effort with each one. Ride 5 min easy. For $\dot{V}O_2$max intervals, ride 6 to 8 × 4 min to HR zone 5, RPE 8 of 10, 4 min easy spin between. Finish at easy aerobic effort and cool down.		

FIGURE 9.8   Sample program for a novice to intermediate triathlete, Half Ironman distance, preparation-level training (continued).

	Swim	Bike	Run	Strength
Wednesday			Run/walk: Walk 3 to 5 min, run or jog 10 min, walk 1 min. Repeat 4 to 6 times. Finish with 3 to 5 min walk. HR zone 1 or 2, RPE 3 to 5 of 10. Or run continuously 40 to 60 min.	30 to 60 min
Thursday	500 drills and warm-up. 1 × 2,000 aerobic. 500 easy as 50 drill/50 swim. Total: 3,000	50 to 70 min aerobic, HR zone 1 or 2, RPE 2 to 4 of 10, at continuous steady effort.		
Friday			Run threshold: Walk 3 to 5 min, run or jog 10 min easy, then 4 × 16 step strides, 1 min walk. On flat or slight uphill, run 2 or 3 × 10 min, 2 to 4 min jog between. At threshold, HR zone 4, RPE 6 of 10. Finish with 3 to 5 min walk. Total run time: 60 to 80 min.	
Saturday	600 choice. 16 × 50 odds, 25 kick (no board)/25 swim. 2 × 600 as set 1 strong aerobic, 30 s rest, set 2 alternate 50 at threshold, 50 as polo drill (swim with head up, hold good body position, and kick). Total: 2,700	60 miles aerobic, HR zone 1 or 2, RPE 2 to 4 of 10, at continuous steady effort. Run off bike for 45 min at aerobic pace.		30 to 60 min
Sunday			Long, steady run: Walk 3 to 5 min, steady run 8 to 10 miles aerobic, HR zone 1 or 2, RPE 4 to 5 of 10. Walk 3 min.	
WEEK 4				
Recovery week: Decrease your volume by 20 to 30 percent from week 1. Take two rest days. Get a massage. Keep all workouts easy and relaxed for this week to prepare your body for the next training phase.				

FIGURE 9.8 **Sample program for a novice to intermediate triathlete, Half Ironman distance, preparation-level training** *(continued)*.

Half Ironman Distance, Race-Specific Training Phase

WEEK 1				
	Swim	**Bike**	**Run**	**Strength**
Monday	Rest day			
Tuesday	300 warm-up. 1 × 1,000, aerobic effort. 10 × 50 sprint, 10 s rest. 500 pull. 200 easy swim and drills. Total: 2,500	Bike tempo: 60 to 75 min aerobic with tempo intervals, HR zone 1 or 2, RPE 2 to 4 of 10. After 20 min warm-up, ride 3 or 4 × 15 min to HR zone 3, RPE 5 or 6 of 10. Ride 5 min easy between. Finish at aerobic effort and cool down.		
Wednesday			Run/walk: Walk 3 to 5 min, run or jog 10 min, walk 1 min. Repeat 4 to 6 times. Finish with 3 to 5 min walk. HR zone 1 or 2, RPE 3 to 5 of 10. Or run continuously for 40 to 60 min.	30 to 60 min
Thursday	500 drills and warm-up. 1 × 1,800 time trial (TT; hardest sustainable effort for the distance), aerobic. 500 easy as 50 drill/50 swim. Total: 2,800 Race prep workout, strategy: Build through first 300, hold steady, and finish strong.	50 to 70 min aerobic, HR zone 1 or 2, RPE 2 to 4 of 10 at a continuous steady effort.		
Friday			Run at half marathon pace: Walk 3 to 5 min, run or jog 10 min easy, then 4 × 16 step strides, 1 min walk between. On flat or slight uphill, run 3 × 10 min at half marathon pace, 5 min jog between. HR zone 3 or 4, RPE 5 to 5.5 of 10. Finish with 3 to 5 min walk. Total run time: 60 to 80 min.	

FIGURE 9.9   **Sample program for a novice to intermediate triathlete, Half Ironman distance, race-specific level training.**

	Swim	Bike	Run	Strength
Saturday	300 warm-up. 1 × 1,000, aerobic effort. 10 × 50 sprint, 10 s rest. 500 pull. 200 easy swim and drills. Total: 2,500 Or open-water swim of 45 to 60 min. If available, open-water swim is the best option. Work on steady aerobic swimming, sighting, and swimming straight.	50 miles at aerobic pace, HR zone 1 or 2, RPE 2 to 4 of 10, at continuous steady effort. Run off bike for 45 min at aerobic pace.		30 to 60 min
Sunday	Transition training: Set up mock transition area in your yard, basement, or a park. With race suit on, run to bike and put on helmet, glasses, and shoes. Run with bike to mount line. Mount bike and take short ride. Hop off bike and rack it. Put on running shoes and number belt and do a short run. Complete this 3 to 5 times.		Long, steady run: Walk 3 to 5 min, steady run 9 to 11 miles at aerobic pace, HR zone 1 or 2, RPE 4 or 5 of 10. Walk 3 min.	
WEEK 2				
	Swim	Bike	Run	Strength
Monday	Rest day			
Tuesday	500 drills and warm-up. 6 × 200 at race effort, 10 to 20 s rest between at 1,800 TT pace. 10 × 50 kick, 10 s rest. 500 pull. 100 easy swim and drills. Total: 2,800	Bike tempo: 75 to 90 min aerobic with tempo intervals, HR zone 1 or 2, RPE 2 to 4 of 10. After 20 min warm-up, ride 3 × 20 min to HR zone 3, RPE 5 or 6 of 10. Ride 5 min easy between. Finish at aerobic effort and cool down.		
Wednesday			Run/walk: Walk 3 to 5 min, run or jog 10 min, walk 1 min. Repeat 4 to 6 times. Finish with 3 to 5 min walk. HR zone 1 or 2, RPE 3 to 5 of 10. Or run continuously for 40 to 60 min.	30 to 60 min
Thursday	500 drills and warm-up. 1 × 2,300, aerobic. 500 easy as 50 drill/50 swim. Total: 3,300	50 to 70 min at aerobic pace, HR zone 1 or 2, RPE 2 to 4 of 10, continuous steady effort.		

FIGURE 9.9   **Sample program for a novice to intermediate triathlete, Half Ironman distance, race-specific level training** *(continued)*.

WEEK 2 (continued)			
	Swim	**Bike**	**Run**	**Strength**
Friday			Run at half marathon pace: Walk 3 to 5 min, run or jog 10 min easy, then 4 × 16 step strides, 1 min walk between. On flat or slight uphill, run 1 or 2 × 20 min at half marathon pace, 5 min jog between. HR zone 3 or 4, RPE 5 to 5.5 of 10. Finish with 3 to 5 min walk. Total run time: 60 to 80 min.	
Saturday	500 drills and warm-up. 6 × 200 at race effort, 10 to 20 s rest between at 1,800 TT pace. 10 × 50 kick, 10 s rest. 500 pull. 100 easy swim and drills. Total: 2,800 Or open-water swim of 45 to 60 min. If available, open water is the best option. Work on steady aerobic swimming, sighting, and swimming straight.	60 miles at aerobic pace, HR zone 1 or 2, RPE 2 to 4 of 10, at continuous steady effort. Run off bike for 45 min, 20 min at aerobic pace, 20 min at Half Ironman (70.3 pace) effort. Walk 5 min to cool down.		
Sunday	Transition training: Set up mock transition area in your yard, basement, or a park. With race suit on, run to bike and put on helmet, glasses, and shoes. Run with bike to mount line. Mount bike and take short ride. Hop off bike and rack it. Put on running shoes and number belt and do a short run. Complete this 3 to 5 times.		Long, steady run: Walk 3 to 5 min, steady run 10 to 12 miles at aerobic pace, HR zone 1 or 2, RPE 4 or 5 of 10. Walk 3 min.	
WEEK 3			
	Swim	**Bike**	**Run**	**Strength**
Monday	Rest day			
Tuesday	500 drills and warm-up. 4 or 5 × 400 at race effort, 20 to 30 s rest between at 1,800 TT pace. 10 × 50 kick, 10 s rest. 500 pull. 100 easy swim and drills. Total: 3,600	Bike tempo: 75 to 90 min aerobic with tempo intervals, HR zone 1 or 2, RPE 2 to 4 of 10. After 20 min warm-up, ride 3 × 20 min to HR zone 3, RPE 5 or 6 of 10. Ride 5 min easy between. Finish at aerobic effort and cool down.		

FIGURE 9.9 **Sample program for a novice to intermediate triathlete, Half Ironman distance, race-specific level training** (continued).

	Swim	Bike	Run	Strength
Wednesday			Run/walk: Walk 3 to 5 min, run or jog 10 min, walk 1 min. Repeat 4 to 6 times. Finish with 3 to 5 min walk. HR zone 1 or 2, RPE 3 to 5 of 10. Or run continuously for 40 to 60 min.	30 to 60 min
Thursday	500 drills and warm-up. 1 × 1,800, aerobic. 1 × 500 pull with paddles and buoy (no kick). 500 easy as 50 drill/50 swim. Total: 3,300	50 to 70 min at aerobic pace, HR zone 1 or 2, RPE 2 to 4 of 10, continuous steady effort.		
Friday			Run at half marathon pace: Walk 3 to 5 min, run or jog 10 min easy, then 4 × 16 step strides, 1 min walk between. On flat or slight uphill, run 1 or 2 × 30 min at half marathon pace, 10 min jog between. HR zone 3 or 4, RPE 5 to 5.5 of 10. Finish with 3 to 5 min walk. Total run time: 60 to 90 min.	
Saturday	500 drills and warm-up. 4 or 5 × 400 at race effort, 20 to 30 s rest between at 1,800 TT pace. 10 × 50 kick, 10 s rest. 500 pull. 100 easy swim and drills. Total: 3,600 Or open-water swim of 45 to 60 min. If available, open water is the best option. Work on steady aerobic swimming, sighting, and swimming straight.	70 miles at aerobic and Half Ironman effort, HR zone 1 or 2, RPE 2 to 4 of 10 for 15 miles. 30 to 40 miles at Half Ironman effort. Finish at aerobic effort to cool down. Run off bike for 60 min, 20 min at aerobic level, 30 min at Half Ironman effort, 10 min to cool down.		30 to 60 min

FIGURE 9.9   **Sample program for a novice to intermediate triathlete, Half Ironman distance, race-specific level training** *(continued)*.

	Swim	Bike	Run	Strength
		WEEK 3 (continued)		
	Swim	**Bike**	**Run**	**Strength**
Sunday	Transition training: Set up mock transition area in your yard, basement, or a park. With race suit on, run to bike and put on helmet, glasses, and shoes. Run with bike to mount line. Mount bike and take short ride. Hop off bike and rack it. Put on running shoes and number belt and do a short run. Complete this 3 to 5 times.		Long, steady run: Walk 3 to 5 min, steady run 11 to 14 miles at aerobic pace, HR zone 1 or 2, RPE 4 or 5 of 10. Walk 3 min.	
		WEEK 4		
	Recovery week: Decrease your volume by 20 to 30 percent. Take two rest days. Get a massage. Keep all workouts easy and relaxed for this week to prepare your body for the next training phase or race.			

FIGURE 9.9   **Sample program for a novice to intermediate triathlete, Half Ironman distance, race-specific level training** (continued).

CHAPTER 10

The Traveling Triathlete

Tara S. Comer

Traveling for triathlons can be fun and exciting. It's a great way to see other cities and connect with the wider triathlon community while experiencing the many amazing venues and courses our sport calls home. The triathlon experience can be greatly enhanced by geography, as there's a little magic in finishing a race on a beach in San Diego, diving into Hawaiian surf, or biking through the Rockies. You can become a citizen of the world through triathlon, but first, you're going to need to learn how to pack!

Traveling to races requires planning and organization skills far in excess of those already needed to shoehorn hours of training into a typically packed schedule. Because you're taking your show (and your bike and wetsuit and shoes and gels) on the road, you're multiplying the possibility for things to go wrong, get lost, and break down by a huge factor, and, however briefly, ceding control over your race prep to an airline, hotel, or interstate highway system. It can be a challenge dealing with the unexpected, but the determination and attention to detail most triathletes exhibit will be a tremendous help during this process. Chances are you'll arrive on time, well rested and prepared to have your best race, but let's not leave it to chance.

USA Triathlon offers travel-related discounts including hotel, car rental, airfare, and bike transport to annual members. Log in to your account or visit www.usatriathlon.org/travel to learn more.

Planning

Choose your race. Seems like this is the simplest thing to do, but as triathlon continues to grow, the race options seem to have expanded exponentially, and just deciding can be tough. Make sure to factor in distance, ease of travel, and race setup and location relative to lodging and transportation. Also, look online for reviews of the race from previous years. You'll want to make sure you're hitting the road for a worthwhile event, and that all of the hard work you put in won't be wasted on a poorly run race over a dangerous course. This time investment up front can save a ton of headaches down the road.

Finding Lodging

Book accommodations early. Sometimes the race has a beautiful host hotel that's convenient, that's affordable, and that stocks those delightful bath gels you love for postrace recovery. Sometimes it doesn't. Get informed about all possible lodging options well in advance so you can make the best choice for your wallet, sanity, and convenience. Resources such as Priceline, AirBnB, VRBO, and Yelp will help identify traditional hotels, but also rental homes or condos, and provide great information about the quality of the stay. Pick a place where you can best relax and prepare, get good sleep, and comfortably recover after the race. An upgrade from the spring break motel to the high-rise well above the crowd may be worth a few more dollars.

Make sure that wherever you're staying is prepared to accommodate your needs. A simple call ahead can help you reserve bike storage, make sure a fridge is in your room for food and fuel, and ensure that you're not sharing a floor with 75 kids on a class trip just dying to keep you up all night! One of the hidden secrets of hotel living is that there are many amenities and services available to the average traveler, but most of us simply don't ask. Often an earnest inquiry to the counter representative can reveal possible upgrades, identify which side of the building is quietest, or yield a better level of service. Remember, the front-of-house staff have an inordinate amount of control over the quality of your stay, and a well-placed $20 proffered to the check-in person can result in any number of benefits. A simple "I'd appreciate anything you could do to make my stay great!" and a discreet gratuity can make you a favored guest and ensure that your race experience is well supported by the hotel.

Once you check in, lay out all your gear. This will enable you to identify anything you may have forgotten, save time later, and confirm the condition of everything post-travel, prerace.

Traveling Internationally

Racing internationally? Traveling with a group such as Endurance Sports Travel can make international racing surprisingly easy and affordable. Using a tri-specific travel agent, while seemingly antiquated by today's book-it-yourself standard, will help immeasurably, as she will have expertise in the specific needs of the triathlete abroad. Destinations have different processes for handling odd baggage such as bikes and equipment, unique customs requirements, and other unforeseen impediments to a smooth travel plan. By letting an agent make your international arrangements, you receive guidance and often expedited service, have someone proficient in handling language or currency conversion concerns, and have someone who understands the importance of what you're doing and how travel can affect your race day.

Traveling Smart

Travel can have a number of effects on your body, and your travel plan should account for those eventualities. Plan to arrive a day or two in advance of the race to become familiar with your surroundings, shake off jet lag or other fatigue, and arrange for proper storage of your gear. The last thing you need is to arrive in haste, be disoriented and rushed, and create stress before your race. Similarly, don't plan to jet out of town hours after you cross the finish line. Allow at least a day after the race to rest, recover, and decompress before cramming your aching muscles into a cramped airplane seat or behind the wheel.

When flying, be sure to request an aisle seat on the plane so you have plenty of room and freedom to get up and stretch. If your race travel involves jetting to a different climate or someplace with a significant time difference, allow more time to let your body compensate and adjust to the new conditions.

Researching the Location

Read the athlete guide and get some local tourism information. The key to a successful race trip is doing your research and gathering as much intelligence about your destination as possible. The athlete guide will give you course maps for review and outline parking, staging areas, and the like; but you need a 360-degree view of your surroundings to make your trip the best it can be. Knowing the local landscape can provide a wealth of benefits, such as identifying pools or beaches for a tune-up swim, locating healthy eating spots, or scouting safe places to run in preparation for race day. Map out the race route because the map in your packet might not be the clearest, and identify the ways in and out of your destination. No one likes fighting traffic or getting lost, but we hate it even more when anxious about an upcoming race and concerned about the location of our stuff.

Another reason to learn about the destination is so you can enjoy yourself if you have some downtime. Traveling for triathlon is about the race, but it's also about seeing new places, taking a break from work and life routines, and using sport as a tool for creating new experiences. Finding out as much about your race location as possible can help your performance, but it can also identify where to get a massage or a triumphant postrace margarita!

▶ Create a Travel Itinerary

Get organized and give yourself peace of mind by creating one document that contains all your travel information. Have a hard copy, but also save a copy in the cloud so it's always accessible. Share your plan with family and friends so they can follow your progress and access contact information in case of emergency.

Key items to include:

- Important contact information for you, the hotel, and the race organizer
- Flight information and confirmation numbers
- Rental car information or shuttle service
- Copies of insurance cards, passports, and visas
- Maps and directions from the airport to the hotel and the race site
- Course maps
- Workout details
- Destination information on parking, swimming pools, bike shops, restaurants, grocery stores
- Packing list of the items you need for traveling
- Gear checklist (see the race day checklist in chapter 11)

Getting Your Bike There

Part of the adventure of traveling to a race is getting your gear there. You've spent months training, your body is at peak performance level, your mental game is strong, your focus is sharp, but your bike is in Des Moines. This is a very real stressor the traveling triathlete encounters. Mitigate your anxiety by having a solid plan in place. Pack your race day essentials (trisuit, goggles, shoes, and helmet) in your carry-on bag and keep it close at all times. This bag represents the core elements of your race gear and is what you most definitely can't live without. If all else fails, you can rent a bike, borrow a wetsuit, and buy gels, but you can't race without your own basic gear. Knowing that those items are always by your side is your security blanket and will keep you ready to race even in the worst-case scenario.

The biggest challenge will be getting your bike to your race destination. You have two options when it comes to getting your bike to a race—use a bike transporting service or fly with your bike.

Using a Service

If you're going to a big race, research whether a local transport service may be shipping bikes to the location. This will allow you to simply hand off your bike to the service and pick it up from the service location once you arrive. Raceday Transport offers bike transport services to many North American races and have a long history of reliability and customer service. You can search for similar services in your area, but make sure they have a strong testimonial record and are fully insured. These services can be worth their cost in several ways.

Unlike the situation with airlines or UPS, this is the only thing these services do, and their expertise is in transporting triathlon bikes. They will be sensitive to your time needs, conscious of the fragile nature of your bike, and tuned in to the specific stresses and concerns of the traveling triathlete. The peace of mind that comes with knowing that the most critical and most expensive of all of your gear is in good hands will alleviate a great deal of anxiety as you move toward the race. Most transport companies make it easy to drop off and pick up the bike and are used by numerous athletes, so you'll be able to easily interface with the company and with fellow customers as you secure your ride. In most cases, the cost is comparable to airline bike fees, but with the added benefit that the people handling your bike get why you're obsessing over it and will make it easy and painless for you to let go of the handlebars when dropping it off. The price in dollars is well worth the value in peace of mind.

Although it's nice not having to build a bike before a race, it's really nice not having to pack it up again afterward.

Flying With Your Bike

Flying to a race with a bike has never been easy. Airlines are now charging excess weight and baggage fees for anyone traveling with a bike—plus, as any frequent traveler knows, airlines' reliability with any baggage, let alone an expensive piece of absolutely necessary equipment, can vary greatly. That's not to say that shipping your bike is a bad idea, but you should analyze the options and determine what gives you the most peace of mind as well as the relative economics of the decision.

First you'll need to invest in a good soft-sided bike travel bag. Soft cases are smaller and much lighter than the traditional hardshell cases and are your best shot at avoiding some of the additional fees. While these are a great option for the wallet, the use of a soft case does involve more than just a bag. The bag alone will not be enough protection for your bike frame and components, so you'll need to buy a set of AlboPads, which are reusable, padded bicycle frame wraps that offer great protection against the hazards of shipping. These will prevent dents, cracks, and chips that can not only ding up your bike but can impede good performance on the course.

If you are going the do-it-yourself route, learning to disassemble, pack, and rebuild a bike is empowering but does take time and skill. In the beginning, it can be less Zen and the Art of Tri Bike Assembly than a case study in frustration, but you will get the psychological reward of knowing you are a self-sufficient tri goddess. If this is your plan, check local bike shops for bike disassembling–assembling and packing classes; this is well worth the time and effort. You'll also need some basic tools to remove wheels, handlebars, seat, and pedals and then reassemble at your destination, so make sure your tool kit is packed and can be taken on whatever means of transport you choose. Take all your bike measurements and list them on your travel itinerary so you don't arrive with a set of bike parts and no blueprint.

Now it's time to learn to disassemble, pack, and rebuild your bike. Don't do this for the first time right before you leave. Plan to test-build your bike at least once to get comfortable and to make any mistakes well in advance. Start by writing down all your measurements, as this is critical to building your bike. Have your tools handy. Use the information you learned in your bike disassembling, assembling, and packing classes.

Allow extra time when checking in with your bike. Bike bags move more slowly than normal luggage. An odd-shaped package full of metal and gears could cause some questions and lead to delays. In addition to your regular luggage tag, attach another ID tag with the travel date, destination, hotel address, and phone number. In case your bike is lost, this makes reclaiming it a bit more efficient. One important thing to remember: Don't travel with CO_2 cartridges, which some riders use to inflate tires. These aren't common to traveler carry-ons and can create confusion and delay with security as the personnel sort out why you have them. If you've researched your race destination, you'll know where the local bike shop is and be able to grab these items easily and cheaply once you arrive.

Make friends with the ticket agent. It's worth asking if you can get a priority tag for the bike. You'll have more leverage if you are a rewards customer in good standing of the given airline. Airline employees often face difficult customers all day and deal with many people who are stressed, hurried, and sometimes rude. A little kindness and understanding can result in a seating upgrade or other amenity that can ease your trip. You're in charge of your travel experience, so don't be afraid to ask for anything you feel would make your flight a more positive one.

Packing for Your Trip

Every athlete has her own system for packing for trips, so take this advice and add your own variations. First lay out all the clothes you think you'll need for the trip, and then take only half with you. Lean toward items that are easy to wash and drip-dry. Use plastic bags to help you separate dirty and clean clothes, and don't waste precious room with toiletries; most hotels offer generous quantities of free product. We use all manner of products and gear to streamline ourselves during the race and lessen resistance, and we need to do the same when we travel. The lighter the load, the easier the trip.

Packing for a Three- or Four-Day Domestic Trip

Pack only the essentials and what you need for the race. It's better to have less stuff to manage so you can focus on the race. In addition to your trisuit, pack a couple of outfits for prerace training sessions. It's a good idea to check local weather to decide on the need for warmer cycling gear and a rain jacket.

Pack your own food cooler with snacks and drinks and whatever food you want for race morning. This will save a trip to the store. Don't forget to bring your race day fuel. To save space, premeasure your drink mix according to the bike rides you will do on the trip, including the race, and store in plastic bags or small containers.

Packing for a Longer International Trip

Consider using space bags. These bags really make a difference when you are packing for a long trip. They allow you to pack several clothing items, zip the seal the way you do with a sandwich bag, and then remove all the air, which significantly reduces the volume of packed items. You can use one bag to pack a full-size pillow in your carry-on for use on long flights or in your checked luggage, as some international hotels have rock-hard pillows.

Don't pack more clothes than you need. Bring clothes in neutral colors that you can mix and match, and pack nonrace shoes that can be worn with multiple outfits. Pack only one pair of jeans, as jeans are heavy. Check the weather at your destination before you leave, and pack accordingly.

▶ Pack Your Wetsuit

Your wetsuit is a durable garment and a critical piece of equipment that should last you a while. Its structural integrity is essential to its utility, and that integrity can easily be compromised by a wayward zipper or misplaced scissors. Take care when packing your wetsuit by using this simple trick:

1. Turn the wetsuit inside out.
2. Place a thick towel down on the floor and put the wetsuit on top of it.
3. Cross the arms of the suit together and fold the suit in half so the head is on top of the feet.
4. Starting at the top, carefully roll the suit so it looks like a jelly roll.
5. Place in suitcase.

This approach protects your suit and minimizes the space it will take up in your bag. You need to carry a ton of gear when traveling for a triathlon, so make efficient use of every square inch of your bag.

Many travel supply companies and launderettes sell small packets of laundry detergent. It takes only a few minutes to wash your clothes in the hotel sink and hang them on a hanger to dry. Freshly washed clothes make waking up nicer and remove some of the transient feelings of life on the road.

The Well-Packed Carry-On

First get a wheeled bag that fits into the overhead compartment. Trying to carry all you need on a plane in only a backpack or over-the-shoulder bag will strain your shoulders, and you could definitely be sore the day after travel. When packing the carry-on, prepare for the worst possible scenario—that your checked bag may not arrive on time or may get lost. Keep vital supplies, flight essentials, and prep and race gear in the carry-on. Barb Lindquist, Olympian and USA Triathlon's College Recruitment Program Manager, suggests packing two separate bags within the carry-on. One bag contains cycling shoes, pedals, helmet, trisuit, goggles, cap, running shorts, socks, and a sports bra. Wear your running shoes on the plane or pack them in your carry-on. The other bag, which you can put under the seat in front of you, contains what you need for the flight: book or e-book reader, earplugs, eye mask, inflatable neck rest, headphones for movies, water bottle, drink mix, pen, food, ball to massage muscles, and contact solution or glasses.

While Traveling

Try to get in a good, solid workout shortly before you head to the airport. This will keep your body loose before you sit in a cramped plane for hours, help ease the anxiety of traveling with all your gear, and remove the stress of wanting to work out as soon as you land. It may also help you relax and sleep if your flight is long. Burning off some excess nervous energy has great mental value as well as keeping you in race shape. It's a better and more efficient use of your time to locate all of your gear and get situated at your lodging upon arrival than having to suit up and run right away.

Treat your tri trip like an exploration into an undiscovered country. Prepare yourself for eventualities such as poor food options, inconvenient vendors, or long delays.

Plan ahead to have healthy food choices on hand and hydration options ready throughout the day. Pack some healthy snacks or a light meal that you can carry with you and some drink powder or electrolyte mix that you can mix with water from a fountain. The best choices are foods that you would normally eat, since you don't want to try any new foods the week of a race. Fruits, veggies, hummus, or simple carbohydrate choices are easy to digest and usually easy to pack ahead. If you're a total planner, call the airline more than 24 hours in advance and order a special meal.

On most flights, your food will come out first, which is a bonus if you are hoping to sleep right away. Triathlon can be all about shaving seconds off your time, and that applies in the air as well as on the course. On the flight, drink plenty of water and avoid caffeine and alcohol. Think about some vitamin C to bolster your immune system, and avoid nasty germs from all the recycled air you'll be inhaling.

Wash your hands frequently. Germs are everywhere, so get in the habit of scrubbing your hands a lot. Keep your hands away from your face. Avoid touching your eyes or biting your nails.

Once in flight, remember to move around the cabin and stretch periodically. It is a good idea to wear compression socks while you travel. These socks can help prevent blood from pooling in your lower extremities and keep your tapered legs ready to race. Distract yourself from thinking too much about the race. Bring some light reading, watch a movie, and get some rest. Make your journey as relaxing as possible, not a chance to obsess for a few hours about your time and race prep. Part of your taper is to relax your body and mind and save your energy for the race.

Once You've Arrived

When you arrive at your destination, immediately follow the new time schedule to help your body adjust. Adjust watches, phones, and other devices so necessary alarms and notifications are delivered at the right time. Sunlight and light exercise also will help you recover from jet lag quickly and allow the tension from your trip to dissipate.

If you traveled with your bike, set it up shortly after you've arrived. Hopefully, everything will be in working order; but if something was damaged on the trip, make it your first priority to find a good bike shop. Refer to your travel itinerary for local bike shops or ask race organizers for recommendations.

Do a course reconnaissance ride via car or bike over as much of the course as is reasonable to get a sense of elevations and hazards and to identify landmarks to measure your race progress. In triathlon, surprises are not enjoyable, so the time you spend familiarizing yourself with the various legs will pay huge race day dividends. This can also ease some anxiety about the race, as the unknown can be a formidable stressor, and invariably, uncertainty about a course is worse than the reality. Chances are, if you're traveling a good distance for this race, you'll find great scenic vistas and natural wonders to be enjoyed, and it's likely that the course will incorporate them. Get the full experience of the race by scouting where you'll run. This will improve your chances of racing well and allow you to appreciate the venue without the pressure of performance.

Follow your regular prerace routine. The point of establishing a routine is that it stays the same no matter where you are. The familiarity of your actions, thoughts, and stretches will calm you, remove the strangeness of your surroundings, and prepare you mentally for the challenge ahead. When you walk out of your room, likely in the dark of the morning, all of your planning, packing, and last-minute frantic searching for your missing sock should ebb, and your focus should sharpen to the task at hand. Remember why you packed all this stuff in the first place, spent all the money on the plane ticket, and holed up in this Holiday Inn—race day. The hard work on the road and the long hours of planning are all in service to this, and you're going to spend the next several hours redeeming all the time and sweat you've invested. Dive in and enjoy!

Mental Travel

One of the last areas I'd like to address is the mental game of traveling for triathlon. It can be overwhelming to remember all the details of gear management, race requirements, scheduling, and sleep, but it's critical to allow yourself a mental break. Additionally, being alone in a hotel room in strange place can leave you staring at the walls with pre-race anxiety. Develop a strategy for some personal time that doesn't involve triathlon. Walk through the local park, find a quiet spot on the beach for meditation, or enjoy a healthy meal at a popular local restaurant. At home, we always have certain things we enjoy to provide relief from the day-to-day; you'll need to do the same when on the go. Find what takes you out of your own head and allows you to relax, and make sure you can accommodate that on your trip. This will lead to better focus, more rest, and improved clarity when it's time to get your race face on. The race is about the finish line, but the trip is about the journey to get there. Take time to enjoy it.

Conclusion

If this seems like quite a lot to consider before traveling, good. The more you think in advance, the smoother your journey will be. The preparation for a race is months in the making, and there are many details about training, nutrition, and gear that you'll be obsessing over, so my hope is to help you take all the thinking out of travel. It's hard enough to get your act together when you're going on vacation; adding the complications of carting race gear, food, and fuel is bound to cause trouble, and that's before you're expecting your body to perform wonders. This chapter, and this book, are about making your triathlon experience the best it can be, allowing you to focus on the sport and lose yourself in it. Distractions are unavoidable, particularly in unfamiliar surroundings, but positive traveling behaviors streamline the process and let you enjoy the trip, run the race, and rest soundly for the trip home.

CHAPTER 11

Race Day Strategy

Melissa Stockwell

Race day can be intimidating for anyone, from the novice to the seasoned athlete. This chapter focuses on race day strategy and what athletes can do to be fully prepared for their race. The chapter also discusses Paratriathletes, or athletes with physical disabilities, and the specific considerations they may need for a race.

A number of factors go into planning a successful race. These include being familiar with the USA Triathlon rulebook (www.usatriathlon.org/rules), race selection, exploring the course, planning both the night before and the morning of the race, practicing transitions, and ultimately crossing that finish line!

Race Selection

The first step in preparing for a successful race is choosing one that matches your strengths. For new athletes, it is best to start out with a shorter sprint-distance race before moving on to the longer, more challenging distances. Big-city races can be crowded and overwhelming for first-time racers. While it's exciting to be among thousands of other athletes, it can cause some added stress. A smaller, local race might be the best bet for a novice.

Before committing to a race, it is always best to check out the course maps, which are typically found on the official race website. Here you can see the course, the elevation chart, the number of laps you need to complete, and other race specifics.

Paratriathletes must make sure the course is accessible. While many athletes with disabilities can compete in any race, it is common practice to e-mail the race director to make sure any specific needs can be accommodated. Paratriathletes will want to know, for example, if there's someone who can help them transfer from their wheelchair to the bike or racing chair or help with prosthetics in transition. An athlete who needs assistance out of the water will need special permission to have a handler at the end of the swim. Among other things, it would be helpful for paratriathletes to know if there are any curbs, if the course is narrow, what type of surface the course has, and if there is enough space in transition. Often race directors have a separate swim wave for paratriathletes to make it easier for them to get out at the water exit. Race directors typically give these athletes additional space in transition as long as these needs are communicated before race day. Paratriathletes need to be proactive about any special considerations required.

Training

Once you have chosen a race, it's time to get busy training and preparing for race day. Work with your coach to determine the best training program for your lifestyle, or choose an online training program that will help you achieve your goals. Along with the swim, bike, and run, it is vitally important that you practice transitions before the race. In the weeks leading up to race day, go to a parking lot, set up your transition area, and practice switching from one discipline to the next, making sure you have everything you need. Practice running with your bike, as once you leave your transition area you will run with it to the mount line and again at the dismount line. You should also know how to do basic bike maintenance and change a flat tire. Plan to carry extra tubes and CO_2 cartridges on the course in case you need them. Some courses have dedicated bike mechanics, but you should always have the knowledge to fix basic maintenance problems on your own. Also spend some time training in the race kit you will be using on race day to make sure it fits your body right and is comfortable.

Developing a nutrition plan is also an important aspect of the race. Research the nutrition that will be available on the course and try it out before race day to make sure it doesn't upset your stomach. If it does, find something that works and plan to carry it with you on the course.

Race Weekend

Once you've done the training, mastered the transitions, and set up your nutrition plan, you are much closer to a successful race. Before you know it, race weekend will arrive and you'll be immersed in the exciting race atmosphere surrounded by other triathletes. If you are traveling to a race, make sure to get to the destination with plenty of time to explore the course and attend the race expo. At the race expo, you will listen to a course talk. Staff will go over the course in detail and point out where the water stops are, whether bike mechanics will be on the course, where the good spectator areas are, and what transportation is available for race morning.

With larger races, public transportation is usually an option, but if you have a personal vehicle and will be driving, find out in advance where you should park and if any road closures are scheduled for race morning. This will prevent unnecessary driving around and undue stress if your usual driving route is closed that morning. Paratriathletes can often get special parking passes or access to a convenient area close to transition to help manage their equipment. Work with the race director if you are worried about transportation issues; they are usually happy to accommodate you if you communicate with them prior to the race.

At the expo, you will hear of any last-minute course changes and get a timeline of events. You will also be given your athlete packet containing your timing chip, race number bibs, a swim cap, and your wristband for race security. These items are vitally important for race morning, so keep them in a safe place. Usually there is a table at the expo where you can verify that your timing chip is working correctly and registered to the right athlete. You can also choose to get body marked at the expo or on the morning of the race. If you get marked at the expo and the numbers fade, it's okay to use your own permanent marker to make them more visible on race morning. Any unanswered questions can be addressed at the race expo; here you can also purchase equipment or race shirts if you'd like.

After the course talk, if you have access to a car, one option is to get in the car and drive the bike course. Even if you've studied the elevation maps online, this will give you a better idea of the elevation changes and hills so you are even more prepared on race day. You may have the option of racking your bike the night before the race. This means less stress on race morning and gives you an opportunity to go into the transition area and check out your spot.

Paratriathletes should make sure that there is enough room in transition for prosthetics or a handcycle and racing chair. Most transition areas are small, with very little space, so be prepared for a tight fit. Athletes in wheelchairs will have difficulty if the transition area is on a hill or in long grass. If this is communicated to the race director before the race, correct accommodations can be made so there are no surprises when you see your transition area for the first time.

The Night Before

By the night before the race, nerves and excitement are at an all-time high. If it's a large race and you are traveling to it, make reservations weeks before at a restaurant of your choosing. Italian restaurants are popular, as carbohydrate loading with some protein is a great choice for a prerace meal. Eat nothing out of the ordinary and eat early so you have time to go back to your room, prepare for the morning, and get a good night's sleep.

After dinner, it's a good idea to set up your transition area and lay everything out as you will the next day. You should always expect the unexpected, and it's good to put a few extra items in your transition bag: an extra pair of goggles, a bike pump, old flip-flops to get to the water's edge, a long-sleeved shirt for warmth before the race, and anything else you think you might need. Along with your race items, it's important to have a headlamp so you can see before the sun comes up, anti-chafing balm, and nutrition. Set out your race kit with your timing chip so it's all ready to go when you wake up. If you use a GPS (Global Positioning System) device, make sure it's charged and ready to go. Many online sites include transition checklists that you can look at while preparing your bag. Make your own checklist, like the one in figure 11.1, before race day.

Set your alarm for a time you are comfortable with. Make sure you plan for eating breakfast and getting to the race with plenty of time to park, set up your transition area, find the portable potties, and get to the swim start with time to spare. This will make things go more smoothly on race morning. Lastly, before you go to sleep, go over the race mentally. Think about all your hard work to get to this point; visualize your swim, bike, run, and transitions and get ready to have a great day!

Race Day Checklist

Swim

___ Tri shorts, swimsuit, or trisuit

___ Two sets of goggles (one tinted and one normal)

___ Swim cap (provided in race bag)

___ Transition towel

___ Anti-chafing balm

___ Wetsuit

___ Flip flops (optional)

Bike

___ Bicycle

___ Helmet

___ Cycling shoes, socks if you wear them

___ Sunglasses

___ Water bottles

___ Chamois cream

___ Nutrition

___ Tool kit: tube, CO_2, levers, multi-tool

___ Bike pump

___ Bar-end plugs

Run

___ Running shoes (two pairs if you have a late start time, one to leave in transition and one to warm up in)

___ Race belt

___ Hat or visor

Other

___ USA Triathlon membership card

___ Photo identification

___ Training device (e.g., Garmin, Timex) and heart rate strap

___ Race belt

___ Sunscreen

___ Body Glide, powder, bandages

___ Warm change of clothes for after the race

___ Postrace recovery drink and snack with 4:1 ratio of carbohydrate to protein

FIGURE 11.1   **Race checklist.**

Race Morning

If you're among the majority of triathletes, you probably haven't gotten much sleep and are up well before the alarm goes off, excited about what the day will bring. You have a few important things to do before you leave the house or your hotel room and make your way to the race.

First, eat a good breakfast. Typically, once you leave the house or hotel, it is still hours before the race begins. Eat some protein, some oatmeal, a banana, a bagel with peanut butter, or something else that's familiar and easily digestible. Many hotels open the breakfast area early when a large number of triathletes are staying there. Make sure you confirm this the day before and know what the breakfast items are. If they are not ideal, stop by a grocery store the night before so you will have something in your room before heading to the race. You should also bring a gel, a small energy bar or similar item to eat about 30 minutes before getting in the water and an extra water bottle to help keep you hydrated before the swim. By an hour before the race, you shouldn't consume large amounts of liquid and should be just sipping your fluids.

Before you leave the house or hotel, make sure you have your bike water bottles filled, and, if you still have your bike, pump those tires up. Don't forget your GPS device, and make sure to remember your timing chip. You've gone over your transition bag the night before, so be confident that you have everything you need for the race and make your way to transition.

Transition Preparation

If you get to transition when it opens, you may find yourself waiting in line with other eager athletes. Security at the entrance of transition will make sure you are wearing your wristband and have your helmet with your bike. If you have yet to be body marked, find the body marking area and have your arms and legs marked. This is a great photo moment, especially if the race is your first one. As you walk toward your area in transition, make a mental note of where the bike out and in are, along with the run out. Once you are settled in transition, it's not a bad idea to walk those routes to avoid any confusion in the middle of the race about where to go.

If you racked your bike the night before, you know where to head once you get to the transition area. Many athletes use balloons or some sort of marker to identify their area. While balloons are not recommended, you could use a bright-colored transition towel to help your area stand out when you are searching for it after the swim. Take note of any particular landmarks that can help you find your way through transition to your spot. Remember that your transition area will be tight, and make sure that you are courteous and are taking up only the room allotted to you. Typically, you are not in the transition area at the same time as the athletes on either side of you, so don't panic if it seems as though the space is too small. If your bike was racked the night before, it's important to pump up the tires, as the overnight air temperature can affect tire pressure. Get your full water bottles on the bike and make sure your extra tubes, CO_2 cartridges, and nutrition are all in place on the bike.

Next, lay out your transition towel. If there is sand from the water exit to T1, many athletes use a small bucket with water or an extra towel to wipe off their feet before they put their bike shoes on. You can choose to place your helmet either on your bike or on your transition towel. Make sure the helmet is unclipped so you can get it on and appropriately sized more quickly. A good place for your sunglasses is in your helmet. That way you won't forget them as you get on the bike and will be less likely to step on them.

Your bike shoes can be lined up next to your running shoes, along with the race belt you will put on after the swim. If you have specific race items such as a good luck charm, ChapStick, prosthetic limbs, or anything else you plan on using during the race, lay those out as well.

If you are a paratriathlete and would benefit from a chair to sit on in transition, ask the race director or a volunteer for a folding chair. At this point, paratriathletes also will have their handlers with them. Hopefully this is not the first time you have met and you have already gone over what they will do for you in transition, such as where they will lay your prosthetics or your crutches, or how they can help you transfer into your handcycle and race chair.

Once you are satisfied with your layout and have organized all the items in the order you will use them, run through the transition in your mind. Then grab your wetsuit, cap, goggles, anti-chafing balm, and your old pair of flip-flops. Leave your area confident that you are prepared for a great race.

Race Start

At this point, it's highly likely that you will need to find a portable potty, due to either nerves or good hydration. Often there are long lines for the bathroom. Rarely are there sex-specific rest rooms, so jump in line with your fellow racers and enjoy meeting new friends or chatting about the course, anything to help you get rid of prerace jitters.

Once you have made it through the line, continue your walk to the swim start. If you feel the need to go to the bathroom again, don't worry, because in a short while you will have your wetsuit on and, if you're comfortable with it, the chance to go again.

Most races have an accessible portable potty on-site for paratriathletes; don't be shy about going to the front of the line. If you are worried about an accessible bathroom, make sure you talk with the race director before the race so any request can be accommodated.

Once you've arrived at the swim entrance with plenty of time before the start, you can perform a prerace warm-up if you want. Not all races allow in-water warm-ups, but when they do, many athletes choose to get in and swim for a few minutes. The advantage is being able to practice your sighting and warm up your arms. The disadvantage, especially on a cold morning, is waiting around in cold temperatures for your wave to start once you get out of the water. If you choose not to get in, you should get your wetsuit on about 20 minutes before your wave starts. Find the wave that has caps the same color as yours and jump in line. As you get close to your start and get on your cap and goggles, it's a good idea to secure your hair (especially if it's long) in a low bun at the base of your neck. This will allow you to put on your helmet quickly in transition, making sure your hair fits into it.

If there is a specific wave for paratriathletes they should head directly to the front of the line for the swim start as they typically go off in the first wave. Typically, the paratriathlete wave is smaller than the others and the race director or swim course director can help direct you to where you need to go. Your handler will be with you and able to assist you in getting into the water. You'll hand over your prosthetics, crutches, or wheelchair for them to be waiting for you at the end of the swim.

At this point, you're almost there! Remember that this is why you put in all those training hours. Believe in your training, do your best, and have fun!

Swim and T1

It's time! You get in the water and your adrenaline is pumping. If it's an early-morning race, take a few seconds to look around, admire the sunrise, and think about what you are about to accomplish. Soon enough the announcer counts down 3-2-1, the horn blows, you start your timing device, and you're off!

If swimming isn't your strength, it's okay to hang back for a few seconds and let the majority of the group get going before you start. In mass starts, an elbow or a kick to the face is common; if you are worried about this, count down from 10 and then start. By now you know the course, you know what color the buoys are and what side they are on, so your only job is to keep moving those arms. At every race, emergency lifeboats or kayaks are in the water, and if you desperately need a rest, it's okay to take a quick break before you keep going.

As you get further into the swim, the group will usually disperse and you'll no longer be closely surrounded by other athletes. You'll start to feel more comfortable, and your only focus is to get into your swimming rhythm, keep those arms moving, and get closer and closer to the swim exit. If you are swimming along the shore, you'll be able to see the crowd as they follow you towards the swim exit. And if you're lucky, you'll spot your loved ones as they cheer you on.

As you near the end, things can get congested again, and it's okay to take your time getting out of the water. Depending on the race, volunteer wetsuit strippers may be there to help you get out of your wetsuit. It's up to you whether to use them. If you do, the stripper will hand you your wetsuit to carry as you run to transition. If not, you are responsible for removing your own wetsuit. Some athletes find it efficient to unzip the wetsuit as they run to transition and then take it off there.

Water volunteers are typically present to help a paratriathlete out of the water, whether it's an athlete with a spinal cord injury who needs to be lifted out and into a wheelchair or an amputee who needs a shoulder to help her up stairs or a ramp. Paratriathletes' handlers will be waiting at the water exit to hand the athlete any equipment they need, and they'll make their way toward transition on prosthetic legs, on crutches, or in wheelchairs.

Once you get to T1, follow the landmarks you noted earlier and head toward your transition area. Once your wetsuit is off, you want to move as quickly and efficiently as possible, making sure to keep your belongings in your area and not disrupt your neighbors' transition area or their race. Put on your bike shoes and race belt, making sure your helmet is on and clipped before you take your bike off the rack. Once your bike is off the rack, your practice running with the bike comes into play. Move toward the bike out and the mount line. Paratriathletes in handcycles are allowed to ride their bikes slowly through the transition area. For upright bikes, race officials at the mount line will make sure people cross the mount line before they get on the bike. Once you are over the line, hop on your bike and start pedaling. Make sure you are aware of the drafting rules and what side you should be passing people on. You've come too far to get disqualified now.

Bike and T2

It's a good idea to get some nutrition within the first 10 to 15 minutes on the bike. Whether with a gel or liquid nutrition, the bike is the best way to stay fueled for the race. There should be at least one water stop along the bike route where you can stop and refill your water bottles if you run out of water. Triathletes are often too concerned about their race time to stop for refills, but hydration is a crucial aspect of a triathlon, especially on a hot day. It's better to take a few minutes to refill than to not finish the race at all.

The best strategy on a bike is to have a high cadence instead of a high gear. If you have a heart rate monitor, you should follow your training zones and know how to monitor your effort level. A higher cadence in a lower gear can save your legs for the run; but if you are set on a high gear, then lower it within the last mile to give those legs a good spin before you get off the bike. Slow down as you get to the end of the bike, as race officials are at the dismount line to make sure you are off the bike before you cross the line. Run your bike back through T2, rack it in your transition area, and get ready for the run.

The bike shoes come off, the running shoes go on. For paratriathletes, either the prosthetic biking leg comes off and the running leg goes on, or the handlers help with transfer from the handcycle to the racing chair.

T2 is a good time to apply additional sunscreen. Remember to keep your race belt on. Bring sunglasses and a hat or visor if you wear one. Follow the signs to run out, and you are on your way to that finish line!

Run and Finish

Stepping off the bike and starting to run can be a tough transition. In your training, you should have practiced this with brick workouts, and you know that your legs can feel heavy for the first half to full mile. Start slowly, and if things feel good, pick up the pace for a strong finish. Your goal is to find your rhythm, and keep moving forward. If necessary, you can do a walk/run pattern, for example, walking for one minute and then running for two minutes.

Walking through the water stops is common, as it's easier to drink the water without spilling it and you get a short rest. Either way, remember that this is your day and smile. Photographers will be positioned along the course, and a big thumbs-up or a smile will make for a great postrace picture.

Keep moving forward toward that finish line and before you know it, it will be in sight. You'll see it, you'll hear the crowds, and if you're struggling, you'll find your feet again and be able to run fast. You'll sprint through the finish chute, motivated by the finish-line atmosphere, proudly cross the line, and you'll be a triathlete!

Walk through the finish area to get your medal, pose for photos, get some important postrace nutrition, and find your family and friends. Take the time to relish the moment and what you've accomplished. Months of training, hard work, and discipline have gone into this moment, and you have succeeded. Be proud of yourself for having had a goal and having accomplished it. You are a triathlete!

Before you head off to celebrate, go back to transition and collect your belongings. Make sure to remember your wetsuit and goggles and all the other items that may or may not be where you left them. Congratulate the other athletes on their races and swap stories about the course, the weather, or whatever happened out there. Today is your day!

As you head for home, hopefully still wearing your medal, think about the race and how great it was. Learn from the race and think about things that could have gone better or what you could have done differently. If you pushed yourself to the limits, you might have finished thinking you would never want to do another triathlon. But as the hours go by and the excitement of being a triathlete shines through, before long you'll be planning your next one.

Conclusion

As outlined in this chapter, a number of factors go into a good race strategy. Choosing the race, previewing the course, and preparing for the race—all play a crucial part in a successful race. It's important to recognize that things won't always go as planned, and that's okay. Learn from yourself at each race so you can make the next one even better. Seasoned triathletes who have done hundreds of triathlons still learn from their experiences and carry these lessons to the next race.

The triathlon community is a small yet powerful one. Triathletes choose to race triathlons as a lifestyle and often inspire others to do the same with their stories of success. Become part of the multisport movement and encourage other women to give it a try, as once they do that, they'll realize what they are truly capable of accomplishing.

CHAPTER 12

Injury Prevention and Recovery

Krista Austin, PhD, CSCS

Our best performance always comes as a result of consistent training over multiple training cycles. Preventing injury is the foundation for consistency in training, especially in female athletes.

In the sport of triathlon, the most common injuries are a function of muscular overuse and underrecovery from training (Migliorini 2011). Accordingly, an athlete's injury prevention plan must include controlling training intensity, learning proper technique, training to prevent injury, and developing strategies to recover the body from the load placed on it during training.

The majority of chronic overuse injuries are a function of running (Migliorini 2011); as a result, swimmers and cyclists who transfer into the sport of triathlon are more likely to become injured because their bodies are not used to the higher impact of running. In addition, women with a swimming or cycling background may maintain body shapes that result in greater impact during running (the lower body, for example, the legs of a cyclist, is often more dense than that of a runner). This chapter first discusses the more prevalent injuries found among triathletes, especially females, and then focuses on how to minimize potential for injury in training and the various methods that can be used to develop your own personal strategy for optimal recovery.

Females and Injury

While sport injuries occur regardless of the athlete's sex, female athletes have been documented to have a higher prevalence of injuries related to bones, joints, and ligaments (Ivković et al. 2007). These injuries are primarily a function of differences in a woman's anatomical makeup. From an anatomical perspective, women are shorter than men and have smaller limbs and a wider pelvis, which results in a lower center of gravity and a greater application of force to the hips, knees, ankles, and feet. Females also have more abundant joint capsules and less muscle mass, which increases joint laxity (joints are looser). As a result, women are more susceptible to bone- and joint-related injuries when participating in sports that require them to carry their body weight over a distance for any prolonged period of time.

Stress fractures are the most common bone injury seen in women. Stress fractures are fractures in the bone resulting from repetitive overload that occurs as a result of force being placed too frequently and rapidly on the bone. Not only is the prevalence of stress fractures higher in women, but also the site of fracture differs (Ivković et al. 2007). While the tibia is the most common site for both men and women, fractures in the femoral neck, pelvis, and metatarsals and navicular bones of the feet are also highly prevalent in women (Ivković et al. 2007). Stress fractures in women, especially those under the age of 30 and postmenopausal women, can also be a function of low estrogen levels in the body (Ivković et al. 2007). In physically active females under the age of 30, chronic stress fractures and low estrogen levels are often associated with inadequate caloric intake resulting in poor bone density and amenorrhea (Ivković et al. 2007). Together, these symptoms are known as the female athlete triad and can become a limiting factor for many female athletes as to their potential for sport development.

Damage to the anterior cruciate ligament (ACL) is another injury that is more common in women than men (Renstrom et al. 2008). The ACL is one of four ligaments responsible for stabilizing the knee. Primary jobs of the ACL are to keep the tibia from sliding forward in relation to the femur and to prevent excessive knee extension and rotation. While it is not well understood why ACL injuries are so common among female athletes, the increased prevalence is attributed to hormone differences, weaker musculature around the knee, and increased force absorbed by the knee given that a female's pelvis is located closer to the ground.

Patellofemoral pain syndrome and patellar tendinitis (jumper's knee) are highly prevalent among triathletes and runners. These injuries are most commonly identified by pain in the anterior (front) portion of the knee, and both injuries are a function of overload to the joint as a result of prolonged running in poor biomechanical position and weak quadriceps. Female athletes who maintain a larger majority of their body weight in the hips and thighs are more prone to developing these injuries given the excessive strain that is placed on the patellar tendon.

Iliotibial (IT) band friction syndrome occurs most frequently in triathletes who perform high volumes of running and do not stretch properly (Migliorini 2011). This syndrome can also occur as a result of biomechanical loading that creates increased friction on the lateral epicondyle of the femur where the IT band inserts. In women, this is frequently a function of their Q angle due to a wider pelvis (wider hips), resulting in a greater angle formation from the quadriceps to the patella and foot. The increased angle results in greater pressure to the epicondyle of the femur, producing increased friction that eventually results in pain or a pulling sensation.

Swimmer's shoulder and lateral epicondylitis, also known as tennis elbow, are the two most common upper-body overuse injuries seen in swimmers and triathletes. Swimmer's shoulder is a function of chronic irritation to the shoulder soft tissues. When athletes have even a slight biomechanical problem or muscular imbalance, these tissues can become impinged and shoulder pain results. Inflammation of the rotator cuff is most likely the cause of swimmer's shoulder when pain is felt primarily during the recovery phase of the stroke. When pain occurs during active pulling, the biceps tendon usually is inflamed. Lateral epicondylitis primarily occurs as a function of chronic wrist extension against resistance (such as pulling a paddle against the water), but can also be a function of chronic overuse by muscles in the neck and shoulder. Pain and tenderness occur at the lateral epicondyle of the humerus, a function of weak musculature somewhere along the chain of wrist, elbow, shoulder, and neck.

The Female Athlete Triad

The most challenging condition that differentiates female and male athletes is the female athlete triad. The triad consists of three primary components: disordered eating, menstrual dysfunction, and osteoporosis, which is decreased bone mineral density (Ivković et al. 2007). Reduced availability of energy intake with high levels of energy expenditure is the primary cause of injuries that characterize the triad (Ivković et al. 2007). When females restore adequate energy intake, bone-associated injuries decline and menstrual function resumes, resulting in improved training and performance (Ivković et al. 2007).

In a sport such as triathlon, in which athletes can benefit from being lighter and in which they compete in form-fitting or minimal clothing, intentional disordered eating is more prevalent than sports that are not highly weight dependent or have participants wear clothing that fully covers the body or that is not tightly fitted. Studies show the prevalence of disordered eating to range between 15 and 62 percent in groups of female athletes, which is significantly greater than the 1 percent identified in the general population (Migliorini 2011). Disordered eating can take on a variety of patterns, from intentional avoidance of food intake to poor food choices because the athlete has not been educated on how to eat for her training load.

When an athlete is not consuming adequate calories and will not intentionally increase food consumption, the disordered eating pattern is termed *anorexia athletica*. Anorexia athletica differs from anorexia nervosa in that the disordered eating patterns are a function of trying to achieve a performance goal rather than body image alone. Athletes willing to increase caloric density in order to achieve adequate caloric intake are not considered to have anorexia athletica.

Anorexia athletica is characterized by an inability of hormones to rise and fall properly in order for menstrual function and normal bone formation to occur. When a female's menstrual cycle is absent for a period of 90 days or more, she is considered to have amenorrhea, which is characterized by low estrogen levels. As a result of these low estrogen levels, bone density is immediately affected, and injury most likely will eventually result. When estrogen levels are too low, osteoclasts within the bone live longer and resorb more of the bone, thus inhibiting the daily rebuilding of bone tissue. Should this occur for a prolonged period of time, the third component of the female athlete triad, osteoporosis—a skeletal disorder resulting in severe decreases in bone strength and density—is the end result. In addition to amenorrhea and decreased bone density, psychological disturbance is also observed in anorexia athletica and includes obsessive food behavior, anxiety, depression, and severe mood swings. Along with food restriction, anorexia athletica may include episodes of binging and purging and increased levels of exercise, especially after consumption of any form of food.

With a lack of appropriate caloric density, athletes with any form of disordered eating also lack nutrient density sufficient to sustain energy metabolism. As a result, stores of critical nutrients such as iron, B_6, B_{12}, folate, vitamin D, calcium, and electrolytes become depleted, resulting in a malnourished state. With declines in nutrients such as iron, B_6, B_{12}, and folate, the formation of hemoglobin and red blood cells is compromised, which eventually results in anemia and a reduced ability to transport oxygen. Thus, one of the primary indicators of insufficient caloric and nutrient density is a continuous decline in training capacity and performance. In addition to anemia, athletes may also present with decreased stores of vitamin D and calcium, which impairs bone remodeling and leads to increased incidence of bone-related injuries.

Preventing anorexia athletica, disordered eating, and the rest of the female athlete triad is not only about nutrition education. It also revolves around the environment, including whom athletes choose as coaches, friends, training partners, and family, as well as the mental outlook athletes have on performance and life. Coaches should help focus their athletes on measures of performance rather than body weight or body composition. Friends, training partners, and family should lend support to optimizing nutrition for performance. Ultimately, an athlete's mindset toward performance will determine her ability to choose the right foods and use them to enhance training and succeed in competition.

Training to Prevent Injury

Preventing injury depends heavily on understanding how to place a training load safely on the body and maintain the body's overall athleticism. The training load can be considered the total amount of stress placed on an athlete's body. Athleticism is the ability of the body to optimize the innate sport characteristics of flexibility, strength, endurance, agility, and explosiveness.

Overloading the body with a higher training load is one of the fundamental principles for improving performance. In the sport of triathlon, when three sports must be improved, too often the load can become too high and injury results. Keys to ensuring that an overtraining injury does not result include improving one sport discipline at a time, using perception of effort to guide training intensity, and manipulating only one of three factors—frequency, intensity, or duration—in the process of loading the body.

Determining the most effective training load on the body is best facilitated through the use of physiological monitoring tools such as power meters and GPS (Global Positioning System) or heart rate monitors in conjunction with a psychobiological assessment such as rate of perceived effort (RPE; table 12.1). In addition, the overall feeling of recovery should be monitored each day to enable full understanding of the impact of training (table 12.2). Together, these methods can then be used with software systems such as TrainingPeaks and Training Load to calculate and monitor a training load or stress score.

TABLE 12.1

Rating of Perceived Exertion (RPE) Scale

RPE number	Breathing rate, ability to talk	Exertion
1	Resting	Very slight
2	Talking is easy	Slight
3	Talking is easy	Moderate
4	Can talk but with more effort	Somewhat hard
5	Can talk but with more effort	Hard
6	Breathing is challenged, don't want to talk	Hard
7	Breathing is challenged, don't want to talk	Very hard
8	Panting hard, conversation is difficult	Very hard
9	Panting hard, conversation is difficult	Very, very hard
10	Cannot sustain this intensity for too long	Maximal

Reprinted, by permission, from K. Austin and B. Seebohar, 2011, *Performance nutrition: Applying the science of nutrient timing* (Champaign, IL: Human Kinetics), 30.

Athletes' optimal training loads or stress tolerances can differ significantly. When training to prevent injury, an athlete and coach must work together to identify how the stress score is best created (e.g., through more aerobic volume or shorter, more intense, or more frequent training sessions) and for how long the stress can be tolerated before a decline in performance occurs (e.g., inability to complete workouts, mood shifts, or sleep disturbances are noted). For some individuals, this could be four to five weeks, while other athletes are able to sustain the maximal training load for only two or three weeks before requiring an unloaded week for regeneration. The ability to sustain training stress for shorter or longer training cycles is not indicative of the performance gains an athlete can obtain, but rather provides a means to create optimal periodization cycles for each athlete.

TABLE 12.2

Recovery Scale

Number on scale	State of recovery
0	No recovery
1	Extremely bad recovery
2	Very bad recovery
3	Bad recovery
4	Bad recovery
5	Moderate recovery
6	Good recovery
7	Good recovery
8	Very good recovery
9	Extremely good recovery
10	Maximal recovery

Reprinted, by permission, from K. Austin and B. Seebohar, 2011, *Performance nutrition: Applying the science of nutrient timing* (Champaign, IL: Human Kinetics), 33.

Training for Athleticism

Triathletes often struggle to balance training for three different sports and as a result may allow one of the most important components of injury prevention, athleticism, to become compromised. However, because specialized training and athleticism are heavily intertwined, triathletes must learn to use auxiliary training that focuses on maintaining athletic characteristics as a preventive training tool.

Training for athleticism consists of balance, flexibility, agility, speed, stamina, strength, reaction time, rhythm, kinesthetic awareness, and spatial orientation.

Maintaining athleticism does not have to be time-consuming. You can accomplish this in one short gym session per week if you keep the content of these sessions highly varied and use exercises that address more than just one athletic skill. For instance, one-legged squats require balance, strength, and flexibility. Jumping rope using different patterns of movement enhances rhythm, reaction time, and agility. Agility drills can be designed to focus on speed, stamina, reaction time, rhythm, and balance. The following is a sample training session designed to address all the athletic skills.

Dynamics

Use these exercises for the warm-up. Perform 25 meters (or yards) of each exercise. Backpedal or jog back for each one.

Knee Hug

Start in the standing position. Step forward with your left leg and lift your right leg up, pulling knee to chest (figure 12.1). Now, alternate by stepping forward with the right leg and lift your left leg up, pulling the knee to the chest. Continue rotating until you have covered 25 meters.

FIGURE 12.1 **Knee hug.**

Hurdle Walk

Stand tall and choose a front leg. Make sure your knee and toe are up. Open the hip and step over an imaginary hurdle (figure 12.2a). As you step forward with your front leg, bring your opposite leg, the trail leg, over the hurdle (figure 12.2b). Typically the leg comes up and through near the armpit and chest area. Do this for a full 25 meters.

FIGURE 12.2   Hurdle walk: *(a)* front leg steps over the imaginary hurdle; *(b)* trail leg follows.

Walking Lunge With Trunk Rotation

Start by standing tall. Step forward into a single-leg lunge (figure 12.3a). Pretend you are holding a medicine ball or something similar. Rotate the imaginary medicine ball (figure 12.3b) from right to left. Alternate legs for a full 25 meters.

FIGURE 12.3   Walking lunge with trunk rotation: *(a)* forward lunge; *(b)* trunk rotation.

Quick Carioca

Stand with feet approximately hip-width apart. Step with the right foot over the left foot (figure 12.4a). Step the left foot to the left, then step the right foot behind the left foot (figure 12.4b). Do this for 25 meters, then switch directions.

FIGURE 12.4   Quick carioca: *(a)* right foot over left foot; *(b)* right foot behind left foot.

Frankenstein

Start by standing tall. Hold your hands out in front, directly from your shoulders. Step forward with your left foot and kick your right leg forward as high as it can go, reaching it toward your hands (figure 12.5). Alternate legs as you cover 25 meters.

FIGURE 12.5 **Frankenstein.**

Backward Lunge

Lift your left foot off the ground and step back. Lower your hips until the right thigh is parallel to the floor (figure 12.6). Once you achieve a 90-degree angle at the right knee, bring your left foot back up to the right one. Alternate legs. For this exercise, you may choose to move back for 25 meters or stay in one place.

FIGURE 12.6 **Backward lunge.**

Skipping

Using leaps or bounds, drive one knee up and forward while pushing off the other foot. Come down and alternate to the other leg.

Side Shuffle

Keep feet approximately 18 inches (45 centimeters) apart at all times. Lower into a squat position with hands near or on the hips. Have the feet straight and pointing out. Reach with the lead foot. Do not bring the heels together. Stay low and shuffle sideways. Go down and back for 25 meters.

Speed Skip

Skip in place, progressively increasing the speed.

Power Skip

Skip with the intent to get lots of height and see how much distance you can cover with each jump.

High Knees

Using your standard running motion, lift the knee of one leg up so it is parallel to the floor (figure 12.7). Alternate legs.

FIGURE 12.7 **High knees.**

Butt Kicker

Place your weight on one foot and raise the foot of your opposite leg to your butt (figure 12.8). Alternate legs as you move forward for 25 meters.

FIGURE 12.8　Butt kicker.

Zigzag Lateral Movement

Moving in a Z-like pattern, shuffle three steps laterally and then push off with the outside foot to follow each segment of the Z. Repeat as you cover the 25 meters.

Proprioception

Proprioception is the body's unconscious ability to know where all parts of the body are at any one point in time. By increasing body awareness, we can help prevent injury and become more in touch with how our body moves while in training. These exercises are also great to perform immediately before the start of your sport-specific training sessions, especially running.

BOSU Wobble Disc

Stand on the wobble disc in a single-leg stance (figure 12.9). Keep the abdominal muscles contracted and use the other leg to create disruptions to alter balance. This might include reaching the opposing leg behind you, using a stork-like stance, reaching down to touch your toes, or even closing your eyes while performing these activities.

FIGURE 12.9   **BOSU wobble disc.**

Box Tapping

Focus eyes on one point on a wall. Alternate left and right foot (figure 12.10), tapping the box as quickly as possible for 30 seconds. Do this three times.

FIGURE 12.10   Box tapping: *(a)* tap with left foot; *(b)* tap with right foot.

Agility and Change of Direction

Agility and change of direction drills help triathletes maintain motor function and work in planes of motion that are not regularly used in training. These exercises help activate muscles that are key to maintaining the integrity of primary movers for running, cycling, and swimming. It is important to ensure that these muscles are regularly activated.

Pro Agility

The goal of this agility exercise is to work on lateral movement. Start in the middle of the lines (5 yards [4.6 meters] on each side of you; figure 12.11). Sprint to the right for 5 yards, turn back and sprint to the left line (10 yards or 9 meters), and turn around and come back to your starting point.

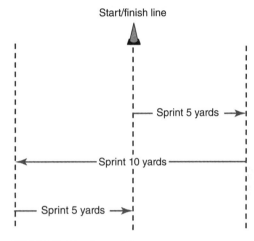

FIGURE 12.11   Pro agility.

Four-Cone Sprint, Back Shuffle

Set up four cones in a 5- × 5-yard [4.6- × 4.6-meter] square (figure 12.12). Begin at cone 1. Sprint to cone 2, then back shuffle to cone 3. Finish by sprinting to cone 4.

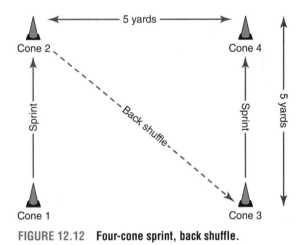

FIGURE 12.12   Four-cone sprint, back shuffle.

Edgren Side-Step Drill

Begin in the middle of a 12-foot-long [3.7-meter] space. Shuffle laterally in a sliding motion for 15 to 30 seconds as fast as you can.

Strength

For each exercise, perform three sets of six to eight repetitions at a rating of perceived effort of four or five. When strength training, focus on technique to ensure safety and maximal benefit while performing the exercise.

Deadlift

This exercise can be performed using a barbell. To do the exercise using a barbell, place your feet shoulder-width apart and right under the bar (figure 12.13a). Facing forward and keeping your back flat and core tight, use a grip that is approximately shoulder-width apart and lift the bar by fully extending the hips and legs (figure 12.13b). Slowly, in a controlled fashion, place the bar back down on the ground.

FIGURE 12.13   Deadlift: *(a)* starting position; *(b)* lift the bar.

Good Morning

Keep your feet shoulder-width apart and place a barbell of appropriate weight evenly across the shoulders (figure 12.14*a*). Make sure your core is tight and that you keep your back straight. Bend at the hips until you can feel the hamstrings in relation to the buttocks (figure 12.14*b*). Do not go so far as to feel pain. Slowly return to an upright position.

FIGURE 12.14   **Good morning: *(a)* starting position; *(b)* bend at the hips.**

Pull-Up

Grasp a pull-up bar with a wide overhand grip (figure 12.15a). Pull the body up toward the bar until your chin is above the bar (figure 12.15b). Lower yourself back down until your arms are in extension. Note: This exercise can also be performed with assistance from a training partner or suitable equipment at the gym that allows you to unload part of your body weight.

FIGURE 12.15   Pull-up: *(a)* starting position; *(b)* chin above bar.

Dip

Use a dip bar. Keep the arms and hips straight with shoulders directly over the hands (figure 12.16*a*). Lower the body until the elbows are at 90-degree angles (figure 12.16*b*) or until you feel a stretch in the shoulders or sternum. Push the body back up until the arms are straight. Note: This exercise can also be performed with assistance from a training partner or suitable equipment at the gym that allows you to unload part of your body weight.

FIGURE 12.16   Dip: *(a)* starting position; *(b)* lower the body.

Technique, Technique, Technique

The technique with which an activity is performed is the most significant factor in determining whether a healthy athlete becomes injured. Working to optimize pulling in swimming, obtaining a correct bike fit, learning to push while pedaling, and running with a stiff midfoot plant and push-off before building training volume are critical to staying injury-free. While swimming, biking, and running all involve unique techniques, the key to optimizing biomechanics for all three disciplines depends on the same factors. In order to optimize technique and enhance the ability to avoid injury, learn the following key factors about how the body functions and the need to develop a strong kinetic chain:

- Correct force production depends primarily on the hips and secondarily on the shoulders. Any form of dysfunction, including a weak supporting musculature or core, results in an increased stress on the lower-body musculature, increasing the risk of knee, ankle, and foot injuries.

- Power from the hips and core to the extremities is a function of midline stabilization. When a strong core is created, the back becomes much like a stiff lever, minimizing any unnecessary forward or backward lean, which also allows the hips and upper body to create a chain that draws on the most powerful muscles of the body in the lower musculature.

- Optimally using the muscles to create power requires the best range of motion a joint can possibly achieve.

- Strength training can help optimize the development of musculature directly linked to the core and further enhance the overall kinetic chain.

Together, correct distribution of stress through the core, back, and lower-body musculature results in improved biomechanical technique and a reduced frequency of injury.

Once a strong foundation has been built to promote the body's overall kinetic chain, athletes can undertake more sport-specific biomechanical analyses to further enhance training efforts. In swimming, evaluation of body position in the water, stroke length and frequency, hand entry, catch, pull, release recovery, and kicking should be evaluated to further refine strength training and muscular imbalances. In cycling, seat height and fore–aft position should be regularly reviewed with increases in strength and power and when overall body musculature or shape has changed. Running analyses should include an evaluation of foot strike mechanics and hip and head position, stride length and cadence, and arm swing.

Building Your Individual Recovery Plan

Building technique and athleticism and optimizing the training load cannot be accomplished without a plan to recover mentally and physically . Underrecovery is one of the greatest limiting factors in the sport of triathlon and one of the major causes of injury. As a result, it is important that athletes develop individualized plans to recover the muscular, energy, and mental systems of the body.

Recovery of the muscular system must not dampen the inflammation response that occurs with training, given that this is critical to inducing training adaptations. However, recovery must be sufficient to restore full range of motion to the limbs and decrease any pain and tenderness associated with training. Recovery of the energy depleted through prolonged or intense training sessions must be designed to enhance restocking of carbohydrate stores in the body, enhance muscle synthesis, and mentally restore the brain's set point for energy status. Mental recovery should involve techniques to relax overall body musculature, support a positive mood, and enhance mental resilience. The recovery methods described here are not intended to be used simultaneously, but rather should be tried and evaluated in order to create an individualized recovery plan.

Muscular Recovery

Muscular recovery can involve daily routines that include self-massage, foam rolling, and stretching and once-a-week exposures to high-level technology including cryotherapy, massage, or compression pants. The most common forms of muscular recovery include hydrotherapies and soft-tissue manipulation.

Hydrotherapy is the use of a fluid medium to improve recovery. Ice baths at temperatures of 55 to 65 degrees Fahrenheit (13 to 18 degrees Celsius) for periods of 15 minutes have been shown to decrease pain from delayed-onset muscle soreness (DOMS) when used postexercise and to decrease the rating of perceived effort when used before training (Versey, Halson, and Dawson 2013). Contrast therapy, in which the athlete alternates between warm- and cold-water immersion, has been reported by athletes to help relieve stiffness and pain, decrease DOMS, improve range of motion, and provide a greater perception of recovery and readiness for training (Versey, Halson, and Dawson 2013). An alternative to hydrotherapy is the use of whole-body cryotherapy, which consists of brief (about 2 minutes) exposures to cold air of −166 to −220 degrees Fahrenheit (−110 to −140 degrees Celsius) in cryochambers. Much like ice and contrast baths, it is reported to help decrease pain and inflammation; however, little research evidence is available to support claims by athletes and companies (Fonda and Sarabon 2013). The greatest benefit of this modality is the brief exposure time necessary to produce an effect similar to that of a more prolonged ice bath.

Self-massage using foam or trigger point rollers and stretching are recovery modalities that can be performed daily to loosen tightened muscles. Self-massage techniques allow acupressure to be applied to targeted muscles, while stretching is typically used to improve range of motion. Assisted massage is an extension of these practices. While there is only anecdotal evidence to suggest that assisted massage may decrease DOMS, improve circulation of nutrients and fluids, increase flexibility, and decrease muscle tonicity, its psychological effects of enhanced mood and overall enhanced feelings of well-being and relaxation suggest that it is of significant benefit to restoring muscle readiness (Brummitt 2008). A more recent novel technology that is similar in approach to massage is NormaTec compression garments. These garments provide dynamic compression and are believed to enhance recovery by decreasing edema, enhancing lymphatic drainage, decreasing pain and tenderness, and restoring a muscle's range of motion.

Energy System Recovery

Training for triathlons can lead to a state of energy depletion. If energy is left unrestored, poor bone and muscle repair and reduced mental recovery can result. Restoration of the body's energy systems is a function of total daily energy intake. Energy deficits greater than 750 calories per day or consumption of less than adequate energy for a prolonged period of time will result in poor performance and also significantly increase the potential for injury.

Achieving the necessary energy intake for the intense and high-volume training associated with triathlon is often best facilitated through the use of a nutrient timing system. This strategy helps the athlete focus the types of nutrients consumed throughout the day and also provides a steady flux of energy all day, especially before, during, and after training.

The first step in developing a nutrient timing system should be to determine the amount of carbohydrate needed before, during, and immediately after training. Once you have determined these amounts, you can develop the carbohydrate content of meals and snacks along with the necessary amounts of protein and fat needed to fulfill total energy requirements. The goal should be to consume energy in small amounts every two to three hours throughout the day, which will enhance overall body homeostasis and promote recovery.

In addition to the consumption of nutrients, optimizing fluid intake to meet daily water needs and replace fluid lost as sweat is critical to restoring body temperature following training and removing metabolic waste from muscle breakdown. Fluid intake is also key to reducing the potential for soft tissue injury since it serves as a critical medium for the transport of nutrients and storage of carbohydrate in the muscle. Hydration status has also been related to mood, energy levels, and cognitive function. When the body is less than two percent dehydrated, mood, energy, and cognition are significantly better, which affects not only work ability but also personal relationships and overall perception of daily activities.

Mental Recovery

Mental recovery encompasses psychological and emotional processes necessary for a healthy lifestyle. Techniques used to enhance mental recovery can range from regular positive social interactions with friends and family to deep muscle relaxation techniques or even enjoying your favorite dessert after a hard day of training. Developing your personal plan for mental recovery should encompass two key types of mental recovery tools: tools used to take your mind off of competition and work, and tools used for mental escape. Both of these should be nonstressful and should produce a more positive mood state. For example, after a hard day of training, my elite athletes will use a deep tissue massage with preferred relaxation sounds and a dinner that is a personal favorite and known for its satisfying taste. At the end of the season, this will even extend itself to a vacation with no training or media or sport related social engagements and vacation components consisting of only their favorite things to do such as scuba diving, horseback riding, and enjoying good food! These tools differ for everyone and should be considered part of a personal plan that applies only to the individual as an athlete.

Sleep

The greatest performance-enhancing physical and mental recovery tool available to athletes is sleep. Athletes who sleep eight or more hours per night are less likely to suffer an injury. This duration of sleep provides a sleep pattern that is sufficient for completion of all the phases of sleep, especially REM (rapid eye movement) sleep, which is needed for muscle repair and the release of hormones to restore the body's homeostatic systems. Sleeping at the same time each night is even more important, since the body operates on a circadian rhythm that must be maintained in order to optimize the restorative process.

Conclusion

Injury prevention is a function of multiple facets coming together in a harmonious fashion to allow athletes continuous training progressions. The training load necessary to improve sport performance must be supported through development of athleticism, proper sport technique, nutrition, and muscular and mental recovery techniques. Each athlete must determine the necessary dose of each preventive tool available and create a unique plan to optimize performance.

CHAPTER 13

Coaching Options for Triathletes

Gale Bernhardt

Whether you're new to the sport of triathlon or a seasoned veteran, having a good coach can have significant positive effects on you and your performance. The right coach can help a beginner triathlete transition into the sport much faster than she could on her own and help her avoid common pitfalls. The right coach can help you improve speed, endurance, and mental toughness while helping you stay healthy.

The structure and accountability that come with training under the guidance of someone else are two of the biggest reasons why triathletes turn to coaches to help them achieve goals. No matter your reasons for seeking the advice of a good coach, the big question is, Where do you begin?

Why Do You Want a Coach?

It may seem like an obvious question, but you must ask, "What do I want from a coach?" The answers may change as you continue your investigation as well as your journey through the sport. A good place to start is with a list or a paragraph detailing why you think a coach could help you. Use first person to write down your reasons.

These are a few common reasons for wanting a coach:

- I want someone to help me stay motivated and on track.
- I need help planning workouts in preparation for a triathlon while avoiding injury and staying healthy.
- A coach can help me learn about the sport faster than I could on my own.
- A coach can explain why I need to do particular workouts at particular times of the season.
- A coach can guide me through the many, many triathlon equipment options available, including gear, fuel, training aids, and bike fit.

- A coach would be a resource on call to answer any sport questions I might have.
- I'd like a coach who is at my workouts to help me with swim technique.
- I need structured training to improve my endurance or speed.
- I don't want a lot of contact from a coach. I just need the structured training so I can follow workout instructions on my own and ask questions from time to time.

These are just a few examples of reasons why people want to work with a coach. You may have several reasons not included on this list.

Why Do You Need a Coach?

Whether a beginner or a seasoned athlete, everyone has room to improve. A good coach wants to help you achieve your goals and has your best interests in mind. Consider the coach your personal cheerleader.

Coaches usually take a baseline fitness measurement or at minimum examine your athletic profile before designing a training program to help you succeed. Where are you now? Where do you want to go? How much time is available to accomplish your goals?

A coach uses this information to plan overall training volume, workout duration, intensity, frequency, power, pace, and other factors in support of your goals. Your coach solves the complex puzzle for you and takes the guesswork out of training. A good coach will pay close attention to health and safety, assisting eager athletes by tempering enthusiasm when extreme goals—such as ramping up race distance too fast or trying to improve swimming, cycling, or running speed at an unreasonable rate—pose a high risk of causing injury.

Good coaches constantly educate themselves on things like physiology, equipment, nutrition, current research, and fads. Their job is to stay up to speed on what it takes to help you achieve your goals while also helping you avoid costly pitfalls. Your coach is your personal reliable resource for the endless information related to triathlon training and racing. Your coach is someone you can trust.

Consider your coach a personal motivator. Having that workout, or multiple workouts, to look forward to each day helps you stay on track and motivated. This planned progression looks far into the future to determine what workouts you need to do today in order to achieve success months from now.

Too often, self-coached athletes end up repeating familiar sequences of training long after the workouts have lost effectiveness and appeal. A coach helps provide variety and structure to keep workouts fresh and gives you ideas for training methods and locations you might not have otherwise discovered.

An enormous volume of information is available in magazines and books and on the Internet. Sample workouts and recommendations can be conflicting and confusing. Great coaches follow time-honored and proven training principles. These principles include gradual progression of volume and intensity or mileage and speed. Coaches know it is wise to build basic aerobic fitness before adding high speed to the mix. They emphasize smart training and are more often holding athletes back than pushing for higher and higher training loads.

Your Budget

After you've outlined what you think you want and need from a coach, begin your investigation process with a monthly budget in mind. As you proceed through your search, you may find that you must modify budget or coaching service expectations.

The fee that a coach charges depends on a combination of the coach's history of success and the services provided. A coach who has many years of success stories and provides highly personalized services demands a higher fee than either a new coach with very personalized services or a highly regarded coach providing limited services.

Triathletes on a tight budget can find detailed training plans designed by highly regarded coaches in books and online. Triathletes with unlimited budgets can have a coach who designs personal training plans and is available on-site for many, if not all, training sessions. This level of service puts the coach one phone call away for advice and support.

Expect to pay $100 to $200 per month for new triathlon coaches or group coaching delivered by experienced coaches. For experienced coaches who have several years of proven results, including podium results at a variety of races, the fee range goes from $200 to $400 per month. Coaches who have proven success working at top levels of the sport, including Ironman, World Cup racing, World Championships, Pan American Games, and the Olympics, charge $400 to $2,500 per month, or more, depending on their resume and the amount of in-person coach contact they provide.

As women rise to the top ranks of the sport, some coaches reduce or eliminate the monthly fee and work for a percentage of the athlete's prize winnings.

Coach's Experience and Formal Education

A coach who has vast and proven experience at successfully coaching athletes has a bigger knowledge base to draw from than someone who has coached only one or two people over a short time. Expect to pay less for coaches who have less experience in the sport and those with limited proven success at coaching other athletes. More specifically, just the fact that someone has achieved a high level of personal success in the sport, such as professional or high-level age-group success, does not mean this person will automatically make a great coach or be the right fit for you.

There are several forms of applicable formal education. The two most common are a college degree and a coaching certification from USA Triathlon, the national governing body for the sport.

For coaches to meet the standards of a degree or certification with a national federation under the watch of the Olympic Committee, they are required to pass a test that exhibits their ability to develop athletes. In the case of USA Triathlon, coaches with the highest levels of certification must provide examples of or proof (written tests as well as practical displays of knowledge) that they have a certain level of experience as a result of successfully coaching athletes over the course of several years.

While there are no guarantees that someone with a degree or a certification is a good coach, both of these provide proof of a minimum level of knowledge.

It is important to distinguish between a personal trainer and a coach. Most often, personal trainers specialize in one area, such as weight training. Training is delivered in one-on-one sessions to only one person or small groups. Typically a fitness assessment is completed before the training, and progress is judged against the baseline mark. Training sessions include instruction, exercise prescription for that session, accountability, and motivation. Often the training result is not time sensitive.

A coach also aims to improve individual baseline performance but is looking at a broader spectrum than the personal trainer is. The coach must have basic knowledge of nutrition, mental skills, strength training, stretching, physiology, and sport skill, as well as the ability to analyze training and race results, to name a few areas. The art of coaching requires that the coach combine many areas of knowledge in order to provide a specific training progression for athletes.

Additionally, most of the time, the coach is concerned about the athlete's positive progression toward a time-sensitive goal. This goal is typically in the form of a race on a specific date. Because some races have cut-off times, it is imperative that the triathlete is trained to achieve race-pace goals in a safe manner. The athlete's progression relies on the coach's ability to plan macro-, meso-, and microcycles of training to help improve the athlete's physical fitness. In addition to physical fitness, the coach must have knowledge of the skills and tactics required for the athlete to become proficient at the sport.

Individual Training Versus Group Training

If you need or want a coach to be with you at workouts to help with form, technique, motivation, or all of these, be prepared to pay more for that high level of personal attention. One way to get personal attention from a coach while keeping your budget under control is to become involved in a group that is coached. These group sessions are a great way for athletes in a particular region or triathlon club to pool resources, receive quality instruction, and develop camaraderie. In this situation, the triathletes may or may not be following the same overall training plan.

If all members of the group are following the same training plan and the coach meets with athletes at the group training sessions, this is an excellent way for athletes to quickly gain knowledge and skills. Depending on the particular situation and the size of the group, the coach may modify the group training plan or help athletes modify the training plan to meet personal needs. In some cases it is left to the individual athlete to make her own modifications.

It is worth mentioning that triathlon teams may have benefits apart from coached workout opportunities. These benefits might include discounts with local merchants, team deals on equipment, and the opportunity to purchase team clothing such as swimsuits, racing triathlon suits, wetsuits, and jackets. For some triathletes, the camaraderie of group training helps motivation and performance. For those who are interested in helping a cause while training for a specific event, some triathlon training groups offer a team training atmosphere while raising funds for a charitable organization.

For experienced triathletes with specific goals, sometimes a group training situation is not the best choice. Athletes with specific and individual goals or those who have reached performance plateaus often need personal attention in order to progress to the next level.

A Highly Personalized Training Plan

If you want a training plan designed to help you achieve your specific goals, address sport-specific performance limiters, and include one-on-one training within the context of your work schedule and other individual issues, expect to pay more for this type of personalized coaching service compared to a ready-to-use training plan or a group training plan.

If you are paying for a highly personalized training plan, be certain that your definition of *personalized* is the same as the coach's. A completely customized plan will be more expensive than a plan modified from a template or a single plan given to a group of athletes. Don't be afraid to ask the coach specifically about how much of your training will come from a template.

Some triathletes are busy professionals who are trying to manage a job with travel as well as family obligations. These athletes are best served by a coach who designs highly customized training that likely does not follow a common pattern. For example, nurses, firefighters, doctors, and airline pilots often work on weekends or have work schedules that follow a rotation other than a seven-day cycle. Work rotations may include long or unusual hours. These triathletes need help structuring a training program that accommodates a busy work schedule with perhaps unusual sleep hours. Typically, these triathletes are best served by a coach who offers highly personalized attention and training plans.

Coach Contact Outside of Training Sessions

If you want to have access to your coach at any time, including a personal cell phone number, and to have priority on that coach's e-mail list, you'll pay a premium for this service compared to limited coach contact or no contact at all. This will require more athlete accountability as well.

Some coaches offer packages with a contract that specifies a limited amount of monthly contact expressed as a certain number of minutes. If you purchase a training package with such an agreement, respect those boundaries and be conscientious about honoring any limitations written into the contract.

Coach Presence at Races or Other Appointments

Is it important to you that your coach be physically present at your races? With some coaching packages, the coach does not attend any races. Some coaches attend a certain number of races while others will attend races, if requested, for an additional fee.

For example, perhaps you plan to do six races this season and your overall coaching package does not include the coach's presence at all races. Perhaps you don't need or want the coach to be present for all of the races, but you do want her there for two of them. Is it possible to pay the coach an extra fee for attending a limited number of events? It doesn't hurt to inquire about this.

There may be occasions when you visit someone other than the coach for a bike fit or nutrition advice, or you visit a sports medicine professional for an injury. It is often good to have an extra set of eyes and ears at these appointments. While you are busy listening to what the professional is telling you, your coach can be taking notes and asking questions about how this appointment affects future training. In addition to being concerned about injury specifics, the coach is evaluating the information provided by the professional in order to best modify training so the athlete can return to play as soon as possible.

Having your coach present at races or other appointments can be very valuable. There is a good chance the coach will notice things that can help you improve. Consider the value of such a service to you and the possibility for additional support within the coaching relationship.

One Coach Versus Multiple Coaches

Some triathletes swim with a masters group, ride with a local bike shop, or run with the running club. These opportunities often include coaches who attend the sessions, but because all of the coaches are different, no one is looking at the overall plan. If you have a multiple-coach situation, it is highly recommended that you have one coach who is overseeing the entire training process. This will prevent you from doing too much volume or intensity, which can lead to illness or injury.

Assessing the Coaching Experience

At the end of three months, six months, or a year, how will you and the coach know that the coach–triathlete experience was successful? This is a question that needs to be asked at the beginning of the coach–athlete relationship and at the end of a race season. A good exercise is to list three ways you will know your coach–athlete relationship was successful at the end of some 3 to 12 months. If your coach does not bring the topic up, share your thoughts with him or her.

Rather than stating that at the end of six months you want "to be a better athlete," get more specific. These are some examples:

- To train and race injury-free the entire season
- To improve running speed by 2 to 3 percent
- To improve timed 500 swim to between 7:00 and 7:10
- To race my best tri event in under 3 hours
- To complete my first 70.3 event
- To improve my 3-mile aerobic time-trial run speed from a baseline of 10 minutes per mile

Notice that all these examples have a result that can be measured. Avoid setting vague and unmeasurable goals.

If you are working with a coach over the course of several months, there is a chance that your goals may change. Each time your training or racing goals are modified, be sure to take another look at defining a successful season and a successful coach–athlete relationship.

So what can you do to improve the probability of a successful athlete–coach relationship? Keys to a successful athlete–coach relationship include honesty, timely feedback (in both directions), cooperative problem solving, and using technology to your advantage.

Do your best to be honest with your coach. Let her know if the training is too hard, too easy, or just right. If you have a sore foot or a slight cold, though it may seem like nothing, let your coach know. She can help you modify workouts in order to minimize downtime, maximize training time efficiency, and improve the likelihood of successful goal achievement.

Another thing you can do is to fill out your training journal within a few hours after each workout. Note your overall rating of the workout. Was it too hard, too easy, just right? How did you feel? Did you have any aches or pains? Was your heart rate or pace normal, lower than expected, or higher than expected?

Life can get busy, and it is convenient to think "I'll post today's workout sometime tomorrow when I have more time." It's easy for one day to lead to two and then, before you know it, you're posting seven days' worth of training all at once on Sunday night. What you lose by posting multiple workouts days after you've completed them are the nuances of each individual workout that might be important. Those nuances might signal your coach to adjust your training load or make other changes to individual workout details that could further help your progress.

Additionally, if you and another 10 athletes are posting 7 to 28 workouts for the coach to review on Sunday night, it's very difficult for her to give all of those workouts a high-quality review. Do yourself a favor and log workouts, including comments, on a daily basis.

You don't have to use every piece of technology available to see results. Your coach can use heart rate, pace, or power data to help you progress. If you have a long-distance relationship with your coach, you can use video tools such as Coach's Eye or Dartfish to discuss technique, form, and equipment fit. Even if you don't have a long-distance relationship, video can be an invaluable tool in assessing your progress.

Coaching Personalities

A wide variety of services are offered by various coaches, and this chapter touches on a few of the important aspects to consider. None of the coach–athlete situations described in the chapter are good or bad; rather, this is a matter of deciding the level of service you want and how much you are willing and able to pay for the various coaching services and experience levels.

In addition to the service options of a coaching relationship, the personality component is also critical to your success as an athlete. You may need or prefer to work with a coach who has a particular type of personality, coaching style, or philosophy. You may want a coach who yells at you during workouts or not.

You may prefer a low-key coach or a highly excitable coach. Be aware of your preferences as you investigate your options. If you are considering a group coaching situation, ask to attend one of the group sessions before signing up with the team. If you can't participate in the session, for whatever reason, ask to attend the session and observe.

If your coaching package does not include personal contact, schedule phone interviews with potential coaches. Before the call, make a list of questions you have for the coach and consider sending those ahead of the scheduled call.

Are You Coachable?

Some triathletes out there are simply not coachable. These athletes do not like someone else telling them how to structure workouts or how to modify current routines in order to succeed. They are unwilling to modify past habits and routines, such as very high training volume, in order to get faster or prevent injuries. These athletes constantly modify, move, or eliminate workouts delivered by the coach, with no interaction with the coach.

If you find yourself constantly modifying the workouts delivered by the coach, discuss with the coach why you are modifying the workouts. Sometimes there is a period of adjustment early in the coach–athlete relationship during which the coach is trying to determine the correct training load. In other cases, you may need a different coach. Sometimes, the problem is you. Consider all possibilities before abandoning the program.

Conclusion

When you begin looking for a coach, take the time to think about how much of a commitment—in both time and money—you can make to your training. Ask yourself what you hope to get out of the relationship, and don't be afraid to ask a potential coach questions about how she or he can help you achieve your goals.

Whether you are looking for a high level of service and reputation or a ready-to-use training plan to follow on your own schedule, there is a coach available to help you succeed.

CHAPTER 14

Training Through Different Life Stages

Wendy Francke, MD

Although I was nervous when approached to write this chapter on training for women through different stages in life, I also was extremely excited about this unique opportunity. Women are different from men, so it makes sense that training considerations will be different, too. As a physician, triathlete, wife, and mother of two young girls, I have knowledge and experience that can help explain the specific challenges women face in training. Women have monthly cycles to take into consideration. There may be times in our lives when we are pregnant or busy balancing young children and jobs. As we get older, we go through menopause. In this chapter, we explore these specific issues and how they relate to women training for triathlons or any endurance sport.

Training and the Menstrual Cycle

I preface this section with the simple but essential observation that every woman is different, and every woman's body behaves differently during her menstrual cycle. Some women have weight gain, water retention, moodiness, fatigue, cramps, or heavy cycles. For others, their cycles don't seem to affect them in their daily exercise and routine. Become more aware of your monthly cycle and see how you feel during the different phases in your cycle. This will help you consider the impact on your training.

Let's first take a look at what is going on in a woman's body during her cycle.

Days 1 to 14

Days 1 to 14 of the menstrual cycle are called the follicular phase. This phase begins on the first day of menses, which for most women can last from 4 to 7 days. Ovulation (release of the egg from an ovary) occurs around day 14. The luteal phase occurs during days 14 to 28 of an average cycle. This is when there is a surge in the hormone estrogen, producing potential metabolic changes that can affect training and performance.

When women are menstruating (follicular phase), they are perfectly capable of training and competing. A female athlete needs to be aware of how her cycle normally flows and prepare accordingly with tampons or pads. Ibuprofen may also help if you tend to have severe menstrual cramps. If you have a big race coming up and want to avoid being on your menses during competition, you can talk to your doctor about manipulating your menses with hormonal contraception. On the birth control pill, patch, or NuvaRing, it is possible to manipulate when your menses occurs. By skipping the placebo week and going straight into a new pill pack, patch, or NuvaRing, you can bypass your menstrual cycle for that month.

Many people believe that blood loss during menses can adversely affect exercise because of the risk of anemia. This is a fallacy about menstruation and performance. The average drop in hemoglobin and hematocrit from one monthly cycle is not significant enough to affect training or performance. Over time, if a woman has heavy menses, she may need iron supplementation to keep from becoming anemic. If you are feeling overly fatigued especially with exercise, in addition to having your doctor check your hemoglobin, check your ferritin level. Ferritin levels can be low before anemia occurs; this indicates low iron stores. Also, if you are taking iron supplementation, taking iron with vitamin C will enhance absorption; however, avoid taking iron supplements with calcium or milk, as these may interfere with the iron absorption.

Days 14 to 28

The second phase of the menstrual cycle is the luteal phase, days 14 to 28. Some metabolic changes during this phase could potentially affect training and performance. During the luteal phase, estrogen surges, which stimulates the body to use more fat and hold on to energy stores more in the form of glycogen. An endurance athlete who is training or racing during this time may need to take in a little more carbohydrate. Extra carbohydrate will make energy more readily available to sustain energy throughout a long training day or race.

Plasma volume can also decrease during the luteal phase. A decrease in plasma volume can cause two issues. First, the blood is thicker, or more viscous, therefore blood flow to muscles can be slower, and that can negatively affect recovery time. Lactic acid that has built up in the muscles may not clear as quickly, so muscles can stay sore longer and need more recovery time. Second, decreased plasma volume in the luteal phase can decrease the amount a woman sweats and increase core body temperature. An increase in core body temperature can lead to overheating, so women should be aware of heat-related conditions during this time. Drinking plenty of fluids and preloading with drinks containing sodium and electrolytes can help increase plasma volume. Also, take care when exercising during extreme heat so as not to overheat.

Effect of the Menstrual Cycle on Training

With all this said, it is still unclear how much a woman's menstrual cycle affects exercise and endurance. Some studies on female athletes during different phases of their cycle have not shown performance changes during a woman's menses. The bottom line is to be aware of your cycle and how your body feels during exercise. Keeping a diary of your exercise and your cycle can show you how your body is affected by menses and can help you plan your training accordingly.

Exercise and Pregnancy

As a physician who does prenatal care, I encourage at least 30 minutes of physical activity a day for my pregnant patients. A woman who is already active and has a good baseline of fitness can continue her exercise but may need to adjust intensity. Those who are not physically active before pregnancy should not start any vigorous activity, but they certainly should get moving by walking, swimming, or performing another lower-impact exercise.

First, if you are pregnant, consult with your physician about your exercise plans and goals. Most physicians have had some training on how to counsel women regarding exercise and pregnancy, but some are more comfortable with endurance athletes and pregnancy than others. If your physician is not comfortable with recommendations on exercise and pregnancy for triathletes, you may want to see if she can recommend someone who has more experience in or knowledge on the subject. Also, when planning your training while pregnant, err on the side of caution when in doubt. You are incubating a baby, which is one of the most amazing feats a female body can perform. This job requires a lot of energy and care. High-risk pregnancy (twins, bleeding, placenta previa, high blood pressure, and so on) require a lot more caution, so listen to your doctor if there are any complications in your pregnancy.

First Trimester

The first trimester of pregnancy (weeks 1 to 13) is the most critical in terms of formation of the baby's vital organs. During this part of pregnancy, many women feel fatigued and may have nausea and vomiting. Shortness of breath may be more common due to increased levels of the hormone progesterone. Some women also experience low pelvic cramping and urinary frequency early in pregnancy. Listen to your body as you are training; if it does not feel good, slow down. Exercise has not been shown to increase the risk of a miscarriage, but if you have any bleeding, stop and contact your physician. During training in the first trimester, the uterus is still very small, so usually there isn't the abdominal discomfort that comes in later stages of pregnancy. Running, biking, and swimming are all safe and generally relatively comfortable to do in the first trimester. If weight training is part of your exercise routine, you can also continue moderate weight training exercises and core strengthening.

Many women who are pregnant want to know if they have to keep their heart rate under a certain level when training. The American College of Gynecology used to have guidelines regarding heart rate and pregnancy, recommending that women keep their heart rate under 140 beats per minute (bpm) when exercising. This is outdated, as heart rate varies from person to person depending on level of fitness. Women can exercise and get their heart rates up above 140 bpm during pregnancy. There is no set maximum heart rate guideline. If you can talk during exercise and not feel too short of breath, this is considered safe. You do not want to be training or racing at 100 percent effort, but 70 to 80 percent effort is generally okay and is not going to hurt the fetus. Some studies have even shown cardiovascular benefits to the baby when the mother exercises regularly during pregnancy.

Second Trimester

By the second trimester (weeks 14 to 27), usually the nausea, vomiting, and fatigue have resolved. Women tend to have more energy, and some women feel very good when exercising. This is also a time when the body is changing; a woman's center of gravity shifts as the baby gets bigger. Running may slow down; swimming feels good, but cycling may become a little more difficult due to the increased abdominal girth and changes in center of gravity. As a woman gets to the middle or end of the second trimester, she may consider going to stationary cycling. There is a reduced chance of accidents on a stationary bike, as it does get more difficult to cycle on a road bike further along in pregnancy due to balance issues. Changing from a road bike to a more upright bike may extend how long you can cycle while pregnant, but certainly stationary and recumbent bikes are more comfortable and safer.

Third Trimester

In the third trimester (weeks 28 to delivery), training is really going to slow down. Running is possible, depending on how comfortable a woman feels. Most switch to walking or to walking and jogging. A woman's heart rate and breathing rate naturally go up in this later stage of pregnancy due to physiological changes in the body. More blood is pumped to the uterus; it is more difficult to expand the chest to get good deep breaths; and the body requires more oxygen for the fetus. Swimming, however, feels great. Being in the water helps relieve a lot of pressure and weight from the growing body.

Considerations for All Stages of Pregnancy

Throughout pregnancy it is vital to keep well hydrated. Always bring water with you when you exercise. Blood pressure naturally goes down in the first part of pregnancy, and keeping well hydrated can help prevent dizziness. Dehydration can also lead to preterm contractions. For comfort, compression or Lycra shorts can help relieve some low-abdominal pressure during exercise in pregnancy. A good supportive bra is also necessary for comfort, as breast size increases in pregnancy, and just wait until you are breast-feeding! Also, remember to bring nutrition when exercising, as some women have low blood sugar if they do not eat frequently while pregnant. The body, which is growing a baby, requires an additional 300 calories daily, so don't skimp on nutrition. Bring an extra energy bar, energy gel, fruit, nuts, and other healthy nutritious snacks, and make sure you eat something an hour before exercising.

It is also possible to race in triathlons during pregnancy; however, you need to be realistic about goals and expectations. Do not expect (or try) to have record-breaking times while pregnant. During my own fairly uncomplicated pregnancies, I exercised and trained throughout much of each one. I did two triathlons during my first pregnancy, one Olympic length at about 8 weeks, and one sprint at about 14 weeks. I also continued to run 5K events up until my third trimester. I raced for the enjoyment and to have a goal to keep some semblance of health and fitness as my body changed with pregnancy. I have also counseled several women in our triathlon club regarding training and pregnancy. One of the women found out she was pregnant (in her first trimester) while training for her first Ironman. She had already planned her trip and had done long swims, bike rides, and runs before she realized she was pregnant. I advised her on race day not to do the entire race and to listen to her body. I thought doing the swim and about half of the bike course would be enough for that day. She was able to do that, and although she did not do the entire Ironman as initially planned, she now has a beautiful healthy son and was back training for some sprint races at four months postpartum.

Remember, when pregnant, consult your physician, be smart, and listen to your body. Pregnancy is not the time to make your fastest times or have your best races. The goal of training or racing during pregnancy is to keep active for a healthy lifestyle and, ultimately, a healthy pregnancy.

Postbaby Training

Many women triathletes are anxious to get back in shape after having a baby. It is hard to balance an active, training lifestyle and being a new mother. You have to look at your short-term and long-term goals as an athlete while caring for a newborn, who is completely dependent on you. With the exception of some elite athletes, most are not going to be in prepregnancy race shape quickly. Take the time to balance your family life and exercise.

You should take many factors into consideration when returning to exercise postpartum. Your body has changed in weight and shape; you have not been vigorously exercising for a few months; you may be breast-feeding; you may have had a difficult delivery or had a cesarean. It takes time and patience to get back in shape. First, take it easy and start by walking. Most women who had a vaginal delivery can start by going for easy to moderate walks at two weeks postpartum; it will take longer after having a cesarean. Your pelvis has changed and ligaments have loosened to accommodate having a baby. If you experience pain while exercising, cut back. Consult your physician regarding when is the best time to start exercising, and give your body a chance to recover and adjust.

When getting back into shape after having a baby, make sure you have appropriate gear. A good supportive sports bra is essential, especially if you are breast-feeding. Sometimes even wearing two bras may be more comfortable. Spandex or Lycra shorts also provide support for the abdominal muscles, which have stretched out. It is a good idea to wear a pad, as urine leakage is very common after delivery, until your pelvic floor muscles are stronger. Pelvic exercises such as Kegels can help lessen any urinary incontinence postpartum. To do this exercise, contract your lower pelvic muscles for 10 to 20 seconds as though you are trying to stop urinating. Repeat 10 sets of these exercises several times a day. Most importantly, always carry a water bottle. Hydration is essential, again especially if you are breast-feeding. You need to keep well hydrated to keep up your milk supply. Make sure your calorie intake is sufficient, too, as breast-feeding burns an additional 500 calories a day. If your food intake is not adequate, your milk supply can decrease. Take care to eat good healthy foods—lots of fruits, vegetables, lean meats, and whole foods, not processed foods.

Having a supportive partner or family member to step in and take care of the baby while you exercise is also vital. Planning your time to exercise involves figuring out when it is best for the baby, the family, and you. Alternating mornings with your partner or getting a workout in while the baby is napping can help you return to fitness. When your baby is small, it is often best to exercise after you have fed him or her. In terms of breast-feeding, your breasts are less full after nursing, so it will be more comfortable for you to exercise at this time. Some lactic acid buildup can occur in breast milk with a vigorous workout. This can potentially make breast milk taste a little more acidic or bitter, so waiting to breast-feed about an hour after vigorous exercise may help if the baby seems fussy when feeding sooner after you have exercised.

If you are not able to get out of the house to exercise, there are some great videos and home exercises that you can do to help with strengthening and conditioning. Little equipment is needed to do many exercises at home, such as planks, sit-ups, squats, lunges, push-ups, burpees, yoga, Pilates, or moves with exercise bands; and many can be done while the baby naps (unless you wisely decide to nap with the baby). Core and strengthening exercises are very important for a triathlete to help regain strength and balance after having a baby. Kegel exercises, planks, bridges, and squats can also help strengthen and realign the pelvis, which may have tilted some during pregnancy. These exercises are very helpful especially if you have experienced some pelvic pain with exercising, particularly with running.

Once you are comfortable walking, start alternating jogging with walking. Again, if you experience pain or discomfort, back off. Swimming is also a good low-impact exercise that can be started as soon as you are healed and have stopped bleeding. As with walking and running, you will be deconditioned, so start slowly in the pool and build up. As for biking, you may want to start on a stationary bike or in a spin class before going out on the road. Breast-feeding women can be a little top heavy, and you need to get reacclimated to your center of gravity and body changes. Again, see how you feel before increasing your intensity in this and all types of exercise.

Consulting with a trainer is a great idea if you are interested in racing or getting back to prebaby shape in the next six months to a year after having a baby. A training plan may motivate you to get exercising, but be flexible. You may not have as much time as you think you will, as new parenting challenges always pop up. Wait to see how you can manage time and exercise before signing up for a race. I have seen many women ambitiously sign up for triathlons four to six months after having a baby. More often than not, they are not ready. Some mothers are hard pressed to get a shower in, let alone exercise, when there is a new baby in the house. Consider starting with a local 5K-goal race before jumping to a multisport event.

As your baby gets a little older, you can start exercising with the baby. At about five or six months (once a baby has good head control), you can start bringing the baby out for a run in a jogger stroller. It is worthwhile investing in a good jogger stroller. There is nothing like pushing a jogger stroller with a baby to get you in shape. (I was probably in my best shape when my children were 2 and 4 after pushing them in the double jogger stroller for 5K races!) Start with shorter distances to see how the baby is in the stroller. Hopefully he or she will enjoy it or, even better, fall asleep. Bike seats can be used at about nine months to a year. These are best mounted on an around-town bike or mountain bike, not your road or triathlon bike. When your child is a little older, a bike trailer is also a great way to get a workout in. Pulling a trailer (30 pounds [13.6 kilograms]) with your child (20 pounds [9 kilograms]) and all the toys and food will certainly make you feel light as feather when you finally get to ride on your own without a trailer.

Balancing Family and Training

A good friend of mine is a physician and a mother of three, and she just qualified for Kona. She gave me a few good suggestions for busy mothers who are getting back into triathlons. Incorporating your family into your training and racing can be fun. Run to the store with your jogger stroller to do simple errands, if possible. Bike with the children in the trailer to bring them to preschool or school in order to get a workout in and spend time with the kids. Bike or run to the park with the children so they can play. Run or bike to a destination such as the beach or a park to meet the family while they drive there. You also can switch and give your partner a chance to run or bike back home.

In the summer, my husband and I go to the beach with the children on the weekend and take turns riding there and back. Then we do an ocean swim with the masters swim group while the children are playing. (Someone is always watching the kids.) Plan longer runs or rides while children are at school so you don't miss time with the family. If you are working when the children are at school, get up and exercise before they wake up because if you wait to exercise until the children go to bed, you may be too tired. To get my exercise in, I wake up at 5:15 every morning and am back by 6:45.

Include your family in race day. First, children love to cheer Mom on. They can have signs, T-shirts, bull horns, or pompoms to cheer you on. Second, moms love to have a cheering section, and there is none better than family. Best is the added benefit of helping your children develop lifelong healthy attitudes toward health and exercise by including them in your exercise and racing.

Triathlon Through Menopause and Beyond

Menopause happens to women no matter what, so we need to learn to deal with it as best as possible. There is no better way to help with perimenopausal symptoms than to stay fit, healthy, and active.

Triathlon training is the perfect complement to going through menopause. Don't let menopause slow down your training. Some women even get faster through menopause. Recently, I competed in a local sprint triathlon in which a 59-year-old woman and I came out of the water together and battled it out on the bike course; then she kept ahead of me on the run. She was first in her age group, and I second in mine, but I am 14 years younger than she. Going through menopause certainly did not slow her down! And if you are menopausal and not active in triathlons, it is never too late to start training for multisport events.

When perimenopausal symptoms start differs from woman to woman. Some women may start early, in their early 40s, but most do not start until they are in their late 40s and 50s. During this time, the normal female hormones estrogen and progesterone are fluctuating and levels are decreasing. Decreases in estrogen can lead to decreases in lean muscle mass, increase in fat storage, and eventually decreased bone density. Perimenopausal symptoms vary, but the most common symptoms are irregular menses, hot flashes, sleep disturbance, fatigue, weight gain, and moodiness.

Hot flashes can come unexpectedly day or night. They generally consist of getting very flushed, getting hot, and feeling uncomfortable. Exercise has been shown to help decrease frequency and intensity of these vasomotor symptoms, but hot flashes can occur during training. If this happens to you, slow down, hydrate, and cool down. The hot flash will resolve, and you can get back to your regular exercise. Cutting back on processed and refined foods can also help with symptoms. There are also natural supplements that can help alleviate or lessen hot flashes. Black cohosh and yam-based or progesterone creams can help, but consult with your physician first. Hormone replacement therapy is still an option for severe menopausal symptoms, but exercise and natural supplements can also help.

Sleep disturbances and fatigue are other common symptoms that can interfere with training. Women can feel more fatigued and may lack their usual energy, which is exacerbated by difficulty sleeping. Again, aerobic exercise can help diminish these symptoms. Women who exercise regularly have better sleep patterns and less difficulty with insomnia. Also, cutting back on caffeine, especially at night, as well as watching your diet by eliminating processed foods and eating more vegetables, whole grains, and lean proteins, can help with insomnia and fatigue. Melatonin is a natural supplement that can help alleviate sleep issues. Again, consult with your doctor if your symptoms are severe.

As for weight gain, exercise is one of the main ways to combat the slowing of a woman's metabolism during menopause. Aerobic activity burns calories and increases metabolic rate. Weight training is also important, as menopause is associated with muscle loss. Trying to maintain muscle mass will keep the metabolism higher, too. Exercise also releases endorphins, which can counteract depression and mood disturbances. Most people feel better during or after exercising, thus the "runner's high." Training for a triathlon also gives you a goal to keep you going on days when you may not feel like getting out and moving. Alternating swimming, biking, and running keeps your entire body fit. As long as you train smart and listen to your body, varying your activity can decrease risk of overuse injury in a maturing body.

Once you have gone through menopause (officially no menses for one year), you may still have symptoms such as hot flashes or insomnia, but they will lessen. Continuing to train and compete in triathlon events is one way to keep you young. Exercise and competition will keep your muscles strong, decrease your risk of osteoporosis, and decrease your risk for heart disease. Including strength training with your aerobic activities will make your bones more likely to remain strong. Incorporating core and balance training such as yoga, Pilates, and tai chi will help to counteract issues with decreased balance. Make sure you are getting enough calcium (1,500 milligrams) and vitamin D (1,000 International Units) in addition to iron and multivitamins. Eating healthy and trying to maintain a healthy weight will also help you continue to train and compete for a long time. The bottom line: Take care of yourself with physical activity and healthy eating, and you can continue to compete in triathlons as long as your body feels good.

Conclusion

This chapter provided an overview and guide to some of the unique issues women face as endurance athletes. An entire book could be dedicated to all the different aspects of being a female athlete. It is possible to train throughout pregnancy and after having a baby while maintaining balance among being a mother, athlete, spouse and or work schedule. Women going through life changes such as menopause can greatly benefit from continued exercise and competition. I strongly encourage women of all ages and stages of life to participate in the sport of triathlon, whether it is for high-level competition, personal challenge, or to keep motivated to stay healthy and strong. Whatever the reason, ladies, let's keep on tri-ing!

CHAPTER 15

Integrating Triathlon Into Your Busy Life

Rebeccah Wassner
Laurel Wassner

By its nature, the sport of triathlon attracts overachievers. After all, participants have to master and compete in not one sport, but three! It would be a lot easier to train for a single sport, right? But it's that alluring element of doing it all that draws people in.

Add a triathlon training program to family, work, school, and various other commitments and you have the perfect formula for a very busy life. Even if all you did was focus on training (as we professionals do), it would still leave you feeling as though you needed a personal assistant. Managing all of these pieces can definitely feel stressful and overwhelming sometimes.

So how do we balance it all and still have a life? Is it even possible to be a triathlete and still devote enough time to kids and spouses, have a social life, and not let bills and unanswered e-mails pile up?

We think it is, but this balancing act is tricky. It could be considered the fourth discipline in the sport of triathlon. It must be carefully considered, learned, and adapted. Think of it like learning to ride with clipless pedals. You will stumble and probably fall, but once you get the hang of it, you don't even think about it anymore. This chapter will show you how to plan and prioritize so that triathlon becomes a natural part of your life without becoming a stress or a burden. Triathlon is a hobby that will lead you to a healthy lifestyle, and the point is to have fun!

Planning

By this point you probably have a triathlon or two on the schedule and are figuring out how many miles you have to run each day or what kind of bike you need to buy. We'll leave the specifics of that stuff up to the other experts contributing to this book. But what we can help you with is figuring out how to seamlessly adapt the triathlon lifestyle.

> ▶ **In Laurel's Words: Turn Your Commute Into a Workout**

Before I was a full-time professional triathlete, I worked as an accountant. After a few days on the job, traveling through bumper-to-bumper traffic to get to the office, I quickly changed my strategy. I started leaving home early, before rush hour, and going for a run around my office before clocking in. Not only did this morning run shorten my commute, it also left me feeling relaxed about getting a workout done while allowing me to focus on my workday. Commuting by bike or running to work is also a great way to fit in workouts. The key to success with this is finding a gym near your office where you can change clothes and take a shower if your office doesn't have facilities. Also, keep a few pairs of shoes and other essentials at the office so that you have less to carry during your commute. No matter how slow or fast these commuting workouts are, they will contribute to your overall fitness.

Weekly Goals

So you signed up for a triathlon and now you're having visions of mastering a flip turn in the pool, going on 25-mile (40-kilometer) bike rides, and tackling running intervals. In order to make these thoughts less overwhelming, we like to visualize each week individually and plan for it in a Monday to Sunday seven-day period.

Every Monday morning we write down a list of triathlon-related goals for the week. These can be process goals or specific workout goals, but we try to keep the list to three or four items that will require a good amount of effort but are within reach. For example, this is a recent list Laurel came up with:

- Swim five times this week or 25,000 yards
- Work on bike position
- Do the Sunday group ride
- Do at least one Pilates class

We find that putting these things on a list helps us stay on course. It's a way to stay focused and feel as though we aren't leaving something behind. When training becomes monotonous, this is a way to measure progress and also get the satisfaction of achieving something. We like to think that the week has been successful if all of these goals are met, regardless of whatever else we did or didn't do.

Timing

Finding the time to train for a triathlon around work, social, or kid schedules is challenging, but it can be done with some careful planning. Going back to the idea of setting weekly goals, get out the calendar and look at the week ahead. Identify the commitments you have, such as chaperoning a field trip or attending a lunch meeting, that you can't miss. Identify the windows of time when you might be able to fit in workouts; for some this is early morning, and for others it's late at night. The best time to exercise is when it works best for you. Identify the opportunities, such as the 30 minutes you have between an appointment and picking up the kids at school, and have your gear ready to go when the opportunity arises. This may mean keeping a bag

> ### ▶ Bec's Spin: Working Out With Kids Versus Me Time
>
> Don't get me wrong—I'm a huge proponent of running with a baby. I've raced my BOB jogging stroller to a sub-21-minute 5K. Not only is tossing the kid in the stroller and pushing 40 pounds (4.5 kilograms) up a hill the sole option sometimes, but it's an incredibly challenging workout. Ever wonder how moms look so good? This is a major reason.
>
> But there's something to be said for going on a run without the kids, when you can focus on you. I find that I do my best thinking while I'm racking up the miles. It's my time to get everything in line and to plan. Actually, on some days, this is my only chance to think clearly at all!
>
> As tired as I am when I finish a run, I feel as though I've solved all my problems and am ready to take on whatever I have ahead. That's why I like to make my training "me time."

with swimming and running gear and granola bars in your car and executing some fast transitions between activities.

Regular Workouts

Planning regular workouts will keep you on task. This could be a weekly group bike ride, a standing running date with a friend, or a masters swim session, even a Pilates or yoga class. These sessions tend to form the backbone of a training week since these are the ones you are less likely to miss and the ones that are the most likely to push you. If you have a coach who gives you workouts, let him or her know about the group sessions you have planned so he or she can work that into your program. With our busy schedules, there's no need to make every session a preorganized affair. Just try one or two of this kind of workout for starters, and then gradually add in more if this works for you. The only caveat is to not overbook yourself with exercise dates.

Fuel

Being a triathlete does not mean having to restrict your diet or eat only bird food. But fueling properly is an important component of the triathlete lifestyle. The more you train, the more you will naturally start integrating more nutritious foods into your day. The tendency toward junk will fade away, replaced by a craving for foods that make you feel ready to tackle your next workout.

We cannot stress enough how essential eating right for training sessions is. Go into a workout hungry, and you could easily blow the workout. Finish a workout and go right to your next activity without a snack, and you'll bonk when you pick up the kids from school. The solution? Plan for meals and snacks. Have a supply of pre- and postworkout snacks on hand and eat nutritious meals before and after big training days. Think of snacks as essential as headphones for running on the treadmill. We like to set aside time during the weekend to go grocery shopping and prepare at least two make-ahead dinners for the week, as well as stock the pantry and refrigerator with staples to make smoothies and quick breakfasts, lunches, and snacks. During those long days of work or with the kids, it's so much easier to have something already prepared. Cooking isn't always an option, but reheating is!

▶ Laurel's Blueberry Ginger Smoothie

There's nothing like a cool and refreshing smoothie on a hot day. One of my favorite combinations is this blueberry ginger smoothie. I mix it up between workouts in order to stay hydrated. Using coconut water as a base for the smoothie keeps things light and provides natural electrolytes, while the Greek yogurt adds protein.

Serves 2

Blend the following ingredients and serve immediately:

1/2 cup Greek yogurt

Juice from 1/2 large lemon

1 bottle (14 ounces [414 milliliters]) plain coconut water

1 frozen banana

1 cup frozen blueberries

1 inch (2.5 centimeters) fresh ginger, peeled and chopped

▶ Bec's Make-Ahead Black Rice Salad With Clementines and Edamame

I like to make a big batch of this rice salad and then eat it throughout the week. It makes a good preworkout lunch because it isn't too spicy and is easy to digest. Add some grilled salmon and you've got a healthy dinner. I use black rice because it has flavor on its own and doesn't need a lot of heavy dressing or sauce to taste good. It also happens to be full of antioxidants. Edamame provides some meat-free protein, and clementines add a fresh element and a little sweetness.

Serves 4

Salad

1 1/2 cups black rice

1 1/2 cups shelled edamame*

3/4 cup fresh curly parsley, chopped

1 large red pepper, finely chopped

3 clementines (or 1 regular orange), each section cut in half

Freshly ground black pepper

Dressing

2 tablespoons lemon juice (from half a lemon)

1 tablespoon olive oil

1 tablespoon maple syrup

1/4 teaspoon cayenne pepper

1/4 teaspoon ginger, powdered

1/2 teaspoon sea salt

Cook the rice in a rice cooker or follow the instructions on the package to cook on the stovetop. This can be done ahead of time. In the bottom of a large bowl, whisk together all of the dressing ingredients. Add the edamame, red pepper, parsley, and clementines and stir to coat. Mix in the cooked rice and finish with a few grinds of black pepper.

* If you use frozen edamame, rinse it under hot water to defrost before adding it to the salad.

Racing

When choosing which races to do, consider the logistics involved. We love racing in the New York City Triathlon because for us, race morning involves a quick taxi ride to the starting line. This is so much easier than dealing with the cross-country travel, hotels, and bike shipments that most of our races involve. We recommend choosing a local race for starters. Once you've gotten into the swing of how things work at a triathlon (race meetings, bike check-in, and so on), try a destination race. If you have kids, consider a REV3 race; these cater to little ones in that the races are at or near amusement parks. Or use triathlon as an excuse to visit a place you've always wanted to go but never had a reason.

Prioritizing

In order to keep a triathlon–life balance, you must set priorities between workouts and other commitments. We feel that it is just as important to plan for nontriathlon activities as it is to make time for triathlon training. Upsetting this balance might leave your family feeling left out or your work colleagues annoyed. We think it's possible to stay on top of it all and keep all parties, including yourself, happy about your triathlon endeavors.

Key Sessions

One way to prioritize is to focus on the key sessions for the week. Plan these for when you expect to be able to rock it, both physically and mentally. You don't want to be distracted or exhausted. For example, you probably don't want to schedule an interval run after spending the morning on your feet working at the co-op preschool. Instead, make it a priority for a morning when you have free time. Likewise, if you are going to a dinner party in the evening, it's probably not a great idea to do a killer bike workout right before. Trying to hold a conversation when you feel like a zombie isn't so fun!

Focus on the Big Picture

Although key sessions are important, we also think it is beneficial to focus on the big picture. Sometimes you won't be able to fit in those key sessions. For example, say you have limited time to train because you're leaving for a five-day work trip and you won't be bringing your bike with you. Instead of worrying about how you are going to keep up triathlon training, take the time to focus on something you can do. You could dedicate the time you would be spending on your bike to improving your running form. The beauty of triathlon is that there are three sports to master, so if your schedule doesn't allow you to get to the pool one day, you can replace that workout with something more convenient. No matter how you look at it, the end result will be fitness in the bank.

> ▶ **Bec's Spin: Help, My Spouse Isn't a Triathlete**

Triathlon is my profession; I get to work out for a living. On the other hand, my husband sits in an office for 12 hours a day. He trained for one Ironman two years ago, qualified for Kona (who does that?), and then promptly retired from the sport. He's obviously a fit guy, but he'd rather exercise to stay in shape and not compete. I live to compete and don't like to exercise for fun. So how do we make it work?

First, leave work at work. I've learned not to talk shop at home. My husband is concerned about how my training is going, and if something is bothering me and I need to talk about it, he's there for me. But he really doesn't need to be bored with every last detail of my swim set or the splits for my 10 × 400s on the track. At the same time, I'm relieved that he doesn't come home from work complaining about his boss or trying to engage me in a conversation about finance.

Second, have triathlon-free time. This is an idea I picked up from professional triathlete Amanda Lovato. What it means is to have time—it could be a day, a weekend, or even a week—during which you leave triathlon out of the picture. This means not toting your bike with you on vacation or even not wearing compression socks to the movies. In all seriousness, it's a good time to focus on all the important things in life other than triathlon.

Third, save some of your energy. It's okay to leave it all out there in some workouts, but try to keep a little oomph for when you are done. It isn't fair to the spouse who doesn't get to work out to come home and be greeted with someone glued to the couch, too tired to get up and say hello.

Most importantly, let him be a part of the journey. You need your spouse to like this sport just as much as you do. You want him to support you. Do what you can to make him appreciate what you are doing. Have him join you for a workout, even if it is just to time you during some intervals. Let him see just how hard you are working toward your goals. When it comes to the races, you are going to need all the help you can get, and having 100 percent support from your spouse makes all the difference. And, of course, don't forget to consult your spouse before planning a race!

Be Efficient

Once you've identified a block of time when you will train during the day, maximize every minute by sticking to the plan. Say you have 2 hours of childcare at your gym. You'd be surprised how much you can fit into 120 minutes if you are efficient about it. Arrive at the gym ready to go, already dressed in workout clothes and with your iPod and playlist in hand. If you are really efficient, you should have time for a quick warm-up, a treadmill workout, stretching, lifting, and even a shower. Then after a quick transition back to regular clothes and a snack, you'll be able to tackle the rest of the day. This is how we handle most of our workouts, with quick transitions on either end. We like to think of this as practice for our race day swim-to-bike and bike-to-run transitions.

Take a Day Off

Your body needs and deserves a day off every once in a while. This could be a planned day off, but it doesn't have to be. If you wake up one morning and feel wrecked, take this as a sign and make it a day off. Don't beat yourself up about taking a day off, either. Even the strictest coach would tell you to listen to your body and let it recharge. It's been our experience that resting when you need to makes you faster in the long run.

Have Fun

We can't emphasize enough how important it is to remember that triathlon is something to enjoy. It isn't something that should cause you stress or make you feel as though you are missing out. It's meant to be something that keeps you active and healthy. Getting too serious about it can bog you down, can run you ragged, and might even start to damage relationships. Here are some tips to help you stay on the right path.

Keep It Social

Triathlon is an individual sport, and the training can be long and lonely. Riding your bike trainer for hours on end in an empty basement may lead you to one place higher in the age-group rankings, but is it worth the possibility of losing contact with your friends? We don't think so. Instead, plan fun workouts with a group of friends. Organize a long ride to a muffin shop. Do a spin class with a friend who isn't a triathlete. Meet friends at the ocean for an open-water swim. You get the idea. Working out with other people is fun and can be very rewarding. You don't all have to be the same speed, either. You can start together and regroup afterward for a postworkout coffee. We've met some of our best friends through fun workouts like this.

If you don't want to organize your own group, join one that is already established, even if it is a virtual one on Facebook or Twitter. This gives you a way to check in and

---

▶ In Laurel's Words: Why I Race With a Smile on My Face

The moment I decided to take my life back after having cancer was when my doctor gave me the all-clear diagnosis. This was on my 5-year posttreatment anniversary and was when my worrying that cancer was going to come back subsided. I was downright sick of being the sick one or the one in bed missing Christmas morning. I was sick of being on the sidelines and having people ask me (or be afraid to ask) if I was okay. I wanted to be the person who could smash a 3-hour swim practice, not the person who had to take a 3-hour nap during the day.

Inside, I was still that vibrant, athletic, competitive person I had been before I got sick, but my body had been wrecked and needed a serious overhaul. My first goal coming back was to run more than 5 minutes and not feel dizzy. I took the recovery slowly, fighting through the setbacks, with the dream of being that healthy person again.

When I turned pro as a triathlete, close to nine years after my diagnosis of Hodgkin's disease, it was my biggest dream come true. Now when I train or compete, I can't help doing it with a smile on my face. I fought to be given another chance in life, and I won. I'll never forget that, and even when workouts or situations get tough, I remember how lucky I am and enjoy the moment.

the accountability you may need to get things done. Groups can be of varying fitness levels and athletic backgrounds. Both of us are on masters swim teams. The teams range from people who have never done anything competitive all the way to Olympians. It doesn't matter what your personal records are, because at that moment everyone is at the pool at the same time, working hard. The support we give each other to bust out that workout each day is invaluable. Triathlon clubs are also a great way to join group workouts and get introduced to individuals who might make good training partners.

Find a Best Training Buddy

This is a universal truth about triathlon: Even though it's such a solitary sport, the miles always seem to go by more quickly when you're plodding alongside someone. It's just so much easier to get out the door when you have someone to meet. Our younger sister Sarah (a super-active mom and runner) met her best training buddy (BTB) through Twitter, and they've been running together consistently for a year. Instead of dreading her Sunday long runs, she actually looks forward to them because she can catch up with her friend, although she assures us that they save the chitchat for the warm-up and cool-down and work it the rest of the way.

Be Flexible

As much as we try to plan every detail, schedules are unpredictable. Try as you might to get out the door for that 4:00 p.m. spin class, there will be days when your darling

---

▶ In Laurel's Words: Do I Have to Give Up My Nontriathlete Friends?

It's a fact, training for a triathlon is going to eat up a lot of your free time. Nights when you would have gone out after work for a few drinks with friends may be replaced by a solo run or a group spin class full of strangers. Too much of that is not my style. I like to make an effort to go out with my nontriathlon friends to see a show or go to a gallery, to do something cultural, at least once a month. However, this group is now dwindling because I've converted most of them into triathletes.

When I first started doing triathlons, my colleagues at the magazine where I worked thought I was crazy. For everyone at the office (including me at one time), Friday mornings were spent hung over and eating greasy bacon sandwiches from the local deli at 10:00 a.m., not swimming and running at 5:00 a.m. When I announced my intention to change careers and become a professional triathlete, no one could quite understand why I was quitting my covetable position at a top publication. Once I started competing (and eventually winning some races), they became my biggest fans. A major victory was seeing a group of friends at the start of the New York City Triathlon. That's 5:53 a.m., by the way. Not long afterward, most of my nonathlete friends were telling me they wanted to learn to run, and a bunch even sign up for a race. It's so rewarding to see that happen, and now I'm honored to offer advice and guidance as they tiptoe into my world.

> ### ▶ Laurel's Top Six Triathlon Lifestyle Tips
>
> 1. Invest in a good coffee pot or electric tea kettle and a good travel mug. There's no time to hit up Starbucks before those early-morning swim practices.
> 2. Always pack an extra set of dry clothes and a cute hat for after workouts. You never know where you may have to go next, and going in bike clothes and helmet hair might not be acceptable.
> 3. Keep a dedicated makeup kit of lipstick, concealer, moisturizer, and sunscreen in your gym bag.
> 4. Put away your laundry organized by complete bike outfits. Do this with your running clothes, too, if you can handle it.
> 5. Join a gym that is convenient, has a cafe, and offers babysitting.
> 6. Opt for the extra foot massage when you get a pedicure.

children or demanding boss may throw a wrench in your normally well-executed plans. What to do? Be flexible. Instead of beating yourself up or sulking over a missed session, quickly do whatever you can. Maybe that's a quick Pilates video or a hard 20-minute run. Maybe it's even using your baby to do arm curls. All you need is a little something to get you by until you find the time to make up the planned workout.

Run Your Own Race

Do not compare your race preparation to anyone else's. Yes, your running buddy may be running 5K personal records in practice, but that's probably not the only way to roll. We used to fall into a trap of feeling inadequate after reading blogs about those supermoms who train for Ironmans while juggling four kids, 10 pets, and a full-time job. That may work for some, but it's not the standard. After all, this is an individual journey, so we have to work within our own means to set attainable goals. Even if your goal of running 20 minutes without stopping seems incomparable to that of someone who runs 18 miles (29 kilometers) regularly, it's still an accomplishment. Keep focused on yourself and celebrate your victories.

Conclusion

We've known women who get completely immersed in the sport of triathlon only to drop it cold turkey after a season or two because it just isn't fitting in with their lifestyle. It's easy for the balance between life and triathlon to shift in the wrong direction, but it is our goal with this chapter to promote longevity for women in triathlon. Through planning and prioritizing while being flexible and having an open mind, triathlon, we believe, can remain a rewarding element of a healthy lifestyle.

CHAPTER 16

Starting Children in Triathlon

Shelly O'Brien

Youth are the fastest-growing demographic within the annual membership of USA Triathlon, representing nearly 30 percent of all members. This growth, coupled with the recent inclusion of women in the National Collegiate Athletic Association, will evoke unprecedented interest in sport programming, education, and competition models. All this is exciting, but it is important to honor the needs of the developing youth athlete and continually seek information about optimizing the potential and the growth opportunities for both athletes and sport development.

At the moment, hundreds of youth programs and teams across the United States are promising to deliver information for children. Unfortunately, there is great variability in the quality delivered. For a parent, the task of finding options and sorting through the list can be daunting. If you are not able to locate a quality program, a later section of the chapter gives sport-specific skill information.

When looking for a team, program, or educational experience for your child, you have many issues to consider and questions to ask:

- How many athletes are in the program, and what is the ratio of coaches to athletes? Although many single-sport teams have 10 to 20 athletes per coach, USA Triathlon requires all national youth and junior camp directors to supply one USA Triathlon certified coach per five athletes. Use your own judgment to determine if adequate instruction can be provided.

- What ages are used to define youth or juniors in the program? As defined by USA Triathlon, youth athletes are ages 7 to 15 and juniors are ages 16 to 19.

- Is sex-specific training provided? Male and female athletes are motivated very differently, in general by a sense of competition or socialization, respectively. The variance is enhanced by age, with the older athletes showing the greatest differences. How is this addressed in the program?

- Is the program specific to these ages, or are young people integrated into adult training? Suggestions and ideas for age-appropriate training are presented later in the chapter.

■ What level of athlete is supported: beginner, youth only (non-draft), youth and junior elite (draft legal)? Today's youth athletes (ages 7 to 15) in youth-only competitions are subject to non-draft or age-group rules with equipment restrictions. For example, if the race is sanctioned as youth competitive or is a USA Triathlon Youth National Championship, all athletes must have a road bike—no aero bars, disc wheels, or aero helmets allowed. (The equipment restriction is not enforced at adult events.) Beginning at age 12, athletes may begin to participate in draft legal events in which they can work together in pelotons or packs on the bike. At age 16, athletes may represent their countries in international competition. This is for non-draft and draft legal in many multisport disciplines and distances.

■ Does the head coach have a certification in youth sport? USA Triathlon has a specific youth and junior certification. Although a multisport certification is optimal, other sports such as swimming and running also offer coaching instruction for those working with youth athletes.

■ Is the team a designated USA Triathlon high-performance team? This title is given to teams with USA Triathlon certified head coaches who have demonstrated willingness to support athlete development and have a working knowledge of youth- and junior-specific training. Also, the team contact has agreed to be a resource for any outside athlete or parent who may want information. A list of designated teams can be found on the USA Triathlon website at usatriathlon.com.

■ Does the program or team focus on development or performance? Triathlon is a late-specialization sport. At the earliest, athletes are in their mid-20s before they physiologically mature enough to maximize sport potential. Thus triathlon requires a more generalized approach to early-adolescent training.

■ How often does the team or program meet for practice? How much of that time is spent in skill development and body awareness training? There is more discussion of this later in the chapter.

■ Is there a development or progression model for those gaining experience and age? How much individual attention is exhibited within a group setting? As an athlete matures in age and experience, what is the opportunity to stay with the group?

■ Is parent education provided? Any youth program should have guidelines and instruction regarding expectations of parents and other individuals in the athlete's support network.

■ If a program isn't available, will you be coaching your own athlete? Often, a team or program is not available or parents are further assessing the needs of their children versus what is offered in training. This chapter discusses further considerations.

Adult Versus Youth Programs

As awareness grows about youth needing to race and train as kids (not adults), it is common to see triathlon parents struggling between training with an active young athlete and trying to do what's best for that child's growth and development. It is acknowledged that youth have different cognitive, social, emotional, and physical needs from adults, but there is also disconnect with solutions.

The beginning of the answer is to let go of a competitive focus and instead remember some of the many benefits, opportunities, and life lessons that sport participation offers:

- Opportunity for family members to support each other
- Friendships that can last a lifetime
- Travel to exciting destinations that can include a family vacation
- Learning communication skills
- Learning about nutrition and proper eating habits
- Learning accountability, for example by keeping a training log
- Learning planning and goal-setting skills
- Acquiring organizational skills such as setting up a transition area
- Learning independence (once the gun goes off, even the youngest athlete must maneuver the course on her own)
- Acquiring problem-solving skills (if an athlete goes off course, what does she do?)
- Gaining confidence associated with accomplishment
- Learning responsibility
- Developing a work ethic
- Gaining a more positive identity through team association, peer interaction, and individual achievement

After reviewing the benefits of sport participation, it is important to clearly define competition relating to youth athletes. In a paper titled "Cooperation Versus Competition: Is There Really Such an Issue?" (Daniels 2007), the author challenges anyone guiding youth training to emphasize cooperative skills like teamwork and achievement motivation such as mastery of skill. This approach works well with any young athlete but especially those who may not be emotionally, mentally, or physically equipped to handle the stress of competition.

To fully understand and employ this approach, we must understand how children look at competition. Youth athletes don't view competitive events in terms of winning or objective outcomes (e.g., podium finish). Depending on age and maturation, their cognitive development doesn't include complex deductive reasoning. Instead, they gravitate toward skill mastery in comparison to peers as a form of competition. For example, ask a young athlete to jump over a set of cones. Soon all the athletes are attempting the challenge because to them, proving that they can accomplish the task is winning.

Therefore, before encouraging an athlete to compete, it is important to ensure that an athlete is ready for the demands of competition. While acknowledging that there are no absolutes, the authors of a study on this topic suggested the following additional guidelines to consider: The sense of social comparison is not achieved until after 6 years of age, and the ability to understand the competitive nature of sport is generally not developed until 9 years of age. At approximately 12 years of age, most children are mature enough to comprehend the complexity of sport tasks and are physically and cognitively ready to participate in competitive sport with appropriate supervision (Patel, Pratt, and Greydanus 2002).

After reviewing, understanding, and discussing youth athlete cognitive development, it is then important to analyze the child's motivation. The primary goal of any development program should be enjoyment. A secondary goal is knowledge of extrinsic and intrinsic influences on emotions. Emotions may be more difficult to analyze, so the following discussion is provided to assist with that process.

During the preschool years, a child learns to regulate and control emotion. Fast forward in time to the age of sport participation, emotional stimulation is a major influence on desire to continue. Unlike the absolutes of cognitive development, emotions can be and are often greatly influenced by the environment of development, social relationships, and surrounding network of coaches, parents, and peer athletes. At the heart of it all, a young athlete wants to know they are being guided to improve performance (developing trust), are gaining skill set proficiency (confidence), and are accepted by key influencers in their life (security). If an athlete begins making statements like "I win triathlon races" or "I am the fastest runner," although possibly correct, they are unfortunately expressing the characteristics of a fragile ego. When such a statement is no longer true, the young athlete may feel frustration or a sense of failure or even experience a personal identity crisis. Such a scenario provides a critical crossroads wherein the support network is key to an athlete's continuation. The network environment must either minimize these negative feelings so that the athlete can maintain interest or teach the athlete to work through the emotion in a constructive, positive manner. It is important to understand that this does not mean a program shouldn't stimulate emotion. Rather, a correctly designed program should offer confidence-building opportunities to develop emotional control and focus (intrinsic influence). For example, all athletes will experience frustration, even anger, which may be channeled into a positive outcome.

Motivation of Youth Athletes

Familial influence is an important component of motivation. Here are three scenarios that relate to this influence:

1. Children may be born into an active family and thus exposed to a fitness-driven lifestyle yet have no desire to be an active participant in sporting activities.
2. They may not be part of an athletically inclined family yet have a desire to participate in sport.
3. Their interests may be aligned with those of the family.

Scenarios A and B can cause frustration in the family because of the disparity in interests and pursuits. Further, that emotion may be compounded by a sibling(s) whose interest is more aligned with family interests. Let's explore a few scenarios. In situation A, siblings may think of or refer to a brother or sister as lazy. Perhaps the so-called lazy sibling doesn't feel confident enough to join the family outing and therefore choses something different. It will help to encourage the child to join in a skill game associated with sport to build confidence. As they master the skill, their interest can be guided to a new skill set. As discussed earlier, no matter the length of time an athlete endeavors in the sport, the skill sets can be far reaching in character development.

In situation B, family members may not know how to support the child. If this sounds familiar, then you're strongly encouraged to seek training, coaching, and positive peer interaction for the sports-minded child.

Unfortunately for families in scenario A or B it is common for children to hear comments that leave a lasting negative impression. It is important to evaluate the impact of such expressions. A parent is encouraged to listen without judgment, then seek a sport program for your child. (We will discuss coaching your own children later in the chapter.) When seeking a coach or training group, be honest with the coach and other parents about challenges and/or concerns. A chosen program should provide guidance and support for yourself as well as the child.

Finally, maintain hope while supporting the interest of the child, effective solutions do exist and if you feel like you're at a crossroads, contact USA Triathlon. A staff member can outline options.

Scenario C, where all family interests align, also has challenges. One of the most common is the role of the parent as coach. At this moment, there is limited data-based research on the relationship between parent-coach and child-athlete. However, even the most educated and passionate parent can struggle with separating parent–child and parent–coach relationships. It is important to understand the separation isn't under the complete control of the parent as the child may have trouble separating your parenting and coaching roles even if you are doing so effectively. In which case it may be important to recognize the need for and importance of allowing someone else to fill the coaching role.

Weiss and Fretwell (2005) interviewed several athletes in an attempt to determine their experience with parents who also performed a coaching role. The athletes reported that, even though the parents strived to be effective in both their parent and coach roles, there were both negative and positive effects on the parent–child relationship. A common positive was having the parents involved. However, a common negative was emotion of disappointment was magnified when the child was corrected (even with constructive criticism) as the child felt as though were letting down both their coaches and their parents.

If you are a parent considering whether you should coach your own child, ask yourself the following questions:

- In your situation, what do you think the negative and positive aspects of coaching your child will be?
- Knowing your child, how do you think he or she will respond to you as a coach?
- Knowing yourself, how well do you think you will able to separate your roles as coach and parent?
- In what ways could you see yourself treating your child differently than other players on the team?
- How do you think members of the team and their parents will respond to your coaching your own child?
- Will you coach your own child? Why or why not?

Given the alignment of familial interests in situation C, the young athlete may likely develop and master skills more quickly than her peer group. The discussion is created because, unfortunately, this can lead to high-volume training such as long training sessions far exceeding the competitive distances of the athlete. Recommended distances for youth athletes is provided in this chapter. At the time of this publication, top youth elite male athletes age 13-15 are racing a run distance of 2.5 kilometer (off a 10 kilometer bike) at 5:30 minute per mile pace. Top females are approximately 6:00 min/mile pace. These are speeds any young athlete is encouraged to develop at much shorter distances such as 400 meters. Once achieved at that distance, then strive to maintain that speed for 600 meters, 800 meters, etc.

Another potential concern is early specialization in sport. Be sure to allow the athlete the opportunity to explore many sports. Longevity in sport depends on this.

Family interests aside, some parents face another challenge—the desire to achieve, which can be known as the "rage to master" (Winner 1997). In a few scenarios, when the rage to master is combined with deliberate practice, a child prodigy may result. We often hear of them in media with their early success in highlights and as a result, these prodigies can be seen as role models setting an often unachievable achievement standard for other developing athletes and their parents which is extrinsic for the athlete (Anders, Krampe, and Tesch, 1993).

Let's discuss the intrinsic or self-driven motivation first. An athlete who exhibits the rage to master and engages in deliberate practice may become obsessive about a particular aspect of training such as nutrition or sport-specific skill development. The focus on these areas supersedes any other which can be a significant compromise to long term athlete development. The rage to master becomes so intense and linear the individual has trouble finding balance amidst all aspects of sport development.

If this describes your child, you may have to slow him or her down and broaden the focus. There isn't a single solution to prescribe for all athletes exhibiting this extreme behavior. However it is fair to say that coaches working with these athletes must understand the intensity in children like this. For all parents facing this scenario, continue monitoring the coach-athlete relationship ensuring it remains positive and confidence building. Further, even in a child with this intensity, cognitive and emotional development will proceed as described earlier, though not necessarily at the same rate.

For some athletes, the rage to master is extrinsic and associated with a desire to please an authority figure in their life. Most often that figure is a parent or coach. If we are applying the scenario to a parent, they may overencourage the young athletes to do well and become overfocused and overbearing about the child's sport performance and progress. "Helicopter parenting" is a term often used to describe this. Coaches may have the same influence especially among more advanced and talented athletes. The intensity described is an extrinsic influence on motivation and has been shown to accelerate burnout in kids.

Physical Development of the Young Triathlete

With all young triathletes, sport diversification is highly encouraged and emphasized. When should an athlete specialize in triathlon training? The simple answer is as late as possible. In recent history, the USA Triathlon youth and junior sport development programs have evolved significantly. This is evidenced by the quality of fields and volume of young athletes participating at the USA Triathlon youth and junior national championships. Further evidence is the depth of identified national talent and USA athlete success at world championships. Evaluation of athletes performing at those levels has demonstrated most didn't specialize before (at minimum) the age of 14 with some waiting until they had fulfilled collegiate scholarship obligations (age 20). As a result of delayed specialization (as compared to other Olympic sports) and thus reduced burnout, they are maintaining performance progression standards as young professionals in their 20s.

Given this background and the success of USA's top athletes, it's easy to become overly focused in a desire to get ahead of the game. Parents and coaches can be heard encouraging sport, in this case triathlon, specialization in the preadolescent athlete, with the thought of giving the child an edge. Unfortunately this approach most often has the exact opposite effect. As exhibited by the army of ghost athletes who showed early promise but got chewed up by the competitive system and ceased all sport by the time they hit puberty.

The position stand of the Canadian Association of Applied Sport Sciences, with supporting scientific background and rationale, summarizes the idea of delaying early sport specialization: "From the physiological and medical point of view, it should be recognized that each child is different in his/her response and tolerance to exercise due to a great range of variability in growth rates, anthropometric indices, gender and state of health, even in children of a similar chronological age. Younger prepubertal children should be encouraged to participate in a wide variety of motor skills, whereas older postpubertal children can become more specialized in their training and sport participation" (Hughson 1986, p.162).

Jayanthi and colleagues (2013) argue similarly: "Some degree of sports specialization is necessary to develop elite-level skill development. However, for most sports, such intense training in a single sport to the exclusion of others should be delayed until late adolescence to optimize success while minimizing injury, psychological stress, and burnout" (abstract).

Dan Coyle and Ross Tucker are widely published and well respected on the topic of athlete development. Dan Coyle summarized the following guidelines quoting Ross Tucker early in the list of recommendations. Quoted from Ross Tucker:

- Delay. "Wait as long as possible before choosing a single sport to pursue. It varies according to sport, but research puts the ideal age for specialization around the early teenage years. (That doesn't mean you start at that age, of course, but rather that you start getting serious.)
- Diversify. Embrace all possibilities to broaden skills. Experiment and cross-train.
- Cooperate. Seek ways to build connections between the silos of individual sports, so that families are not forced to choose one over the other too soon."

Dan Coyle (2014) then offers the following addition:

- Connect. One of the main reason specialization is hard to resist is the parental peer pressure that comes with joining any elite team. The point is not to bash specialization, but to bash *mindless* specialization, and to point out that it carries costs. To ask, how many kids quit the sport rather than join elite teams?

Diversifying sport participation allows optimization of development during different stages of physical growth. Figure 16.1 contains a model, now widely accepted, that uses peak height velocity (PHV) to determine windows of optimal trainability specific

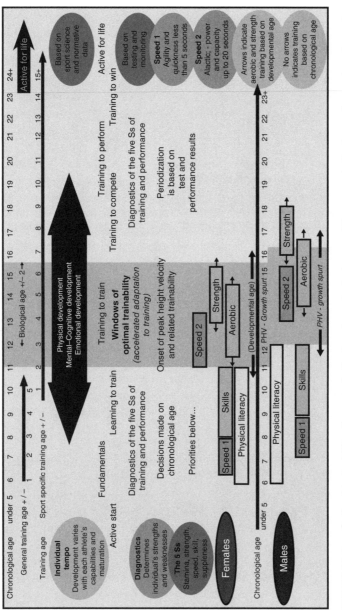

FIGURE 16.1 Optimal trainability. No arrow indicates chronological age, while arrows indicate moving scales, depending on the onset of PHV. Before the onset of PHV and after maturation (postpuberty), simple testing can determine training priorities, taking into consideration the windows of accelerated adaptation to training. ABCs = agility, balance, coordination, speed; RJT = run, jump, throw; KGBs = kinesthesia, gliding, buoyancy, striking with object; CPKs = catching, passing, kicking, striking with body.

Reprinted, by permission, from I. Balyi et al., 2009, *Karate for life* (Montreal, Canada: Karate Canada), 58.

to the central nervous and energy systems. This model is a guide and can be easily adapted to sport and individual athlete demands.

The sport of triathlon offers the opportunity for sport sampling given the swim, bike, and run components. Even so, shortcomings relating to athlete development remain. For example, swimming, biking, and running are all linear sports (forward in movement). The combination fails to develop lateral awareness. In addition, triathlon relies solely on individual sport performance as a measure of success. Team sport participation (e.g., basketball, soccer, lacrosse) requires relationship building and multiplanar sensory acuity. Other sport suggestions include gymnastics or martial arts to train body spatial awareness.

While the common message is late specialization, younger athletes are supported and encouraged to seek and master the skill components of triathlon. Technique should be the focus of any program.

Swimming

The first step in developing any youth or junior swim program is to differentiate between children who are learning to swim and those who are ready to begin a triathlon swim program. Ideally, all children have completed the first three levels of an American Red Cross swim program or equivalent: introduction to water skills (getting in, getting wet, and going under), fundamental aquatic skills (floating and getting around in the water for short distances), and development of the front and back crawl strokes. At the completion of these programs, athletes should have basic skills of blowing bubbles, treading water, floating and kicking on their backs, and swimming without goggles. In addition, they should have spatial awareness relating to other swimmers in the water. If for any reason a child has anxiety while performing basic skills, the skills should be reviewed and the child should master them before proceeding. Until then, uncertain swimmers can pose a safety concern for themselves and other swimmers.

When the basics have been achieved, specific stroke mechanics can be taught. The instructional approaches are as varied as the coaches standing on deck. However, an emphasis on technique is fundamental. Although the swimming culture is slowly changing in the United States, it is common to emphasize volume or to chronically impose long swim sets on the developing athlete. Unfortunately, as growth occurs, the athlete's skill execution is compromised and, unless corrected, remains so.

There are many ways to advance an athlete's swim development besides merely swimming. Games are a great option. Common swim games include sharks and minnows, diving for an object on the bottom of the pool, wheelbarrow (one swimmer in front, the swimmer behind holding the ankles and kicking), leapfrog (must be able to stand in the water; the last person in a line dives under the legs of the other athletes and then surfaces, and so on), and bottle brigade (swimming across the pool pushing an empty plastic bottle with the feet). Search online and you can find numerous suggestions.

Workouts on deck (dryland training) include strength training through the use of body weight, functional movement, and the use of resistance tubing. Dryland training is a great way to aid in the child's body awareness and to support the various aspects of growth.

Triathlon offers the additional challenge of swimming in open water (no pool). To prepare, athletes should be able to swim 1.5 times their suggested event distance without stopping, have gained an understanding of sighting, and have mastered the basic safety skills discussed earlier.

Many athletes do not have the ability to swim in an ocean, lake, or other open-water environment, so there are preparatory workouts that can be done in a pool. A simple way to prepare for athlete awareness is to place three athletes in a 2.13-meter lane (approximately 6.5 feet), one on the right, one on the left, and one on the black line. All three swim in those positions, which requires them to sight and to experience body contact. Discourage racing or fast sets to avoid head-on collisions.

Much of the best open-water preparatory training is done with the lane lines removed. The open-water triangle is a swim test that can be adapted for individual needs.

50- or 100-Meter Open-Water Triangle

In a pool, set up a triangular course using three anchored turn buoys (figure 16.2). The base is 16 meters; the sides are 17 meters each. The swimmer starts at the bottom left corner. One lap around the course is 50 meters; two laps is 100 meters. The swimmer's objective is to swim the 50 or 100 meters for her best time while executing three or six open-water turns.

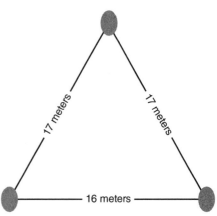

FIGURE 16.2 **Triangular course for open-water triangle swim test.**

Cycling

Proficiency on the bike is a combination of proper equipment, skill, proper training, and awareness of one's environment. Equipment is one of the most important components, with an appropriate bike at the top of the list. USA Triathlon competitive youth rules prohibit the use of aerobars, disc wheels, or aero helmets (USA Triathlon 2014).

Each youth triathlete needs the following equipment:

- Properly fitting bicycle with two wheels (not a recumbent) that is in good working order. This includes quality tires, effective braking, and proper shifting.
- Appropriate helmet with a sticker on the inside indicating approval by the U.S. Consumer Product Safety Commission. When buckled, the helmet should sit properly and securely on the child's head.

- Cycling shorts made of snug-fitting Lycra that won't catch on the saddle during mounts and dismounts. Many children use swim jammers, although these shorts do not have padding and are not optimal for that reason.

- Cycling shoes. Many young athletes use athletic shoes. It is advisable for those who use athletic shoes to also have cages on the pedals for safety and security during pedaling. As athletes progress, they may adapt the use of cycling shoes.

- Clothing that covers the shoulders. T-shirts, cycling jerseys (best option), jackets, or any other clothing that covers the shoulders is advisable to reduce the risk of road rash in case of a fall.

- Tire changing kit that includes a tube, patch kit, CO_2 cartridge and adapter, identification, and saddle bag. It is easy to rely on a coach for these items, but there are several wheel sizes, so tubes may be unique to your athlete.

Bike fit is absolutely essential, and for children it should be checked every three months by a specialist. If the child has grown significantly, a fitting will probably be needed sooner than three months. A parent can perform a few checks to determine if a fit is needed sooner. For safety and accuracy, these are best performed on a bike trainer.

- Check saddle height. While sitting on the saddle, the athlete places her heel on the pedal at the bottom of the stroke or the point closest to the ground. There should be a soft bend in the knee. If not, adjust saddle height to achieve this position. Note that this effectively changes the saddle fore (down) or aft (up).

- Be sure to check handlebar reach. While sitting in the saddle, the athlete places her hands on the handlebars where they are most often positioned during a ride, allowing a soft bend in the elbows. Imagine a straight line from the ear through the elbow to the ground. If not, you can adjust the saddle forward or back, but the same inverse relationship occurs as with saddle height (down or fore, or up or aft).

- Finally, the athlete should be able to easily reach the brake levers. Small hands may have a hard time with this. There are equipment options to bring the levers closer to the bars, as well as the option of placing additional brakes near the stem.

Resist the urge to buy a larger bike than needed with the idea that the child will grow into it. Bike handling is critical to a safe, confident rider, and a large bike can make skill achievement difficult. Many teams have swap programs or groups of parents who are shifting athletes to different frame sizes. This is an economical way to get a bike that is the correct size for your athlete.

Once proper equipment is acquired and bike fit complete, training can begin. Before joining a team, the athlete should be able to mount, pedal, stop, and dismount confidently in a parking lot by herself. When these skills are achieved, more advanced training can begin:

- Turning and cornering. See the following drills for sample exercises.

- Bike maintenance. This is the key to safety and the longevity of equipment. Many bike shops offer free classes.

- Traffic safety. At some point athletes will encounter vehicular traffic while training. All athletes need to learn the rules of the road. Practice in a parking lot.

- Communication. The outside voice is critical to safety for other cyclists when riding. It is important for athletes to practice alerting others on the road when stopping, slowing, turning, coming alongside, and coming inside and to warn of potential hazards (holes, gravel, and other dangers).

180-Degree Turn

On a closed street or in a parking lot, set up a 300-meter out-and-back course. Place a set of cones 150 meters perpendicular from the start–finish line to mark the turning point (figure 16.3). Athletes start clipped in both pedals with a volunteer holding the seat for balance. The athlete's objective is to ride the 300-meter course for best time, making a clean 180-degree turn at the far end.

90-Degree Turn

On a closed street or in a parking lot, set up a 300-meter course with a 90-degree right turn (figure 16.4). Use cones to mark the turn if a safe street corner is not available. Mark a start and a finish point 150 meters from the corner of the turn, such that the lines between these points and the corner would form a right angle. The athlete's objective is to ride the 300-meter course for best time, making a clean 90-degree turn.

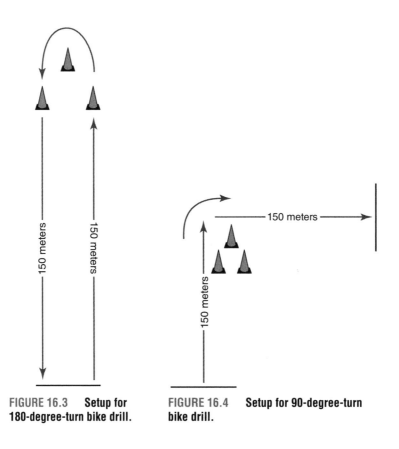

FIGURE 16.3   Setup for 180-degree-turn bike drill.

FIGURE 16.4   Setup for 90-degree-turn bike drill.

300-Meter Bike Slalom

On a closed street or in a parking lot, set up a 300-meter course with five slalom turns (figure 16.5). Set the first cone 25 meters from the start line on the center line of the course. Set the second cone 25 meters left of center and 75 meters from the start line. Set the third cone 25 meters right of center and 150 meters from the start line. Set the fourth cone 25 meters left of center and 225 meters from the start line. Set the fifth cone 25 meters from the finish line on the center line of the course. The athlete's objective is to ride the 300-meter course for best time while making clean turns.

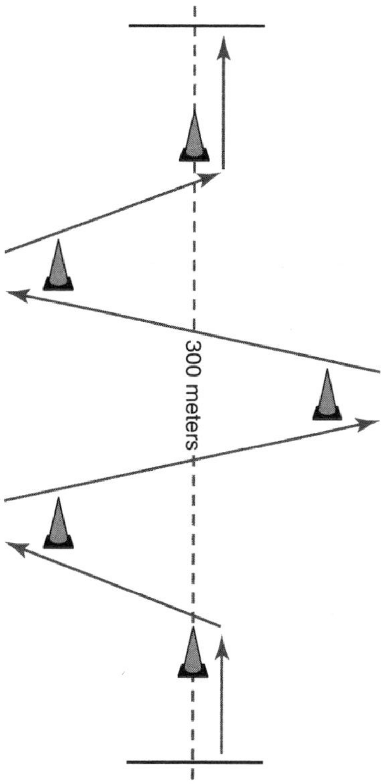

Running

For running, proper shoes are at the top of the equipment list. Unless a pediatric podiatrist has made specific suggestions for the child, children's running shoes should have minimal stability components and should offer maximal freedom of movement. Only if a young athlete is diagnosed (by a medical professional) with a structural pronation or supination deviation should stability run shoes be worn. Most foot mechanical changes are a by-product of growth, strength, and stability changes that need to be developed in skill training.

FIGURE 16.5 **Setup for 300-meter bike slalom drill.**

During growth, expect gait mechanics to change. Any corrective component of the shoe will influence those changes, and potential negative effects should be minimized. With this word of caution, seek a quality shoe retailer to assist with your purchase.

Running is the most challenging of the triathlon sports to develop. Unfortunately, running is often viewed as an innate ability that needs to be trained only through endurance. However, run proficiency is highly skill based and in youth athletes is largely dependent on growth, including peak height velocities, sex, and body somatotype development. The greatest challenge is sustaining the patience to develop and maintain a skills-based approach to run development throughout the growth years. Limiting volume and incorporating body awareness, strength, and flexibility training are important.

Young athletes often view competition based solely on peer interaction and immediate gratification. To optimize the development of running skill while maintaining enjoyment, participation in team sport is highly recommended. Also young athletes should perform alactic or peak velocity work to maximize the opportunity to develop neural biomechanic integration. In other words, the ability to be fast. To ensure longevity in sport, fun has to be at the forefront of practice. So try putting a soccer ball in front of a team and watch the high-quality interaction that fulfills the needs of the coach, the parent, athlete performance development, and the individual.

For some athletes, team sport may not be an option for developing run skills. *Athletics 365: Challenges and Curriculum* (England Athletics, British Athletics 2013) identifies and progresses through a series of run skills. A PDF download with color-coded progressions is available. Go to http://www.englandathletics.org/shared/get-file.ashx?id = 3913&itemtype = document to download. In addition, the following benchmark tests can be adapted to fit individual needs.

300-Yard Switchback Run

On a football field, set up a switchback run course (figure 16.6). Chose a sideline and place the first cone on the 50-yard line at that sideline edge of the field. Place the second cone on a goal line 18 yards from the same sideline edge. Place the third cone on the opposite goal line directly between the sidelines. Return back to the original goal line and place the fourth cone 18 yards from the secondary sideline edge. The fifth (and final) cone is placed on the on the 50-yard line at the secondary sideline The athlete's objective is to run their best effort while making three near 180-degree turns. Record the athlete's time for 300 yards.

100-Meter Run, Steer, Rack

Set up a course on the 100-meter straight of a running track. Center transition racks at the 30-meter and 70-meter marks (figure 16.7). Place the bike with the front wheel facing out at the center of the first rack. The athlete starts at the start line for the 100 meters in the center lane. The athlete runs to the bike, puts on a helmet, runs with the bike to the second rack (pushing and steering by holding the saddle), places the bike on the second rack, places the helmet in the basket, and runs to the finish. The athlete does not mount the bike during this test.

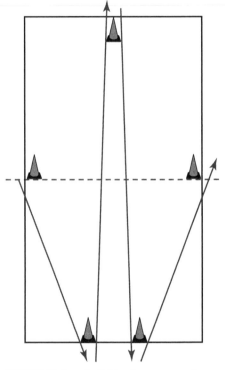

FIGURE 16.6 **Switchback run course for the 300-yard switchback run.**

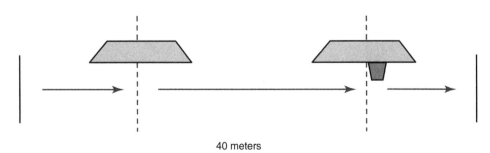

40 meters

FIGURE 16.7   **Setup for the 100-meter run, steer, rack test.**

Racing

When an athlete is ready to begin competition, it is important to maintain age-appropriate distances (table 16.1). In addition, most youth athletes should spend 75 percent of the time in training and only 25 percent in competition (Balyi and Hamilton 2004).

When looking for a program, look for USA Triathlon Skills and Select Camps and USA Triathlon certified youth- and junior-specific coaches, or try the local YMCA, local sport clubs, swim teams, USA Triathlon high-performance triathlon teams, and IronKids events.

Conclusion

The basis of any program or sport pursuit for young athletes is an inherent emphasis on fun and the promotion of a lifetime of fitness and health. Athletes at all levels of development, from children to elites, need to enjoy their training and racing. Training variety, positive social interactions with coaches and fellow athletes, the development of new skills, and an emphasis on improvement can help to foster a fun atmosphere. Positive experiences motivate young athletes and keep them from leaving the sport. Triathlon and its component sports can be part of a healthy and fit lifestyle from childhood to senior age. However, an athlete's long-term health must never be jeopardized to achieve a short-term gain in sport, for example through the use of performance-enhancing drugs or competing in the presence of a serious injury.

A study conducted by doctors at the Youth Sport Institute at Michigan State University showed that of 10,000 students, 45 percent participated in sport while growing

TABLE 16.1

Recommended Competition Distances for Youth and Juniors

Racing age is determined as of December 31 of the year in which the event takes place.

Racing age	Category	Swim distance	Bike distance	Run distance
7 and 8	Youth	50 to 100 m[1]	2 km	1 km
9 and 10	Youth	100 m[1]	3 km	1 km
11 and 12	Youth	200 m[1]	5 to 7 km	2 km
13 to 15	Youth elite[2]	400 m	10 km	2.5 km
16 to 19	Junior	400 to 750 m	15 to 20 km	5 km
16 to 19	Junior elite[2]	50 m	20 km	5 km

[1]Pool swim recommended.

[2]Youth elite and junior elite races are draft legal; are typically staged on multilap, closed courses; and are officiated using International Triathlon Union competition rules.

Reprinted from USA Triathlon, 2011, *Youth and junior coaches manual* (Colorado Springs, CO: USA Triathlon).

up (Ewing and Seefeldt 1990). Of the group that participated in sport, 50 percent had dropped out by the age of 18. These were some of the reasons given for discontinuation:

- I lost interest.
- I was not having fun.
- It took too much time.
- The coach was a poor teacher.
- I was under too much pressure.
- I wanted more sport activity rather than competition.
- I was tired of it.
- I needed more time to study.
- The coach played favorites.
- The sport became boring.
- There was an overemphasis on winning.

Pushing children too early in training and competition appears to keep many from continuing in sport for a lifetime. The ideas presented in this chapter can help your young athlete avoid becoming a ghost of performance past.

CHAPTER 17

Succeeding in Off-Road Triathlons

Melanie McQuaid

Off-road triathlon is to road triathlon what snowboarding once was to skiing: a new, intense challenge that takes a sport in a different and exciting direction. Born in 1996, the first off-road triathlon was contested in Maui by a mix of the top athletes in triathlon with the best mountain bike racers. The organizer's vision was to create an event in which mountain bike, Ironman, and short-course triathlon athletes would race against each other on a course that featured elements from both triathlon and mountain biking. Off-road triathlon is a short-course, Olympic-distance triathlon on that takes place on trails and in forests. Since 1996, the sport has been defined as its own discipline under the umbrella of triathlon. This discipline of triathlon requires the strength of long-course triathlon, the power and speed of short-course triathlon, and the technical skills of mountain bike racing. It is exciting, dynamic, and challenging.

What Is Off-Road Triathlon?

XTERRA may be the brand of off-road triathlon most familiar to athletes in North America, but these events are only one brand of competition available. Worldwide, organizers are creating events that incorporate an open-water swim, an off-road bike course, and a trail run. These are the three elements that define this discipline of triathlon.

Most often, an off-road event includes an approximately 1,500-meter swim, 30-kilometer mountain bike, and 10-kilometer run. At many of these events, a half-distance race is offered to beginner participants competing for the first time, thus many sprint-distance off-road triathlons are held in conjunction with longer events. The exact distances are often approximate, as most courses are laid out according to what the terrain dictates. If the course is very hilly or technical, the bike segment of the race may take longer, and thus the distance would be shorter. In general, the course is designed so each segment would contain the best athletes in the field at least as long as the equivalent road triathlon would take. The swim is generally 1,500 meters but at some venues this is not always the case. There are no strict rules or restrictions on what a course will be, so each event is unique. Most off-road triathlon races are laid out according to the venue, so from race to race there is unlikely to be any reliable consistency in terms of distance.

The International Triathlon Union (ITU) has an off-road format labeled cross triathlon with specific rules on the layout of the race course that serve to define these events. In ITU cross triathlon, the courses are a bit shorter, with a 1,000-meter swim, 20-kilometer bike, and 6-kilometer run, although these distances can also vary from one venue to another. The race is held in a multiloop format; that is, the swim, bike, and run are multiple loops. The ITU cross triathlon is shorter, is more spectator-friendly, and places the amateur, professional men's, and professional women's fields in separate starts. This is a departure from the format of XTERRA, in which the event often begins with a mass start of the entire competitive field or wave starts rather than separate events.

All off-road events are draft legal. This means there are no penalties for drafting behind another competitor in any category. In general, the low speeds used on a mountain bike do not create much advantage to a trailing rider.

Although the specific training for a shorter cross triathlon event is different than for the longest XTERRA events, in general, the considerations for off-road triathlon are the same. For the remainder of the chapter, the term "off-road triathlon" refers to all styles of off-road triathlon event that you may consider racing.

Swim

Most often the event begins with a mass start, with all competitors entering the water to start the race at one time. If the swim entrance is narrow or if it is unsafe to start all competitors together for any reason, wave starts are determined by age category.

XTERRA and ITU follow the USA Triathlon guidelines for water temperature. The temperature at which wetsuits may not be worn is much lower than for World Triathlon Corporation's Ironman events. There also are separate rules for professional and amateur competitors; a swim will be non-wetsuit for the professional field and wetsuit for the age-group field if the temperature falls between the cutoff for professionals and that for the amateurs. In XTERRA racing, wetsuits are allowed based on water temperature measured the day before the event and confirmed the day of the event. If water temperatures are close to the limits, the decision is made one hour before the start of the first swim. Professional and elite athletes are allowed to wear wetsuits if the water temperature is below 68 degrees Fahrenheit (20 degrees Celsius). Age-group athletes can wear wetsuits if the water temperature is below 72 degrees Fahrenheit (22 degrees Celsius). For all athletes, wetsuits are mandatory if the water temperature is 57 degrees Fahrenheit (14 degrees Celsius) or below, and challenged athletes are allowed wetsuits at any water temperature.

The rules for swimskins are different for XTERRA and ITU. XTERRA allows swimskins (worn over race clothing) and they may be removed after the swim in transition. The ITU rules for cross triathlon require athletes to race in the same suit as for swimming, so if a swimskin is worn, it cannot be removed at any point in the race. In general, this means no swimskins at all in ITU racing, and all swimskins approved on the USA Triathlon website are allowed in XTERRA. Ironman events limit legal swimskins to those manufactured with textile fabrics.

Bike

One of the greatest differences in off-road triathlon to other triathlons is the bike segment. Mountain biking is a radical departure from racing a road bike or a time-trial bike. Differences include, but aren't limited to, wheel size, tires, and position. Additionally, the variable terrain, obstacles, elevation, and race dynamics create numerous challenges in off-road triathlon that make it a fun test of endurance and patience. Athletes cannot do all of the training on a road bike and expect it to transfer effectively to a mountain bike; instead they need to adapt their training to address both physical and technical challenges.

The original rules for XTERRA, from the inaugural race in 1996, stated that only mountain bikes were legal for competition. Cyclocross bikes still are not allowed in XTERRA or in ITU cross triathlon. No drop handlebars or aero bars are allowed, and a minimum tire width on the bike eliminates the option of cyclocross tires. All bikes must have 26-inch, 27.5-inch, or 29-inch wheels. Bar extensions or grips off the handlebars may not exceed 5 inches (12.7 centimeters), and all bar ends must be capped (this is a safety issue).

There are two kinds of mountain bike: one with front suspension forks only (a hardtail) and one that has suspension both in the front forks and at the rear of the bike (a dual suspension). As far as deciding between a hardtail or a dual-suspension bike, it comes down to the rider. Dual-suspension bikes are more forgiving in bumpy and technical terrain but generally are heavier than hardtail bikes. Beginners will feel much more comfortable if they start out with a dual-suspension bike, as this bike makes riding technical obstacles and terrain much easier compared to a hardtail. Technically skilled athletes could weigh the decision based on the course. A more technical course would be more easily navigated with a lower energy cost on a dual suspension, but racing a very steep and hilly course might call for the weight advantage of a light hardtail bike. If technical ability represents the greatest challenge in the race, most likely a dual suspension is the best choice to give the rider maximum confidence on the course.

The next decision for a new athlete would be what diameter of wheels to try. The industry standard used to be 26-inch wheels, but the mountain bike industry has shifted to the option of 29-inch or 27.5-inch wheels for cross-country racing. Endurance mountain bike racers have been experimenting with a new 27.5-inch wheel as a novel way to split the difference in size and ride. There isn't a clear choice, as some of the top elite athletes racing the UCI Mountain Bike World Cup have still been winning on 26-inch wheels. Wheel diameter preference is based on efficiency and control, as each wheel diameter is legal for all versions of off-road triathlon. The 26-inch wheel size has been virtually abandoned in elite cross-country mountain biking, since 27.5- and 29-inch wheels are faster. Smaller wheels tend to accelerate faster with less power, which means that smaller riders may find they can get up to speed much faster on smaller diameter wheels. Larger wheel diameters hold momentum with less effort and roll over obstacles more easily. An athlete might be faster on 29-inch wheels on a flat course but need smaller wheels for a very steep or technical course. These are all decisions to be made based on the size, strength, and experience of the rider and the terrain most likely to be encountered.

Run

Although the run course in off-road triathlon would be expected to be off the pavement, rules in off-road triathlon do not state that the event needs to take place exclusively on trails. Many races combine paved and off-road sections in the run segment, so shoe choice can vary with the race course and can be a critical planning decision.

Depending on where the race is held, the course can vary from steep mountain trails to a network of park or forest trails connected by paved streets. Most often, race flats, trail racing shoes, or lightweight trainers are a good choice. For more steep and rocky races, a trail racing flat or a shoe with a protective sole might be a better choice.

Clothing

In most full-distance XTERRA events, it takes between 2 1/2 and 3 hours for the fastest athletes to complete the course. In order for the rider to remain comfortable for the duration of the event, technical, breathable, and well-fitting clothing is important. A trisuit with legs, rather than a swimsuit, is advised for women. Off-road courses can be unpredictable and can have a lot of low-hanging foliage that can scratch and scrape. There is also a higher risk of crashing in off-road events, so some minimal protection in the form of a full trisuit is a good option. A swimsuit is not as comfortable on a longer bike course, and having some Lycra covering the midsection can help prevent chafing, scrapes, and sunburn.

The increased chance of crashing also makes wearing gloves a very wise decision in off-road racing. Most athletes' first instinct is to put their hands out to break a fall, so having some protection on the hands is a good idea.

Many people place dry socks in transition areas to be put on after the bike or before the run, as it is difficult to run in hilly terrain and avoid blisters. If the choice is to forgo using socks, spreading some baby powder and Vaseline inside the shoes can prevent chafing on the feet.

Training for Off-Road Triathlon

A good training plan maximizes strengths and deemphasizes weaknesses. In general, off-road triathlon favors strong, all-around athletes. Training should focus mostly on the strength component, as off-road triathlon is rarely fast and occurs predominantly in hilly or rolling terrain, and the event is a start-to-finish time trial. Emphasizing the strength component in training and paying attention to specific technical skills are the gist of a good off-road triathlon program. As in Ironman racing, strength on the bike improves running ability, so a lot of emphasis on the bike portion of the race often results in better overall ability.

Versatility is an asset for an off-road athlete. Having a strategy in advance for how to pace the course is essential. There are no steady efforts in off-road racing; what is steady is a depletion of the power in the engine. Many find that pacing is the most difficult part of planning for the race.

Swim Training

Training for the swim in off-road triathlon is really no different than swim training for any other triathlon. A strong program will provide enough mileage to train the athlete to comfortably swim for 1,500 meters and will include some practice in open water so she can get used to swimming in a large pack. Strong pack swimming skills are critical and should be incorporated into your training plan, since some of the waves in off-road racing can be very large. Always bring a wetsuit even if the forecast for the water is borderline too warm. There have been numerous instances in which a swim that is always non-wetsuit becomes a wetsuit swim at the last minute because of unusually cold water. The wetsuit isn't that large an item, so pack it in the race bag for every race.

Mountain Bike Training

Physically, mountain biking differs from road riding in the position, the terrain, and the technical emphasis. This makes it necessary in training for you to address position on the bike, climbing strength, and technical skills on the trails in order to be confident on race day.

When you consider bike position, extrapolating the position on a mountain bike directly from a road bike may not be optimal. Visiting a local bike fitter with a good reputation is well worth the money.

One of the first challenges that road cyclists face in mountain biking is the climbing. In general, traction is the biggest difference between road and off-road riding, highlighted by cornering and climbing. Strong mountain bikers constantly reposition their body weight to maximize traction and steer the bike rather than relying solely on their tires or handlebars to navigate the trails.

With notable exceptions, it is generally more efficient to remain seated while climbing in a mountain bike. In off-road racing, it is preferable to minimize anaerobic efforts to save the legs for the run, so training to climb seated and using climbing out of the saddle for strong accelerations to pass is a good way to conserve power while racing. It takes thoughtful weight placement to maintain traction on the rear tire (where power transfer occurs) to stand out of the saddle when climbing. Keeping the center of gravity over the rear wheel helps to maintain traction.

Try this workout. Start with 5-minute efforts with 2 or 3 minutes of rest, climbing in a big gear (large chain ring if possible) in which your cadence is approximately 55 to 65 revolutions per minute. This is more a strength workout than a cardiovascular workout, so your heart rate will likely be a bit lower than it would be if you were doing hill repeats at a higher cadence. Using a big gear helps you focus on applying power evenly through the pedal stroke while thinking about pushing and pulling in circles with each leg.

Once you are comfortable with the big gear hill repeat, advance the workout by dropping into a much easier gear and spinning at 100 percent effort for the last minute. This will tax your cardiovascular system when your legs are tired and mimic a race effort when you are pre-fatigued, thus addressing 2 energy systems in one workout. You can also try standing for the last 30 seconds of the repeat to mimic accelerating over the top of the climb.

Start with 3 repetitions and build to 5 or 6, keeping in mind that quality is always preferable to quantity in any training session. This workout is best done on a dirt climb on a mountain bike.

Some events require specific preparation in order to meet the challenges of the race. For example, the Ogden XTERRA event starts at 4,500 feet (1,372 meters) of elevation and climbs up to 7,700 feet (2,347 meters). As a predominantly uphill event on the bike and much of the run, the race offers topography requiring good climbing skill and strength. These course conditions make it wise to focus preparation on longer climbs and to add an altitude adaptation protocol to prepare for the elevation.

Run Training

Off-road running is often more a strength effort than a truly fast run. The terrain does not allow constant, steady pacing, so a strong hill runner who can tolerate numerous incline changes has the advantage. The race courses dictate constant pace, direction, and elevation changes. The following are some suggested additions to base training to help you maximize your strength for a hilly and technical 10 kilometers off the bike.

Hill Repeats

Hill repeats allow you to train uphill strength and downhill speed. Running downhill is frequently overlooked but can be the toughest part of the event. Keep in mind that running an uphill after a downhill effort is even more difficult. Keep the hill intervals short. The uphill and downhill efforts together become the effort. Run the downhill relaxed, focusing on quick turnover rather than forcing the speed. Downhill runs are meant to train the body to default to high turnover and withstand the force of the downhill while still recovering.

Try this workout to incorporate some uphill and downhill training into your program. Warm up and start with 6 repeats of 30-second intervals on an 8 to 10 percent grade, with a loose and relaxed run down to recover. The key to these hills is to run with high cadence, a good forward lean, and strong arms to keep cadence high. The intervals should get longer as training progresses, up to 2 minutes on the run up while maintaining loose, relaxed, and quick turnover on the run down. Rest for 1 to 2 minutes and then repeat the circuit 4 or 5 times.

Training Over and Under Threshold

Undulating terrain demands efforts that are above and below hard race pace as the terrain alternates between uphill and downhill. Training the body to adapt to this inconsistency is important in order for you to perform a strong bike and run split in your race.

Try this workout. After a solid warm-up, run for 20 minutes, alternating 5 minutes at a hard race pace (maybe slightly under 10K pace) followed by 5 minutes at a comfortable tempo (at approximately half-marathon pace) and repeat twice. It is better to do this on rolling and undulating off-road terrain to make it more specific to off-road racing. To progress this workout, increase the length of the workout 5 minutes at a time until the session reaches 40 to 50 minutes. Cool down with an easy 5- to 10-minute jog.

Core Strength

Core strength is key to power development for all levels of athletes. Riding off road constantly challenges balance and reflexes, and a strong core will improve the platform from which the body moves with the bike and on the run. In addition, riding a mountain bike requires huge amounts of torque and power that is generated from the core. A strong core, hips, and lower back generate more power and reduce the chance of injury from high-intensity training.

Add a program with plank poses in all 4 directions. This is a simple way to start to work on hip and core stability. Start with 30 seconds on the left side, front, right side, and back, resting on your elbows, alternating for 2 minutes. Over the course of a few weeks, work up to 10 minutes per day, every day.

Putting It All Together on Race Day

Many athletes testing themselves in off-road triathlon have trained as well as possible for the coming race but find that there are last-minute decisions to make that can affect the outcome of the race. Here are some factors to consider in the days leading up to the event.

Should I Preride On The Race Course?

In off-road triathlon, getting familiar with the course generally allows athletes to race it at higher speed. An off-road course tends to have more corners and tricky sections that will mostly likely be ridden faster with some practice. Knowing a race course can build confidence before race day, but the logistics of a preride can be challenging. In point-to-point events in which the start and finish are separated, the preride can take a significant amount of time and energy. It is important to time a preride on the course allowing adequate opportunity to recover for race day. Some off-road bike courses are very long loops. Mountain bike rides longer than two hours within one or two days of the event are long for many athletes. Knowing the downhills is very important, but so is maintaining freshness before race day. The benefit of course knowledge is lost if a preride results in flat and fatigued legs on race day. In general, it is a good idea to keep the two days before the race short. Three days or more before is a better time to plan to ride the course if it will take a significant amount of time to get through it.

An option is to ride just the key downhill sections. This can be challenging depending on the course layout, but if you can access the more technical sections without riding the entire course, opt for that. In the end, fitness trumps course knowledge, so honor the training by remaining as fresh as possible.

What Tires at What Pressure?

Tires are a major consideration in off-road racing, and tire choice should match the terrain of the race. This is a matter of trial and error that comes with experience on a variety of different tires. Just as summer tires don't drive well in the snow, tires designed for dry conditions on a mountain bike are not as effective in the mud. Knowing what sort of course conditions exist at the race will help inform these decisions. In off-road racing, most athletes race with tubeless tire systems in which the tire is mounted on the wheel without a tube. Liquid latex suspension is used inside a tire to protect against pinhole punctures. Some athletes use tubular mountain bike tires glued to the rim, but this is less common in triathlon. In general, tubes are not recommended, as the risk of punctures and pinch flats in tubes is very high. It is not expensive to convert almost any wheel to a tubeless setup.

The pressure at which tires are run can change their performance. Lower pressure improves traction but may increase rolling resistance and risk of punctures if tires are run too low. Course conditions, rider weight, suspension setup, and tire choice are all factors that influence tire pressure. In general, experimenting in training with different pressures in a variety of conditions will help you determine the optimal setup.

Racing Flats or Trail Shoes?

Off-road triathlon is one of the few triathlons in which tread on a shoe can make a difference. The top professional athletes run in everything from lightweight trainers to race flats or trail racing shoes. A bit more stability around the ankle can be an asset in rocky terrain, but a race flat can be adequate for hard-packed trails connected by paved roads. In general, the shoe should match the run course.

The terrain in off-road triathlon is widely varied, and different courses suit different athletes. A better strength runner will enjoy the steeper hills; a fast road runner will excel in flatter and less technical races; and the nimble trail racer will excel on technical single-track events. Each venue offers a challenge suited to different athletes.

Nutrition Plan

Fueling for an off-road event depends on how long the race is going to take. Some events are 2 hours; others can take up to 4 hours. The climate will dictate how much hydration and nutrition are required. Take easy-to-digest carbohydrates and some kind of electrolyte drink. The challenge is planning where and how to facilitate fueling. Off-road courses can be very rough and can make it difficult to eat and drink while navigating technical sections on the bike. Since the run can be very intense, plan to get most of your required nutrition on the bike. In general, use your course knowledge to plan to feed wherever the course is smoother or more open. Riding with a hydration pack helps to facilitate drinking on a more regular schedule.

Off-road races are from 20 percent up to 50 percent longer than Olympic-distance races. In order to finish strong, you will need to properly fuel on the bike. Practice eating and drinking on a mountain bike at race pace in the trails. Try to consume 60 grams of carbohydrate per hour as this will significantly improve your ability to maintain a fast pace on the run. The run courses are often quite hilly, causing major spikes in heart rate, so often athletes will find it difficult to consume calories during this leg of the race. This makes fueling on the bike a very important part of racing well.

Conclusion

Off-road triathlon is an exciting and dynamic discipline of triathlon. The distance and terrain make for a race with some of the speed of short-course racing with a slightly longer duration, offering a test of strength and terrain that challenges skills. With some practice riding and running hilly trails, these races can be a fun addition to a triathlon season. The focus of training should generally be on climbing and strength; this will be very beneficial on any terrain. Using off-road triathlon to build more power and speed for long-distance racing works well, and short-course athletes will find that racing off road improves their strength and endurance in shorter events. Overall, off-road events encourage triathletes to be well rounded and to develop great bike skills, two characteristics that define a strong and versatile triathlete.

CHAPTER 18

Careers in Triathlon

Celeste Callahan
Brenda Barrera

It's no secret in the business world—triathletes make great employees. Why? Triathletes are goal oriented, thrive on competition, and understand the importance of teamwork. Who wouldn't want to hire someone disciplined enough to juggle a full-time career, family responsibilities, and add an additional 15 hours of training for a grueling endurance event to their week?

Now, let's turn the tables and imagine the possibility of extending one's passion for triathlon so that it's not just fun time, but also work time. Is that thought only a daydream during a swim set of 5 × 400s, a century bike ride, or a leisurely 10-mile run? Good news—it can be a reality! There are many career opportunities for women within the sport of triathlon in addition to racing. To start off, volunteering or getting an internship is an excellent way to gain experience and get a foot in the door; it also gives you an opportunity to assess whether the triathlon industry supports your career goals.

In this chapter we outline some careers in the fields of coaching, event management, governance, media, professional, as well as retail and manufacturing. Each section includes a Q & A with insight and advice from outstanding women professionals: Jennifer Hutchison, Kat Donatello, Melissa Merson, Julie Deardorff, Barb Lindquist, and Nicole DeBoom. This is an opportunity to learn from and be inspired by those who have competed in the sport and also found a successful, fulfilling career that includes the triathlon industry. Take the time to explore the opportunities presented, whether you are a competitor or are compelled to share your passion and keep triathlon one of the fastest-growing sports. Table 18.1 lists several resources that will help you on your path to the triathlon career of your choice.

Coach

So, you've been competing in triathlons for several years with impressive results, and you are the go-to person for newbies seeking answers to questions such as "How many hours a week should I train for a sprint race?" and "Should I invest in a wetsuit?" If sharing your expertise and helping people reach their triathlon goals seems appealing, maybe it's time to take that interest to the next level and become a triathlon coach.

TABLE 18.1

Resources for Triathlon Careers and Interests

Category	Resource
Coaching	USA Triathlon Coaching (www.usatriathlon.org/audience/coaching) USA Cycling Coaches (www.usacycling.org/coaches) USA Swimming Coaches (www.usaswimming.org) USA Track & Field Coaching Education (www.usatf.org/Resources-for---/Coaches.aspx) Team USA Coaching Education (www.teamusa.org/About-the-USOC/Athlete-Development/Coaching-Education) Road Runners Club of America (RRCA) Coaching Program Overview (www.rrca.org/programs/coaching-program-overview)
Sports nutrition	Academy of Nutrition and Dietetics (www.eatright.org/BecomeanRDorDTR/content.aspx?id=8143) Sports, Cardiovascular, and Wellness Nutrition (SCAN) (www.scandpg.org)
Training	American College of Sports Medicine (ACSM) (www.certification.acsm.org/health-fitness-certifications)
Event management	USA Triathlon Race Directors (www.usatriathlon.org/ racedirectors) Road Race Management (www.roadracemanagement.com)
Governance	USA Triathlon (www.usatriathlon.org) USA Triathlon Governance (www.usatriathlon.org/governance) USA Triathlon Regions (www.usatriathlon.org/regions) International Triathlon Union (www.triathlon.org) Team USA Careers (www.teamusa.org/Careers)
Media	USA Triathlon Magazine (www.usatriathlon.org/magazine) Association of Women in Sports Media (www.awsmonline.org) Endurance Sportswire (www.endurancesportswire.com) Triathlete (www.triathlon.competitor.com)
Professional triathlete	USA Triathlon Elite Membership (www.usatriathlon.org/elitemembership) USA Triathlon's Certified Training and Performance Centers (www.usatriathlon.org/certifiedcenters)
Business	U.S. Small Business Administration (www.sba.gov/writing-business-plan) Entrepreneur (www.entrepreneur.com/businessplan/index.html)
Other	Outdoor Industries Women's Coalition (www.oiwc.org) Sports and Fitness Industry Association (www.sfia.org) Triathlon Business International (www.triathlonbusinessintl.com) Women's Sports Foundation (www.womenssportsfoundation.org)

Being a coach is certainly an alternative to working a traditional 9-to-5 job, but self-employed colleagues will attest to the importance of the hard work and long hours needed to grow a successful coaching business. A good starting point is a realistic business plan. Next, familiarize yourself with the history of the sport, the industry, and coaching resources like books, videos, seminars, and conferences. Networking with other coaches or even having your own coach will certainly be valuable.

One of the first steps to becoming a triathlon coach is to acquire USA Triathlon coaching certification, which has different categories: Level I, Level II, Level II Endurance, Level III, and Youth and Junior Certification. Expect to budget for the cost. The certifications involve written examinations. USA Triathlon webinars are available, ranging from topics such as motivating triathletes to understanding iliotibial band syndrome, and many can be used to obtain CEUs (continuing education units) for recertification. In addition, liability insurance comes with the certification, plus inclusion in the coaches' online directory, a first stop for athletes looking for a coach. At the time of this publication, there were more than 2,200 USA Triathlon certified coaches. For additional information see chapter 13, "Coaching Options for Triathletes."

Background

Four-year degree, ideally in kinesiology, sports medicine, sport nutrition, exercise science, or a similar field

USA Triathlon coaching certification

Other certifications such as USA Cycling, USA Swimming, USA Track & Field, Road Runners Club of America

Certified personal trainer

National Academy of Sports Medicine Certified Personal Trainer (NASM-CPT)

CPR/AED certification

Skills

Building and maintaining your brand; honesty; integrity; interpersonal communication skills; knowledge of fitness, cardiovascular training, and proper nutrition; motivation skills; multitasking; organizational skills; time management; and understanding of essential tools and equipment to swim, bike, and run.

Q & A With Coach Jennifer Hutchison

Jennifer Hutchison, RD, CSSD, CSCS, LDN, has more than 14 years of USA Triathlon coaching experience and is one of only 20 coaches in the United States to earn the highest USA Triathlon coaching certification, USA Triathlon Level III Elite. Since 2006, Jennifer has served as USA Triathlon Florida's regional athlete development coordinator (RADC); her role as RADC is to serve as the Florida region's primary resource for young athletes, parents, and coaches who wish to learn about USA Triathlon's athlete development Olympic pathway as well as explore and train for the draft legal race format. She is also a registered dietitian, board certified as a specialist in sport dietetics, a USA Cycling Level 2 coach, and a competitive age-group triathlete with more than 100 races of all distances to her credit including being a three-time Ironman World Championship qualifier and finisher.

How did you get started as a triathlon coach?

I started out as a registered dietitian working with athletes and then added full-time coaching because there was a need in the area. I have to credit two women with helping me get my start: Diane Berberian, a triathlete who is now a paratri-athlete, and 86-year-old Jackie Yost, one of my first clients.

Can you share some advice for someone who wants to become a coach?

It is important to be grounded in exercise science and physiology. Continue your education by taking classes and make time to learn from other coaches through practical observation. Reach out to other female coaches; it's worthwhile to find a mentor. Find your niche as a coach. Target a population you are passionate about, whether it be first timers, youth, or seniors. There's a market to coach women who are first timers and looking for an avenue to a healthy lifestyle.

Is there a misconception about what makes a good coach?

Just because someone is a fast or highly competitive triathlete does not auto-matically make her a good coach. Some of the best coaches might be mid- or back-of-the-pack competitors who know how to break down the complicated and confusing science into practical, relatable terms so the client can focus on what she needs to do to achieve her goals.

How do you balance coaching with your own athletic endeavors?

As a former competitive age-group athlete, I discovered as I grew from coaching part-time to full-time that it's difficult to be competitive. I find it nearly impos-sible to give my athletes the support and feedback needed if I'm competing in the same race. What does work for me is I balance my personal time by racing during my client's off-season.

Event Management

A career in event management draws people from a variety of backgrounds. An event manager could be a triathlete with years of racing experience who was tapped because of her firsthand knowledge as a participant. Sometimes she's a road race director who has had success at managing running events and is expanding her resume to include multisport. Either way, it's a daunting responsibility that requires stamina and atten-tion to detail along with a broad spectrum of skills.

Writing a business plan with a realistic budget should be at the top of the list, as well as securing key stakeholders such as community partners and sponsors. The planning stages include choosing a location and race date. Then you will need to design a course, get permits from local authorities, and plan logistics. Just the fact that you have built it does not guarantee they will come, so promotion is also an important component to the success of an event.

Obviously, one person cannot do it all, so it's essential to have key personnel with expertise in overseeing operations, a medical team, a timing company, and a volun-teer coordinator. If the participants have a safe and positive race experience, you can build on your success.

USA Triathlon offers multiple benefits and extensive resources for anyone interested in becoming a USA Triathlon certified race director for adult and youth races, camps, and clinics. A USA Triathlon certified race director must complete a 16-hour educational training class that includes information on the latest in race-directing methods, insurance and risk management trends, and USA Triathlon sanctioning compliance.

Background

Four-year degree

Experience in event management, race operations, or related position

Ability to manage and produce a safe event from inception through postrace

Skills

Event management requires leadership, communication, attention to details, the ability to handle multiple tasks and budgets, the ability to negotiate contracts and permits, strong management skills, a willingness to troubleshoot, the ability to remain calm in high-pressure situations, and understanding of timing and race registration, plus database management.

In addition to these skills, an event manager needs to build relationships with stakeholders such as local governing bodies, municipalities, police, medical and safety providers, sponsors, vendors, and volunteer staff.

Types of Jobs

In addition to race director, job opportunities including working in these areas:

Charity partners

Communications

Community relations

Information technology

Marketing and promotion

Operations and event production

Race results and timing

Sales and sponsorship

Volunteer coordinator

Q & A With Kathleen "Kat" Donatello

With the help of veteran triathletes from her training group, Kat Donatello, a USA Triathlon certified race director, put on the inaugural Pumpkinman Triathlon in 2007. The event has since grown into the Pumpkinman Triathlon Festival, which includes a Half Iron distance (Maine's first and only). In addition to being a USA Triathlon All-American since 2010, she has finished several Ironman races including the Ironman World Championships (2013). She has served as chairman of the USA Triathlon New England board of directors, vice chairman of the USA Triathlon Age-Group National Committee, and served on the USA Triathlon Hall of Fame Executive Committee. She is also a member of Triathlon Business International.

When you put on the first race, did you have any race management experience?

I had assisted in the direction of the Sea to Summit, an endurance adventure race. My experience came from racing all over the world, and I wanted to put on a race that I wanted to participate in.

What lessons have you learned along the way? What advice do you have for any women interested in getting into race management?

Work closely with local officials, politicians, neighbors, and main street businesses. They want you to succeed, but they also want a production that reflects their community. Don't be afraid to think outside the box. I brainstorm year round with my team, but also with athletes, community members, school teachers, and police officers. We are constantly thinking of improvements and how to do things better. If you go cheap, your athletes will know it! Don't be afraid to say "I screwed up." Mistakes happen, so you need to take ownership and you will earn far more respect.

What's the biggest misconception about being a race director?

That I make a lot of money. Our event currently is a nonprofit, and we donate all the proceeds to local student-athlete–based charities and scholarships. We also use money to help fund police safety projects in town.

Being a race director can be demanding. What are the rewards?

Watching someone dramatically change her life by participating in our event. I take pride in knowing we helped numerous people in our town and community add years to their lives. In addition, I feel I have become an excellent role model to the young girls in our community.

Staff and Governance

If you are interested in being part of the team that supports athletes, races, directors, coaches, club officials, and the sport overall, an exciting career option is a job or position on the USA Triathlon staff or in the governance of the sport. A caveat: If you want to be a USA Triathlon staff member, you might be required to live in Colorado—often voted one of the best places to live in the United States. Not a bad place to work, right? Before you pack your bags and book a flight, note that career options in triathlon governance also include volunteer opportunities to serve on a regional, national, or international (International Triathlon Union, ITU) level with opportunities on a variety of committees.

Whether you are advancing a career or jump-starting one, the benefits of serving on a governing board or committee vary. One can develop and expand skills, build a professional portfolio, showcase expertise, and find a mentor. It's also rewarding to give back to the triathlon community—an opportunity to pay it forward. Before making a commitment, however, be sure you have the time and are clear about what you can give and also what you want to get from the experience.

USA Triathlon serves as the National Governing Body for triathlon, which is the fastest-growing sport in the world. This signals growth and opportunity. A board of directors governs USA Triathlon, and additional leadership opportunities are drawn from the

10 regions with various committees and commissions. Governance positions require election or appointment, and staff job listings are available on the website. College students have the opportunity to gain experience through a U.S. Olympic Committee internship program, which includes areas such as broadcasting, development, human resources, journalism, marketing, Paralympics, sports administration, sports medicine, and strength and conditioning.

It can be helpful to see how a career path develops. Follow Kathy Matejka's career from college to her current job as a part of the USA Triathlon staff. She graduated with a degree in physical education and a coaching emphasis in team sports; taught elementary through high school; transitioned into the parks and recreation field; worked for a municipal parks and recreation department; volunteered for triathlon; served as president of two triathlon clubs; competed in more than 150 events from sprint to ultra-distance triathlons; was assistant race director for a Kona qualifying race; became a USA Triathlon certified official in 1997; and joined USA Triathlon in 2004 as the event sanctioning manager. As of 2014, she is event services director and staff advisor to committees including the USA Triathlon Women's Committee.

Background

Administration

Coaching

Communications (print, online, social media)

Development and fund-raising

Finance

Marketing

Public policy

Sports administration

Sports medicine

Sport performance

Sport science

Skills

A person in triathlon governance should be responsible and show accountability; be effective at making decisions; exercise good judgment; and demonstrate integrity, leadership, and the ability to negotiate.

Q & A With Melissa Merson

Melissa Merson, a triathlete who has raced every distance from sprint to Ironman, is a USAT coach, race director and race official, a youth and junior coach and event director specialist, an ITU Continental official, and the only U.S. woman and the second American ever to serve on the ITU executive board. In addition, she served on the former USA Triathlon Women's Commission and International Relations Committee as chair, the Pan American Triathlon Confederation Women's Committee as a member and North American Sub-Continental representative, and the USA Triathlon Mid-Atlantic Council as secretary. For nearly a decade she has coached a school-based youth program. She now leads Triathlon Family USA Inc., a family business that produces youth triathlons, camps, and clinics.

You have been part of USA Triathlon governance in one way or another for decades. What is your background that led you there?

While my professional life, which included Senior Communications Official in the congressional budgets office, trained me for governance leadership, my heart beats for youth sport development and their Olympic dreams. I joined the USA Triathlon Mid-Atlantic Region in the 1990s and worked for about a decade to help build our region into a great triathlon community. Having worked so close to government in my professional life, I felt I had a valuable understanding of representational democracy and protecting the rights of minorities. Athletes in the Olympic pipeline are young and vulnerable, and we in sport governance have an obligation to protect and support them as they strive toward their Olympic dreams. I worked in Washington, DC, with people from all over the world, teaching them about U.S. democratic processes, so I had international relations skills. In 2000, I was selected for the U.S. Olympic Committee's Project GOLD (Guaranteed Olympic Leadership Development) program. The more I learned about Olympism and sport development, the more I felt obligated to try to make a difference. I felt there was an opportunity here where I could contribute in a way that would help our age-group and elite athletes, women, and our sport overall.

What do you think is your greatest accomplishment in governance?

It would be easy to say that it was being elected to the ITU board, because ITU is one of a very few international federations led by a woman president. It is the only one also with a woman secretary general, a woman vice president, and several more women on the board. Being part of the women-led, fastest-growing sport in the Olympic movement was a significant accomplishment. While that was important personally, it was more important to the sport that I was able to bring USA Triathlon and ITU closer together, where U.S. cities are now hosting prominent races, and we are contributing to the growth of the sport internationally. The other elements that made that a great achievement for me were giving our elite athletes the opportunity to race at the highest levels on U.S. soil and bringing ITU, USA Triathlon, and WTC (World Triathlon Corporation) together to work on anti-doping and rules harmonization When I arrived on the USA Triathlon National Board in 2007, no one was willing to talk about any of these things, and it is enormously satisfying to see how far we've come since then.

Why is it important for women to get involved in aspects of the sport in addition to racing?

Like most other sports in the United States, triathlon is run by a largely volunteer organization. USA Triathlon relies on thousands of volunteers who contribute as coaches, officials, race directors and support personnel, and in governance positions. Women make up about half of the triathletes who participate in our sport, so they also should be represented in all of these other areas of the sport in equal measures.

Any advice for women interested in sports administration or governance?

My view is that women should bring the many skills and great expertise they have accumulated in other areas of their lives and share them with the sport community. Women who are teachers and counselors make great coaches and officials. Women who run businesses and organize events make great race directors. Women who are in elected offices or work in various parts of federal, state, or local government would be great board and committee members and leaders. Those of us who are in positions as coaches, officials, race directors, and in governance need to extend a welcoming hand when we meet women with these needed skills and help them see how their contributions are valued in sport.

Media

A career in sports media is certainly a dream job for someone with a passion for sport. The triathlon market is a narrow niche, and jobs are not as plentiful as they are in more mainstream sports such as football or college athletics, but they do exist. In many cases, it is necessary to think outside the box and explore opportunities at the regional and local level. For anyone interested in this career field, an educational background and some experience are a prerequisite for most jobs. Volunteering or freelancing is most often the ticket to learn firsthand what to expect, find out what skills are needed, and network with those in the position to hire even if the job is not full-time but is a fulfilling part-time or a steady freelance job.

Background

Four-year degree

Experience in journalism, communications, and public relations

Experience in various mediums (broadcast, print, online, digital)

Types of Jobs

Editor (broadcast, print, online, digital)

Graphic designer

Media relations

Producer (film, video)

Photographer

Radio or television broadcaster

Researcher

Social media

Sports commentator

Writer

Q & A With Julie Deardorff

Julie Deardorff is an award-winning writer, journalist, and health expert and an ACSM (American College of Sports Medicine) certified personal trainer with more than 20 years of experience as a journalist. She currently serves as a writer/media relations specialist at Northwestern University. A two-time Ironman finisher with more than 15 Half Ironman distance finishes, she is not racing now but still finds time to run, bike, swim, and do strength training, yoga, and Pilates. Her most memorable race was the 1999 Philippine Half Ironman in Matabungkay Beach because she went alone, managed to finish the race despite heat stroke, and ended up being the overall women's winner.

For someone interested in working in triathlon (multisport) media, what basic skills and work experience would you recommend?

A journalism degree helps but it isn't essential. Some of the best journalists I know have been trained as teachers, musicians, or lawyers. The key is to write and write often, to read, and to get published. For someone who isn't a journalism major, a journalism or communication course can help students get comfortable with cold-calling people or approaching strangers for interviews. Being able to conduct effective interviews is an essential skill, regardless of the career. Though there's no such thing as a dumb question, there are ways to ask good ones so you get better responses. Journalists learn this, but often more by doing rather than studying technique. I also think anyone going into this field needs to be strong in social media and video, as well as reporting.

Do you need to be a rock star, All-American triathlete to cover the sport?

Political reporters don't have to be politicians, and few sportswriters are professional athletes. Many of them are drawn to the job because they are interested in the topic and wanted to be around the excitement. It helps to have done a triathlon or be training for one especially if you are writing for an educated crowd. But there's always a need for a fresh perspective, and someone who is too immersed in the triathlon world may use jargon that is off-putting to beginners. So a fresh perspective is always good, no matter what you cover. That said, the more educated you are about a topic, the more informed your writing can be.

If someone wants to land a job covering the sport of triathlon, is freelance the best way to get a foot in the door?

Jobs covering triathlon specifically are going to be few and far between. But there's great opportunity in writing stories about the people who do triathlons for a wide variety of traditional and new media. I started as a freelance writer, and it's a good way to get your name out there and start working with editors. But keep in mind, it's also very difficult and competitive if you need stability or regular income.

Professional Triathlete

Most Americans have grown up watching professional women's sports such as basketball or soccer, and it is no secret that those opportunities are limited to a select few athletes. Every four years marks a Summer Olympic Games, and across the country, girls can now watch and aspire to be an Olympian in the sport of triathlon—but what about the chance to add professional triathlete to your resume? Is it possible to parlay this passion into a full-time job?

Becoming a professional triathlete is possible but requires a combination of talent, the desire to win, and the financial resources to support oneself with alternative sources of income, since the prize money, while available, is small compared to that in most professional sports.

It's fine to draw inspiration from professionals such as Gwen Jorgensen, who left a job in accounting to pursue a professional career and can now add Olympian and ITU World Champion to her resume; but it's equally important to be realistic about making the leap to a full-time occupation. A professional triathlete needs to factor in time outside of training and recovery for sponsor engagements, public speaking, media interviews, and building a personal brand. Professional triathletes also incur costs related to recovery such as massage, physiotherapy, sport psychology or mental skills training, and medical coverage for injury prevention and treatment.

Background

Professional triathletes come from a variety of backgrounds. Many excel at swimming, running, or cycling and were collegiate standouts in one or more of these sports. They may have been successful at national or international competition or were top age-group athletes who may have excelled in high school or come up through the USA Triathlon Junior Elite or Under-23 program.

Skills

In addition to talent, one needs determination, hard work, discipline, commitment, passion, and persistence.

Q & A With Barb Lindquist

Barb Lindquist began her athletic career as a swimmer. She competed for Stanford University and medaled at the Pan Am Games in 1987 and 1991. In 1996, she began her professional triathlon career. Lindquist was a member of the USAT World Championship team for 10 years; and in 134 career races, she won 33, stood on the podium 86 times, and finished 114 times in the top 10. She was ranked first in the world from February 2003 through 2004 and placed ninth at the 2004 Olympic Games. Though she retired from racing in 2005, she continues to contribute to the sport as the USA Triathlon Collegiate Recruitment Program manager and serves on the USA Triathlon Women's Committee.

Approximately how many hours should one expect to train per day or week in order to be successful as a professional?

Depending on the time of year, 20 to 30 hours per week of just swimming, cycling, and running. Add an extra 5 hours for strength training, foam rolling, massage, preparing proper food, and napping, all of which can add more time to the week.

A lot of top amateurs dream of becoming a professional. What is the biggest challenge they should expect?

An amateur needs to realize that once she gets her elite card, it does not mean the floodgates of sponsorship are completely opened. Even when I was ranked number one in the world, my husband-manager still had to knock on doors for sponsorship. My race results made it much easier for him to get sponsorship deals, but they still weren't cold-calling him.

Can you recommend a few tips for longevity as a professional?

Take care of your body and mind. Have a long-term plan. When athletes want something too fast, they get into trouble with injury. Pay attention to the little things between workouts to keep healthy.

Do most professionals also coach on the side to make additional money?

Not at the highest level—at least I never did, but now I do coach athletes who are coaches themselves. They realize they need a coach even if they are a coach themselves. This is important. Also, I think some athletes strive for earning their elite card so they can use the title "professional triathlete" in order to get more business.

Any advice for women who aspire to be professional triathletes?

Make a business plan. The Internal Revenue Service calls a business a hobby if you haven't made money in three years. Make it a business without taking the joy out of making it a passion.

Retail and Manufacturing

So many factors have contributed to the growth of the sport of triathlon and the triathlon industry, including careers in retail and manufacturing. The market for women-specific products and apparel has spurred opportunities for women worldwide. Long gone are the days when the only choice for women was to purchase equipment and apparel from companies that would shrink it and pink it to appeal to the market. Today, most major sport brands offer women-specific products, from bicycle frames to apparel lines, that appeal to women of all backgrounds, sizes, and shapes who participate in our sport. This has created an opportunity for an entrepreneur to land a niche market.

Popular brands for women from women-owned businesses and companies started by women include Betty Designs, Coeur, Moving Comfort, Oiselle, Shebeest, Sheila Moon, Skirt Sports, Smashfest Queen, SOAS, Sturdy Girl, and Title Nine.

Background

Apparel

Design

Marketing

Product brand manager

Product design

Sales representative

Skills

A person in this field needs to have strong communication skills and attention to detail, must be able to meet deadlines, and do well working with a team.

Q & A With Nicole DeBoom

Nicole DeBoom, founder and CEO of Skirt Sports, is a prime example of the unintentional businesswoman, a collegiate swimmer turned professional triathlete whose love and passion for running led her on a pursuit to evolve women's running apparel and thus launch Skirt Sports. She competed in more than 100 triathlons including six Ironman competitions; she won the 2004 Ironman Wisconsin while wearing the first-ever women's running skirt. Business honors include 40 Under 40, SGB, SportsOneSource Group (2009), and Boulder County Business Report (2011).

What lessons have you learned as you grew Skirt Sports from an idea to the success it is today?

Having a positive outlook is necessary. In order to succeed, there is no room for doubt. You need to believe 100 percent with your entire heart, mind, and soul that there is no other alternative than success. This is the only way to stay positive during the very hard times, and there will definitely be very hard times in business. Everything always costs more and takes longer than you think it should.

How did being an athlete help you in launching your business?

I used what I learned as an athlete to build the foundation for Skirt Sports. When I started the business, I was simply exploring a "new sport" which would later become a women's clothing brand. After I decided to move forward, I approached it as if I were training for a race. I started by building a foundation, in my case based around the creation of the running skirt. Over the years I've enjoyed many peaks and valleys, much like a long triathlon racing career, taking the aid station approach to business. I have my sights set on the finish line, but I am going one mile at a time, analyzing my performance at each aid station, refueling, and then checking to make sure I'm still on the correct course.

Can you share any advice for getting into the sport apparel or retail manufacturing business?

Many people have ideas, but very few follow through with them. My first advice is to explore beyond the product you are dreaming up and consider how you will get that product to market. Today, there are so many unique ways to launch a business, from crowd-sourcing (crowd-designing) products, to setting up innovative online shopping platforms, to specifically targeting key customers and developing a customized strategy for them. In the end, you never know what you can do until you try. Once you have the basic plan, go for it, but don't quit your day job until you know it's going to work.

How important is it for women to mentor other women?

I didn't have any women mentors in the triathlon industry, but I did have phenomenal women mentors from other industries. The most notable was Lara Merriken, the founder of LÄRABAR. We met at a trade show before her business was even operational. We became friends, and I was fortunate to closely watch her progression, from branding to manufacturing to financing and more. I learned secondhand that the road would not be smooth but it could still be incredibly fulfilling.

Any additional thoughts you would like to add or share?

Building your team is critical for success and happiness. Remember, you can choose whom you want to work with. I have two requirements. First, I hire athletes. They don't need to be fast, but they need to understand how to set goals, work hard, and chase dreams. Second, I hire people with whom I would enjoy going out to dinner!

Conclusion

Participation in the sport of triathlon has been steadily rising since 1974 when 46 people launched the first official race in San Diego, California. Today, triathlon is one of the fastest-growing sports in the world; and career opportunities have also increased, making it possible to turn a passion for triathlon into a profession. In this chapter we have outlined background and skills needed for several career options and included advice from successful women in the field. Have we sparked your interest? Whether it's your first venture into the workforce or a midlife job switch, familiarize yourself with the resources available; network with industry professionals at race expos; attend educational seminars to learn best practices and new trends; and seek out an internship or volunteer position, since both are sure ways to garner on-the-job experience. When it is time to dive into the water, go right ahead and take that leap of faith to combine a healthy, active lifestyle with a rewarding career in the triathlon industry.

REFERENCES

Allen, H., and A. Coggan. 2010. *Training and Racing With a Power Meter.* Boulder, CO: VeloPress.

Anders Ericsson, K., R.T. Krampe, and C. Tesch-Römer. 1993. The role of deliberate practice in the acquisition of expert performance. *Psychol Rev,* 100(3): 363-406.

Balyi, I., and A. Hamilton. 2004. *Long-term Athlete Development: Trainability in Childhood and Adolescence. Windows of Opportunity. Optimal Trainability.* Victoria: National Coaching Institute British Columbia & Advanced Training and Performance Ltd.

Bisson, D.L., G.D. Dunster, J.P. O'Hare, D. Hampton, and M.D. Penney. 1992. Renal sodium retention does not occur during the luteal phase of the menstrual cycle in normal women. *Br J Obstet Gynaecol,* 99: 247-252.

Boisseau, N. 2004. Gender differences in metabolism during exercise and recovery. *Sci Sports,* 19: 220–227.

Brummitt, J. 2008. The role of massage in sports performance and rehabilitation: Current evidence and future direction. *N Am J Sports Phys Ther,* 3(1): 7-21.

Burd, N.A., J.E. Tang, D.R. Moore, and S.M. Phillips. 2009. Exercise training and protein metabolism: Influences of contraction, protein intake, and sex-based differences. *J Appl Physiol,* 106(5): 1692-1701.

Burke, L.M. 2010. Fueling strategies to optimize performance: Training high or training low? *Scand J Med Sci Sports,* 20(suppl. 2): 48-58.

Coyle, D. 2014. Hey parents quit raising specialists and start raising omnivores. Available: http://thetalentcode.com/2014/02/06/hey-parents-quit-raising-specialists-and-start-raising-omnivores/

Daniels, A.M. 2007. Cooperation versus competition: Is there really such an issue? *New Dir Youth Dev,* Fall(115): 43-56.

Devries, M.C., M.J. Hamadeh, S.M. Phillips, and M.A. Tarnopolsky. 2006. Menstrual cycle phase and sex influence muscle glycogen utilization and glucose turnover during moderate-intensity endurance exercise. *Am J Physiol Regul Integr Comp Physiol,* 291(4): R1120–R1128.

England Athletics, British Athletics. 2013. *Athletics 365: Challenges and Curriculum.* Available: www.englandathletics.org/shared/get-file.ashx?id=3913&itemtype=document [September 9, 2014].

Enns, D.L., and P.M. Tiidus. 2010. The influence of estrogen on skeletal muscle: Sex matters. *Sports Med,* 40(1): 41–58.

Ewing, M.E., and V. Seefeldt. 1990. *American Youth and Sports Participation: A Study of 10,000 Students and Their Feelings About Sport.* North Palm Beach, FL: Athletic Footwear Association.

Fonda, B., and N. Sarabon. 2013. Effects of whole-body cryotherapy on recovery after hamstring damaging exercise: A crossover study. *Scand J Med Sci Sports,* 23(5): e270-e278.

Friel, J. 2004. *The Triathlete's Training Bible,* 2nd ed. Boulder, CO: VeloPress.

Henderson, G.C., J.A. Fattor, M.A. Horning, N. Faghihnia, M.L. Johnson, M. Luke-Zeitoun, and G.A. Brooks. 2008. Glucoregulation is more precise in women than in men during postexercise recovery. *Am J Clin Nutr,* 87(6): 1686–1694.

Hughson, R. 1986. Children in competitive sports—a multi-disciplinary approach. *Can J Appl Sport Sci,* 11(4): 162-172.

Ivković, A., M. Franić, I. Bojanić, and M. Pećina. 2007. Overuse injuries in female athletes. *Croat Med J,* 48(6): 767–778.

Jayanthi, N., C. Pinkham, L. Dugas, B. Patrick, and C. Labella. 2013. Sports specialization in young athletes: Evidence-based recommendations. *Sports Health,* 5(3): 251-257.

Kriengsinyos, W., L.J. Wykes, L.A. Goonewardene, R.O. Ball, and P.B. Pencharz. 2004. Phase of menstrual cycle affects lysine requirement in healthy women. *Am J Physiol Endocrinol Metab,* 287(3): E489–E496.

Migliorini, S. 2011. Risk factors and injury mechanism in triathlon. *J Hum Sport Exerc,* 6(2): i-vi.

Myles, K., and J.W. Funder. 1996. Progesterone binding to mineralocorticoid receptors: In vitro and in vivo studies. *Am J Physiol,* 270: E601-E607.

Oosthuyse, T., and A.N. Bosch. 2010. The effect of the menstrual cycle on exercise metabolism: Implications for exercise performance in eumenorrhoeic women. *Sports Med,* 40(3): 207–227.

Paik, I.Y., M.H. Jeong, H.E. Jin, Y.I. Kim, A.R. Suh, S.Y. Cho, H.T. Roh, C.H. Jin, and S.H. Suh. 2009. Fluid replacement following dehydration reduces oxidative stress during recovery. *Biochem Biophys Res Commun,* 383(1): 103-107.

Patel, D.R., H.D. Pratt, and D.E. Greydanus. 2002. Pediatric neurodevelopment and sports participation. When are children ready to play sports? *Pediatr Clin North Am,* 49(3): 505-531.

Paulsen, G., K.T. Cumming, G. Holden, J. Hallén, B.R. Rønnestad, O. Sveen, A. Skaug, I. Paur, N.E. Bastani, H.N. Østgaard, C. Buer, M. Midttun, F. Freuchen, H. Wiig, E.T. Ulseth, I. Garthe, R. Blomhoff, H.B. Benestad, and T. Raastad. 2014. Vitamin C and E supplementation hampers cellular adaptation to endurance training in humans: A double-blind, randomised, controlled trial. *J Physiol,* 592(pt 8): 1887-1901.

Peternelj, T.T., and J.S. Coombes. 2011. Antioxidant supplementation during exercise training: Beneficial or detrimental? *Sports Med,* 41(12): 1043-1069.

Renstrom, P., A. Ljungqvist, E. Arendt, B. Beynnon, T. Fukubayashi, W. Garrett, T. Georgoulis, T.E. Hewett, R. Johnson, T. Krosshaug, B. Mandelbaum, L. Micheli, G. Myklebust, E. Roos, H. Roos, P. Schamasch, S. Shultz, S. Werner, E. Wojtys, and L. Engebretsen. 2008. Non-contact ACL injuries in female athletes: An International Olympic Committee current concepts statement. *Br J Sports Med,* 42(6): 394–412.

Sims, S.T., N.J. Rehrer, M.L. Bell, and J.D. Cotter. 2007. Pre-exercise sodium loading aids fluid balance and endurance for women exercising in the heat. *J Appl Physiol,* 103: 534-541.

Sims, S.T., N.J. Rehrer, M.L. Bell, and J.D. Cotter. 2008. Endogenous and exogenous female sex hormones and renal electrolyte handling: Effects of an acute sodium load on plasma volume at rest. *J Appl Physiol,* 105(1): 121-127.

Stachenfeld, N.S., D.L. Keefe, and S.F. Palter. 2001. Estrogen and progesterone effects on transcapillary fluid dynamics. *Am J Physiol Regul Integr Comp Physiol,* 281: R1319-R1329.

Stachenfeld, N.S., A.E. Splenser, W.L. Calzone, M.P. Taylor, and D.L. Keefe. 2001. Sex differences in osmotic regulation of AVP and renal sodium handling. *J Appl Physiol,* 91: 1893-1901.

Strobel, N.A., J.M. Peake, A. Matsumoto, S.A. Marsh, J.S. Coombes, and G.D. Wadley. 2011. Antioxidant supplementation reduces skeletal muscle mitochondrial biogenesis. *Med Sci Sports Exerc,* 43(6): 1017-1024.

Tarnopolsky, M.A., M. Bosman, J.R. Macdonald, D. Vandeputte, J. Martin, and B.D. Roy. 1997. Postexercise protein-carbohydrate and carbohydrate supplements increase muscle glycogen in men and women. *J Appl Physiol,* 83(6): 1877–1883.

Tucker, R. 2013. Long-term athlete development: Foundations and challenges for coaches, scientists and policy-makers. Available: http://sportsscientists.com/2013/02/long-term-athlete-development-foundations-challenges/ [December 10, 2014].

USA Triathlon. 2011. *Youth & Junior Coaches Manual.* Colorado Springs, CO: USA Triathlon.

USA Triathlon. 2014. USA Triathlon Supplemental Youth Rules. Available: www.usatriathlon.org/about-multisport/rulebook.aspx#supplemental [September 9, 2014].

Versey, N.G., S.L. Halson, and B.T. Dawson. 2013. Water immersion recovery for athletes: Effect on exercise performance and practical recommendations. *Sports Med,* 43(11): 1101-1130.

Weiss, M.R., and S.D. Fretwell. 2005. The parent-coach/child-athlete relationship in youth sport: Cordial, contentious, or conundrum? *Res Q Exerc Sport,* 76(3): 286-305.

Winner, E. 1997. *Gifted Children: Myths and Realities.* New York: Basic Books.

INDEX

PLEASE NOTE: Page numbers followed by an italicized *f* or *t* represent figures or tables found on those pages, italicized *ff* or *tt* represent multiple figures or tables found on those pages, respectively.

A

acidosis 22
ACL. *See* anterior cruciate ligament
aerobars 10-11, 10*f*
aerobic, definition of 114
aerobic exercise 40
aero helmets 13
Allen, Hunter 93
American College of Gynecology 203
ankle bands 85-86
anorexia athletica 171-172
anterior cruciate ligament (ACL) 170
antioxidants 48-49
apparel
    compression clothing 15-16, 156
    considerations before buying 16
    cycling shoes 16
    for off-road triathlon 240
    for postbaby training 205-206
    running shoes for children 233
arm movement 104-105, 104*t*
armpit breathing 90
Association of Applied Sport Sciences (Canada) 227
athletes. *See* coaching options for triathletes; paratriathletes
Athletics 365 234

B

BCAAs. *See* branch-chain amino acids
Bec's Spin (side bars)
    Bec's make-ahead black rice salad 214
    my spouse isn't a triathlete 216
    working out with kids 213

bicycle exercise 70, 70*f*
bicycles. *See also* apparel; cycling-specific training
    aerobars 10-11, 10*f*
    bike fit 9, 9*f*, 10*t*
    for child triathletes 230-232
    cycling training tools 13-15, 15*t*
    electronic shifting systems 11
    Global Positioning System 14-15, 15*f*
    heart rate monitor watches 14
    helmets 13, 13*ff*
    for off-road triathlon 239
    power meters 14
    road *versus* triathlon 6-7, 6*f*, 7*t*
    stack and reach 8-9, 9*f*
    stationary trainers 14, 15*t*
    triathlon-specific 7
    triathlon time trial (TT) bike 115
    wheels 11, 12*t*
bike tests
    field testing 22, 22*f*
    lactate profiling 20, 20*f*
    power ramp testing 21
bilateral breathing 80
black rice salad 214
blood lactate profiling 19-21, 20*f*-21*f*
blood sugar fluctuation 43-44
blueberry ginger smoothie 214
body position for swimming 80-81
Borg scale 116
BOSU wobble disc 181
bow exercise 71, 71*f*
box tapping exercise 182, 182*f*
branch-chain amino acids (BCAAs) 38
breathing patterns 80, 90

brick intervals 109
brick workout 111
bridge exercise 30, 31*f*
bridge with leg lift 72, 72*f*
butt kicks drill 108

C

cadence 104, 104*t*
camel with side bend 73, 73*f*
Campagnolo electronic shifting systems 11
carbohydrates
    intake goal per day 44
    role of 39-41
    sources of 41, 42*t*
careers in triathlon
    coaching 247-249
    event management 250-252
    professional triathlete 257-258
    retail and manufacturing 258-260
    sports media 255-256
    staff and governance 252-255, 253*t*
careers in triathlon, Q & A's
    on coaching 249-250
    on event management 251-252
    on professional triathletes 257-258
    on retail and manufacturing 259-260
    on sports media 256
    on staff and governance 253-255
catch-up drill 81
children in triathlon
    adult *versus* youth programs 222-224
    benefits of sport participation 223
    cycling 230-233, 232*f*-233*f*
    early specialization in sport 226-229, 228*f*

children in triathlon *(continued)*
 familial influences on 224-226
 issues to consider 221-222
 physical development of 226-229, 228*f*
 racing 235, 235*t*
 reasons for discontinuation 235-236
 role of the parent as coach 225
 running 233-234, 234*ff*
 swim games for 229
 swimming 229-230, 230*f*
clamshell exercise 67, 67*f*
classic long run workout 111
clothing. *See* apparel
coaching options for triathletes
 assessing the coaching experience 198-199
 budgeting for 195
 coachability of athletes 200
 coach contact outside of sessions 197
 coaching personalities 199
 coach presence at events 197-198
 coach's experience and education 195-196
 individual *versus* group training 196
 need for a coach 194
 one coach *versus* multiple coaches 198
 personalized training plans 197
 reasons for wanting a coach 193-194
Coggan, Andrew 93
communication
 between body and mind 102
 for cycling safety 232
 positive key phrases 56
compression clothing 15-16
compression units 18, 18*f*
Computrainer 21
confidence 58-59
"Cooperation Versus Competition" 223
core strength 24. *See also* exercises, core strength
Cori cycle 22

corpse pose 77, 77*f*
Coyle, Dan 227
creatine kinase 49
crescent lunge 63, 63*f*
cycling-specific training
 aerodynamic positioning 99-100
 fast pedal drill 96
 goal of 95
 group rides 94-96, 95*ff*
 nutrition and hydration plans for 98
 principles of 91-92
 progression from sprint to half Ironman 115
 racing to your strength 99-100
 riding on dirt 96-97
 spin classes 115
 training *versus* racing 97-98, 97*f*-98*f*
 training with power 92-93
 in the zone 100
Cyclocross bikes 239

D
Daniels, A.M. 223
Deardorff, Julie 256
DeBoom, Nicole 259-260
disordered eating 171-172
DNA (deoxyribonucleic acid) damage 48-49
dolphin diving 88-89
Donatello, Kathleen "Kat" 251-252
downward-facing dog exercise 68, 69*f*
dryland training 230
dual-suspension bikes 239

E
emotions 224
Empfield, Dan 8
endorphins 208
energy systems 91
equipment. *See also* apparel; bicycles
 ankle bands 85-86
 band exercise 27, 27*f*
 barbells 184-185
 BOSU wobble disc 181
 for child cyclists 230-231
 compression socks 156
 compression units 18, 18*f*

Computrainer 21
Cori cycle 22
cycling training tools 13-15, 15*t*
 foam roller exercises 28, 28*f*
 foam rollers 18
 Global Positioning System 14-15, 15*f*, 161
 goggles 2, 2*f*, 3*t*
 hand paddles 85
 heart rate monitor watches 14
 helmets 13, 13*ff*
 jogger stroller 206
 kickboards 84-85
 massage sticks 18
 physioball 26, 26*f*
 power meters 14, 93
 pull buoy 85
 race day checklist 161
 swim caps 1, 2*f*
 swim fins 85
 swimming snorkel 85
 swim paddles 5, 5*f*
 swimsuits 2-3, 3*f*
 tempo trainer 86
 towel exercise 27, 27*f*
 wetsuits 3-5, 4*f*, 154
exercise and pregnancy
 considerations for all stages 204-205
 first trimester 203
 postbaby training 205-206
 second trimester 204
 third trimester 204
exercises, alternative. *See also* stretching
 bicycle 70, 70*f*
 bow 71, 71*f*
 bridge with leg lift 72, 72*f*
 camel with side bend 73, 73*f*
 clamshell 67, 67*f*
 corpse pose 77, 77*f*
 crescent lunge 63, 63*f*
 downward-facing dog 68, 69*f*
 front plank with leg lift 64-65, 65*f*
 pinwheel pigeon 76, 76*f*
 reclining twist 76, 76*f*
 revolved head-to-knee 75, 75*f*

side plank 66, 66*f*
squat with twist 74, 74*f*
warrior III 64, 64*f*
exercises, core strength
    bridge 30, 31*f*
    hip flexor-glute toe raise 30, 30*f*
    single-foot plank 29, 29*f*
exercises, strength training
    lean-back hip flexor and quad stretch 32, 32*f*
    leg raise 33, 33*f*
    overhead squat with foam roller 28, 28*f*
    side lunge with band 27, 27*f*
    single-leg wall squat 26, 26*f*
    standing lunge 26, 26*f*
    towel lunge 27, 27*f*
exercises, warm-up
    backward lunge 178, 178*f*
    butt kicker 180, 180*f*
    Frankenstein 178, 178*f*
    high knees 179, 179*f*
    hurdle walk 175, 175*f*
    knee hug 174, 174*f*
    quick carioca 177, 177*f*
    skipping 179
    walking lunge 176, 176*f*
    zigzag lateral movement 180
eyewear for bike and run 17, 17*f*

F
fast pedal drill 96
fatigue 208
fat intake 44
FDA. *See* Food and Drug Administration
feedback 93
field testing
    about 21
    bike field test 22, 22*f*
    run field test 23, 23*f*
    swim field test 23-24
fist drill 82
flexibility
    crescent lunge exercise for 63, 63*f*
    through yoga and Pilates 62
flying with your bike 152-153
foam rollers 18
focus
    blocking out distractions 57
    on body awareness 102

    worrying about competition 57-58
Food and Drug Administration (FDA) 48
foot strike 103, 103*t*
Fretwell, S.D. 225
Friel, Joe 105-106
front plank with leg lift 64-65, 65*f*
functional lactate threshold 22-23

G
Garmin Forerunner 920XT 15, 15*f*
gastrointestinal (GI) distress 47
gliding 81
Global Positioning System (GPS) 14-15, 15*f,* 161, 172
glycogen 40
glycolysis 22
goals
    arm swing goals 104*t*
    cadence goals 104*t*
    carbohydrate intake per day 44
    of cycling-specific training 95
    of development programs for children 224
    leg swing and foot strike 103*t*
    outcome-related 56
    postural 103*t*
    protein intake per day 44
goggles 2, 2*f,* 3*t*
group rides 94-96, 95*ff*
guidelines
    for early sport specialization 227-229, 228*f*
    for prerace swimming 87
    for run training safety 101

H
hand paddles 85
heart rate
    during a bike field test 22, 22*f*
    during a bike test 20, 20*f*
    described 93
    during pregnancy 203
    during a run test 20, 21*f*
heart rate monitors 14, 117-118, 172
helmets 13, 13*ff*

high hand recovery 90
hip flexor-glute toe raise 30, 30*f*
hip flexor muscles 25
Hodgkin's disease 217
hormone fluctuations 35, 37-38
hot flashes 207-208
Hutchison, Jennifer 249-250
hydration
    for cycling-specific training 98
    during exercise 37
    fluid intake for recovery 190
    and fuel for Olympic racing 50-51
    and fuel for 70.3 to Ironman racing 51-53
    for Olympic racing 50-51
    during postbaby training 205
    separating hydration from fueling 47-48
    sodium stores 46-47
    sports drinks 46-47
    for 70.3 to Ironman racing 51-53
    during training 46
    while traveling 155
hydrotherapy 189
hyponatremia 51
hypovolemia 47-48
hypoxia 47-48

I
iliotibial (IT) band friction syndrome 170
injuries. *See also* training for athleticism
    anterior cruciate ligament 170
    energy system recovery 190
    female athlete triad 171-172
    iliotibial (IT) band friction syndrome 170
    lateral epicondylitis 171
    mental recovery 190
    muscular recovery 189
    osteoporosis 171-172
    patellofemoral pain syndrome 170
    sleep, for recovery 191
    stress fractures 170
    swimmer's shoulder 170-171
    training to prevent 172-173, 173*tt*

In Laurel's Words (sidebars)
    Do I have to give up my non-triathlete friends? 218
    Laurel's blueberry ginger smoothie 214
    Laurel's triathlon lifestyle tips 219
    turn your commute into a workout 212
    why I race with a smile on my face 217
integrating triathlon into your lifestyle
    flexibility for 218-219
    fuel for 213-214
    keeping it social 217-218
    Laurel's triathlon lifestyle tips 219
    prioritizing 215-217
    racing 215
    regular workouts 213
    run your own race 219
    timing 212-213
    training buddy 218
    weekly goals 212
international traveling 150
International Triathlon Union (ITU) 238
intrinsic motivation 226
ITU. *See* International Triathlon Union

J
Jayanthi, N.C. 227
jogger strollers 206
jumper's knee 170

K
kickboards 84-85

L
lactate profiling 19-21, 20*f*-21*f*
lactate threshold, functional 22-23
lactate threshold interval training 91-92
lactic acid 20
lateral epicondylitis 170-171
Laurel's blueberry ginger smoothie 214
lean-back hip flexor and quad stretch 32, 32*f*
leg raise exercise 33*f*
lifestyle nutrition plan 41, 42*t*-43*t*

limiter, definition of 105
Lindquist, Barb 155, 257-258
Lombardi, Vince 90
long easy brick workout 111
long run workout 111
Lovato, Amanda 216

M
massages 189
massage sticks 18
Matejka, Kathy 253
melatonin 208
menopause 207-208
menstrual cycles. *See* training and the menstrual cycle
mental travel 156-157
Merson, Melissa 253-255
metronomes 86
mitochondria 48
motivation 226
mountain bike helmets 13
mountain bikers 96-97
mountain bike training 241-242
movement awareness 102-103
muscle glycogen synthesis 40
muscle glycogen utilization 40

N
National Collegiate Athletic Association 221
negative body response 58
negative self-talk 55
NormaTec compression units 18, 18*f*, 189
nutrition
    antioxidants and supplements 48-49
    carbohydrate sources 41, 42*t*
    critical elements of 38-39
    for cycling-specific training 98
    disordered eating pattern 171-172
    hydration and fuel for Olympic racing 50-51
    hydration and fuel for 70.3 to Ironman racing 51-53
    lifestyle plan 41, 42*t*-43*t*
    nutrient timing system 190
    for off-road triathlon 244
    during postbaby training 205
    protein bars 47
    resources for 248*t*

role of carbohydrate 39-41
sample eating plan 44-46
separating hydration from fueling 47-48
for training and racing 46-47
triathlete diet 39
for the triathlete lifestyle 213
while traveling 155

O
off-road triathlon
    bike segment 239
    clothing for 240
    core strength development for 243
    described 237
    hill repeats 242
    mountain bike training for 241-242
    nutrition plan for 244
    preriding the course 243
    run segment 240
    run training for 242
    shoe choices for 244
    swim segment 238
    swim training for 241
    tire pressure for 243-244
    training over and under threshold 242
osteoporosis 171-172
overhead squat with foam roller 28, 28*f*
overload principle 91, 172
oxidation 48
oxidative stress 49

P
pacing 109-110
paratriathletes
    bike and T2 strategies 166
    parking passes and race access 160
    race selection for 159-160
    strategies for the race start 164-165
    swim and T1 strategies 165-166
    transition areas for 161
patellar tendinitis 170
patellofemoral pain syndrome 170
peri- and postmenopausal women 37-38
perimenopausal symptoms 207

periodization 114

physioball 26, 26*f*

Pilates 24, 61-63. *See also* exercises, alternative

Pilates, Joseph 61

pinwheel pigeon exercise 76, 76*f*

plasma 37

PMS. *See* premenstrual syndrome

positive body response 58

postbaby training 205-206

postexercise recovery 36-37

posture 103, 103*t*, 108

power, definition of 92

power data 92

power meters 14, 93, 97, 98*f*, 172

power ramp test 21

pregnancy. *See* exercise and pregnancy

premenstrual syndrome (PMS) 37

productive thinking 58

progesterone 37

protein 42-44

protein bars 47

protein intake 40-41

protein use during exercise 36-37

pull buoys 85

Q

quick cadence 90

R

race day strategy

    bike and T2 166

    the night before 161, 162*f*

    race selection 159-160

    race start 164-165

    race weekend 160-161

    run and finish 166-167

    security 160-161

    swim and T1 165-166

    training 160

    transition preparation 163-164

Raceday Transport 152

race security 160-161

rage to master 226

ramp tests 21

rating of perceived exertion (RPE) scale 116, 172, 173*t*

during a bike field test 22, 22*f*

described 19

RPE at threshold 20-21

during a run test 21*f*

reach, definition of 8

reactive oxygen species (ROS) 48-49

reclining twist 76, 76*f*

recovery 92

recovery boots 18, 18*f*

Recovery Pump recovery boots 18*f*

recovery scale 173*t*

recovery tools 18

revolved head-to-knee exercise 75, 75*f*

road helmets 13

rollers, foam 18

ROS. *See* reactive oxygen species

RPE. *See* rating of perceived exertion (RPE) scale

Rudy Project sunglasses 17, 17*f*

run field test 23, 23*f*

runner's high 208

running shoes 16-17

run tests 20-21, 21*f*

run training

    analyzing workouts and races 107

    arm movement 104-105

    brick intervals 109

    build strength 109

    butt kicks drill 108

    cadence 104

    choosing a race 118-119

    develop speed 109

    endurance training 110-111

    foot strike 103, 103*t*

    guidelines for safety 101

    identifying strengths 106

    identifying weaknesses 105-106

    know when to stop 106-107

    long easy brick workout 111

    long run workout 111

    measuring intensity 116-118, 117*tt*

    movement awareness 102-103

    pacing 109-110

    periodization 114

    posture 103, 103*t*

    progression from sprint to half Ironman 116

    race strategy 118-119

    running well off the bike 107

    short pace progression run off bike 108

    standing postural practice 108

    strength training 116

    use proper intensity 111

    walking lunge drill 108

S

safety strokes 89-90

self-driven motivation 226

self-talk 55

Shimano electric shifting systems 11

short pace progression off bike 108

side bars. *See* Bec's Spin; In Laurel's Words

side lunges 27, 27*f*

side lunge with band 27, 27*f*

side plank exercise 66, 66*f*

single-arm drill 83

single-foot plank 29, 29*f*

single-leg wall squat 26, 26*f*

single-side breathing 90

skin lubricants 17

Skirt Sports 259

sleep, for recovery 191

sleep, quality 38-39

sleep disturbances 208

sleeveless wetsuits 4-5, 4*f*

snorkels 85

Snow, Cait 8*f*

sodium stores 46-47

spin classes 115

sports drinks 46-47

squat with twist exercise 74, 74*f*

stability 24

stack, definition of 8

stack and reach 8-9, 9*f*

standing lunge 26, 26*f*

standing postural practice 108

strategy. *See* race day strategy

streamline position for swimming 81, 81*f*

strength training. *See also* exercises, core strength; exercises, strength training

    about 24-25

strength training *(continued)*
developing glute strength 25, 26f-28f
hip flexor strength and stability 32, 32f-33f
improving core strength 29
nutrition for training and racing 46-47
stretching 34
stress
effect of gut microbiota on 39
oxidative stress 49
stress fractures 170
stretching
downward-facing dog exercise 68, 69f
importance of 34
success, visualization of 59
supplements 48-49, 202
swim caps 1, 2f
swim field test 23-24
swim fins 85
swimmer's shoulder 170-171
swimming. *See also* off-road triathlon
body position 80-81
breathing 80
the catch part of the stroke 82, 82f
catch-up drill 81
dolphin diving 88-89
editing your strokes 90
equipment and tools for 84-86
the finish part of the stroke 84
fist drill 82
prerace guidelines 87
progression from sprint to half Ironman 114-115
the pull part of the stroke 83, 83f
recovery part of the stroke 84
safety stroke 89-90
sighting 89
single-arm drill 83
start of the race 87-88, 88f
streamline position 81, 81f

swim games 229
Tarzan drill 86-87
triathlon races 79
swim paddles 5, 5f
swimskins 3, 3f, 238
swimsuits 2-3, 3f

T
Tarzan drill 86-87
tempo, definition of 114
tempo trainer 86
tennis elbow 170-171
testing. *See* bike tests; field testing; performance testing
The Triathlete's Training Bible (Friel) 105-106
threshold, definition of 114
towel lunge 27, 27f
training. *See also* strength training
individual *versus* group 196
plan design for 197
postbaby 205-206
Training and Racing with a Power Meter (Allen; Coggan) 93
training and the menstrual cycle. *See also* exercise and pregnancy
days 1-14 (follicular phase) 201-202
days 14-28 (luteal phase) 202
effect of on training 202
training for athleticism
agility and change of direction 183, 183ff
exercises for warm-up 174-181, 174f-180f
importance of technique 188
proprioception 181-182, 181f-182f
strength 184-187, 184f-187f
training intensity 116-118, 117tt
Training Load software 172
TrainingPeaks software 172
transport services 152
traveling for triathlons
finding lodging 150

flying with your bike 152-153
international traveling 150
mental travel 156-157
nutrition and hydration 155
once you've arrived 156
packing carry-ons 155
packing for international trips 154-155
packing for your trip 153-154
planning 149
researching the location 151
transport services 152
traveling smart 150-151
travel itinerary planning 151
triathlon group rides 94-96, 95ff. *See also* off-road triathlon
triathlon time trial (TT) bike 115
True, Sarah 9f
Tucker, R. 227

U
underwater pull 83, 83f

V
visualization, of success 59
VO₂max, definition of 114

W
walking lunge drill 108
warm-up exercises. *See* exercises, warm-up
warrior III exercise 64, 64f
watts, definition of 92
Web sites
Athletics 365 234
resources for careers and interests 248t
for swim equipment 5
Weiss, M.R. 225
wetsuits 3-5, 4f, 154, 238
wheels 11, 12t
wobble disc exercise 181

X
XTERRA racing 237-238

Y
yoga 61-63. *See also* exercises, alternative
Youth Sport Institute 235-236

USA Triathlon is proud to serve as the National Governing Body for triathlon, as well as duathlon, aquathlon, aquabike, winter triathlon, off-road triathlon and paratriathlon in the United States. Founded in 1982, USA Triathlon sanctions more than 4,300 races and connects with nearly 500,000 members each year, making it the largest multisport organization in the world. In addition to its work with athletes, coaches, and race directors on the grassroots level, USA Triathlon provides leadership and support to elite athletes competing at international events, including International Triathlon Union (ITU) World Championships, Pan American Games and the Olympic and Paralympic Games. USA Triathlon is a proud member of the ITU and the United States Olympic Committee (USOC). Visit www.usatriathlon.org to learn more and to join our community of members.

Tara S. Comer is a training and development specialist with more than 15 years of experience in progressive social change in women's health, sports, leadership, and professional development. She is the chair of the USA Triathlon National Women's Committee and a member of the Ironman Women for Tri advisory board, leading national efforts to support and increase the number of women in triathlon.

Tara has been an endurance athlete for more than 20 years, competing in triathlon, road, bike, and adventure races all over the United States. She turned her passion into her profession and has coached hundreds of athletes in achieving their goals and breaking down barriers to success. Tara has developed local and national programs and partnerships that benefit public health and fitness initiatives, including cofounding the Triathlon Club of New England. She is a frequent presenter at high-profile yoga and wellness centers and corporations such as RI Obesity Symposium, Irongirl, Danskin Women's Triathlon, USA Triathlon Coaching Symposium, American Heart Association's Go Red for Women, and ShapeUp RI.

Through her various leadership roles, Tara has developed key programs that empower women in business and health. Tara is a USA Triathlon certified coach, advanced yoga teacher (E-RYT 500), and founder of womenRYSE.

Tara lives in Warwick Rhode Island with her husband and their two sons.

Krista Austin, PhD, CSCS, is a physiologist who has worked for the United States Olympic Committee, the English Institute of Sport, and England's cricket team. She is a consulting physiologist for the U.S. Army, USA Triathlon, and USA Taekwondo. Austin has done endurance coaching for distance runners and triathletes at all levels and provided performance nutrition to various populations, including elite athletes and those with chronic medical conditions. Austin's clients have included elite distance runners such as Meseret Defar, Kara Goucher, Amy Yoder Begley, Dathan Ritzenhein, and 2009 New York City Marathon champion Meb Keflezighi. She has also worked with top-tier triathletes such as Lesley Patterson, Matt Chrabot, Sam McGlone, and Laura Bennett. Austin is the author of the book *Performance Nutrition: Applying the Science of Nutrient Timing*, in which she approaches nutrition from a performance. She frequently contributes to online media such as *Lava* magazine and is frequently interviewed for training and nutrition advice by *Sports Illustrated*, *Running Times*, *Runner's World*, *Competitor*, *Inside Triathlon,* and *Triathlete* magazines. As a member of the American College of Sports Medicine and National Strength and Conditioning Association, Austin regularly writes for accredited industry publications and is a referee for multiple scientific journals. Austin was an associate editor of the *International Journal of Sports Nutrition and Exercise Metabolism*. She earned a bachelor of arts degree in physical education, master of science degree in exercise physiology, and PhD in exercise physiology and sport nutrition. She is a certified strength and conditioning specialist.

Brenda Barrera, a writer and editor with more than 20 years of experience in the publishing industry, has covered triathlon as editor of *Chicago Athlete*, *RunMidwest*, and *Washington Running Report* (now *RunWashington*). Since 1985 she has competed in many triathlons and qualified for the USA Triathlon Age Group National Championships several times. Brenda is the author of the *Chicago Running Guide* and has been an invited speaker for sports organizations on the topic of working with the media. She currently is working on sports books for girls, writes for regional running and multisport publications, and serves on the USA Triathlon Women's Committee as communications and social media lead. Follow her on Twitter @brendajbarrera.

Gale Bernhardt was the USA Triathlon men's and women's team coach at the 2003 Pan American Games and 2004 Athens Olympics. She's worked as a World Cup coach and delivered coach education training for the International Triathlon Union's sport development team. She has coached Olympic road racers, World Cup mountain bike riders, and Leadville 100 racers. Bernhardt coaches athletes for and has personally raced triathlons of all distances. She enjoys trail races, mountain bike races, and alpine and Nordic skiing. Bernhardt is the 12th woman in history to win the prestigious 1,000-mile Leadville 100 Mountain Bike Race belt buckle.

Celeste Callahan starting jogging in 1977 and ran her first marathon in New York in 1980. She has since completed 11 marathons. Her first triathlon was in 1984, and in 1987 she participated in her first nationals, where she placed fifth. She is a three-time Kona finisher; her personal best earned her fifth place. Celeste was the national duathlon champion in 2004 and the world triathlon champion in 2002. She served three terms on the USA Triathlon national board of directors and was on the founding team of CWW Triathlon 501.ce for novices. Earning the title of Top Triathlon Volunteer from USAT and IOC as well as the inaugural Award of Excellence in Sport from the Women's Committee of ITU, Celeste is a two-time record holder in the Race Across America. She is a level II coach and race director for USA Triathlon. She received her bachelor of arts degree from Creighton University and her master's degree from Denver University. Currently she is a candidate for a PhD in theological studies.

Rachel Sears Casanta is a USA Triathlon certified coach and co-owner of Hypercat Racing, an endurance sport coaching, bike fit studio, and retail shop based in Ventura, California. A retired professional triathlete and duathlon age-group world champion, Rachel is a veteran of 10 world championships, including Ironman Hawaii. She is a graduate of Syracuse University and the S.I. Newhouse School of Public Communications and School of Arts and Sciences. She also earned a master of arts degree in sport management from the University of San Francisco. When she is not training, racing, or coaching, Rachel is busy with her most important job of taking care of her son and spending time with her husband and their cats and dogs. You can reach Rachel at rachel@hypercat.com and the Hypercat Racing website at www.hypercat.com.

Tara S. Comer is a USA Triathlon certified coach, advanced yoga teacher (level E-RYT 500), and chair of the USA Triathlon Women's Committee. Since becoming a certified coach, Tara has trained more than 200 athletes to achieve their goals. She has more than 1,000 hours of teaching performance workshops, multisport clinics, yoga classes, and retreats. Tara cofounded the Triathlon Club of New England in 2010, leading it as president and serving as head coach for three years. The club has grown into a vibrant community of more than 200 athletes and a force in triathlon throughout the region. She is known for delivering innovative training programs that use the mind–body connection in service to performance, mental strength, and achievement in triathlon.

Wendy Francke, MD, is originally from Duxbury, Massachusetts. She has bachelor's and medical degrees from Georgetown University. She completed her residency in family practice in Ventura, California, and a one-year fellowship in obstetrics and gynecology. Married with two daughters, Wendy has been working in full-spectrum family practice since 2001. Wendy is an amateur triathlete and has run seven marathons and multiple road races. She has coached youth track and youth cross country since 2011.

Sarah Haskins grew up in St. Louis and began swimming at a very young age. She swam on the Parkway Swim Club for nine years and ran cross country and track in high school. Sarah was a Missouri state champion in cross country and swimming while attending Parkway South High School. At the University of Tulsa Sarah competed in cross country and track. She has a bachelor's degree in elementary education and a minor in mathematics. Sarah competed in her first triathlon in St. Louis in June 2003 after graduating from college. She was invited to the Olympic Training Center in Colorado Springs in 2004 and became the U23 national champion later that summer. Sarah placed 11th at the 2008 Olympics. Since then she has had 35 professional wins, two Pan American Games medals, and a silver medal from the ITU World Championships. Sarah has one daughter.

Lindsay Hyman is a professional-level coach with Carmichael Training Systems, a personal coaching company that has improved the performance of more than 10,000 athletes since 2000 in the disciplines of cycling and triathlon. She is also a sport physiologist for the United States Olympic Committee in Colorado Springs and a USA Triathlon level II certified coach. Hyman earned her master's degree in exercise physiology from the University of Colorado with a focus on software training analysis of long-course elite triathletes. Her interest in the sport began in the early 1990s as a participant in the IronKids program and continued to grow through the USA Triathlon junior programs and professional racing. Today Hyman still enjoys the excitement of endurance racing and competes in ultraendurance events.

Siri Lindley was the 2001 ITU world champion and two-time ITU series winner. Ranked as the top triathlon athlete in the world at the time of her retirement from competition in 2002. Since then, Siri has coached athletes to four Ironman world championship crowns, three Ironman 70.3 world championship crowns, and Olympic selection and Olympic medals. Siri graduated from Brown University in 1991 with a degree in psychology. She Lives in Boulder, Colorado, with her wife, Rebekah Keat.

Melissa Mantak is a USA Triathlon level III and USA Cycling level I certified coach and has a master's degree in sport science. In 2013-2014 she was a USA Triathlon national development coach. Melissa teaches multiple clinics in the individual sports of triathlon and presents at USAT coaching certification clinics. She was also an ITU World Cup Series overall champion and 2010 USAT National Coach of the Year. Melissa was the official coach of the Tri for the Cure Triathlon, an all-women's sprint triathlon in Denver. Melissa empowers athletes of all abilities to take their triathlon training and racing to the next level. Contact her at melissa@empoweredathlete.com or www.triathlontraining-coach.com.

Sara McLarty has been in the sport of triathlon since 1990 when she competed in her first race at 7 years of age. The only break she took from triathlon was during her collegiate swimming career at the University of Florida. After narrowly missing the 2004 Olympic team, Sara returned to triathlon to compete for USA Triathlon on the ITU world circuit. Since becoming a professional triathlete in 2005, Sara has competed all over the world, trained under knowledgeable and experienced coaches, and represented the United States at multiple world championships.

Sara is known as the fastest female in triathlon because of her strong swimming background. She shares her swimming tips and techniques with her U.S. masters swimming team in Central Florida and around the country at clinics and seminars.

Melanie McQuaid has been a professional athlete since 1994 and has competed internationally in mountain biking, road cycling, off-road triathlon, and road triathlon. Her career began in mountain bike and road racing with multiple appearances at the UCI Cross Country Mountain Bike World Championships and one trip to the UCI Road World Championships Road Race. After seven years of traveling the world competing in pro cycling, she turned her attention to racing off-road triathlon in 2001. In the Xterra World Championships she has three titles, three second-place finishes, and one third-place finish. She has one ITU Cross Triathlon World Championship title and one second-place finish at the ITU Cross Worlds. In 2012 she began to focus on the half Ironman discipline of triathlon and now has five half Ironman titles and more than 10 podium finishes. McQuaid continues to race as a full-time professional triathlete with a focus on stepping up to full Ironman distance. A graduate of University of Victoria with a major in chemistry and a minor in biochemistry, Melanie applies her science background to coaching athletes and contributing to sport-specific magazines.

Shelly O'Brien is a USAT level III elite and certified youth and junior coach, the SMW regional athlete development coordinator, a USAT national youth and junior camp director, USAT certified race director, and USAT coach certification instructor. In addition, she holds a BS in sports medicine and is a certified strength and conditioning specialist. She is the founder and head coach of IconOne Multisport, a USA Triathlon certified high-performance junior team that has supported many athletes to national and world championship titles. She shares her passion for education and support of athlete and coach development through clinics and camps. For more information visit www.icon1multisport.com.

Sage Rountree is an internationally recognized authority on yoga for athletes and an endurance sport coach specializing in athletic recovery. Sage is the author of five books, including *The Athlete's Guide to Yoga* and *Racing Wisely*. Sage is an experienced registered yoga teacher at the highest level (E-RYT 500) with the Yoga Alliance and is on the faculty at the Kripalu Center for Yoga and Health. Her nationwide workshops include weekends on yoga for athletes, training for yoga teachers on working with athletes, and running and yoga retreats. Her students include casual athletes, Olympians, NBA and NFL players, and many University of North Carolina athletes and coaches. Sage competes in running races from the 400-meter to the ultramarathon and triathlons from the supersprint to the Ironman. A member of PowerBar Team Elite since 2008, she has also been an Athleta Featured Athlete and is an ambassador for prAna. She holds coaching certifications from USA Triathlon and the Road Runners Club of America, and she writes for publications such as *Runner's World*, *Yoga Journal*, and *USA Triathlon* magazines. She lives with her husband and daughters in Chapel Hill, North Carolina, and co-owns the Carrboro Yoga Company and the Durham Yoga Company, where she heads the 200- and 500-hour yoga teacher training programs.

Margie Shapiro took up triathlon on a whim after finishing her collegiate running career at Georgetown University. The pastime grew into a passion and then profession as she won the Age Group World Championship Overall in 2005. She was a member of the U.S. national team and qualified for two U.S. Olympic Trials in the ITU format. In 2012 she returned her focus to nondrafting racing with a specialty at 70.3 distance. Margie coaches runners and triathletes and co-owns Potomac River Running, a chain of nine running specialty stores in the DC metro area. She lives in Herndon, Virginia, with her husband and two kids.

Stacy T. Sims has contributed to the environmental exercise physiology and sport nutrition field for more than 15 years as both an athlete and a scientist. Her interest in sex differences and performance has been the focus of her academic and consulting career. Stacy worked as an exercise physiologist and nutrition scientist at Stanford University from 2007 to 2012, specializing in sex differences in environmental and nutritional considerations for recovery and performance. Before working at Stanford, she was a senior research scientist in clothing and textile sciences at Otago University, where she transferred her PhD work to investigating the interactions of human performance, fabrics, and extreme environmental conditions. An elite athlete herself, Stacy has extensive experience working with athletes at the highest levels of sport worldwide, including the Olympics and Tour de France.

Melissa Stockwell is a U.S. Army veteran who became the first woman to lose a limb in active combat. In 2004 Melissa was on a routine convoy through Central Baghdad when her Humvee was struck by a roadside bomb. The blast took her left leg above the knee.

After a year of rehab at Walter Reed Army Medical Center, she swam in the 2008 Paralympics and carried the American flag into the closing ceremonies. In 2009 Melissa turned to triathlon and is a three-time paratriathlon world champion and an Ironman competitor. She is a certified prosthetist with Scheck and Siress Prosthetics, where she fits other amputees with artificial limbs. She is the cofounder of the Chicago-based Dare2tri Paratriathlon Club. Melissa is a member of the Mideast

Triathlon Council, the USAT Women's Committee, and the USAT Foundation. She also does motivational speaking and is on the board of directors for the Wounded Warrior Project. Learn more about Melissa at www.melissastockwell.com or follow her on twitter: @MStockwell01.

 **Rebeccah Wassner** and **Laurel Wassner** are twin sisters and professional triathletes. Rebeccah turned pro in 2004, leaving behind a career as a certified public accountant (CPA). In 2004 she was named USA Triathlon Rookie of the Year, and in 2009 she was named USA Triathlon's Non-Drafting Athlete of the Year. Specializing in the Olympic distance, Rebeccah has won the New York City Triathlon three times and the Philadelphia Triathlon four times. She welcomed her first child in January 2013. She and her husband, John, divide their time between New York City and New Paltz, New York.

Laurel Wassner turned pro in 2008 after battling Hodgkin's lymphoma, becoming the first triathlete to turn pro after surviving cancer. In 2008 she was named Rookie of the Year by USA Triathlon. Laurel has tackled every distance and format of triathlon racing. In 2012 she finished as the top New Yorker at the New York City Ironman, her first of that type of race. She has stood on the podium at several high-profile professional races. Before turning pro as a triathlete, she was a photo editor at several magazines in New York. Laurel splits her time between New York City and Santa Monica, California.

In 2012 the twins launched the blog AthleteFood.com. With a close friend who is a food writer and a graduate of culinary school, they share anecdotes and create recipes about the nutritious food that fuels triathletes . The blog, featuring Laurel's photography, was named *Triathlete* magazine's favorite food blog and was a finalist in *Parents* magazine's Top Blogs of the Year contest in 2013.

You'll find other outstanding triathlon resources at

www.HumanKinetics.com/triathlon

In the U.S. call 1-800-747-4457

Australia 08 8372 0999 • Canada 1-800-465-7301
Europe +44 (0) 113 255 5665 • New Zealand 0800 222 062

HUMAN KINETICS
The Premier Publisher for Sports & Fitness
P.O. Box 5076 • Champaign, IL 61825-5076 USA